HOWARD HAWKS

INTERVIEWS

CONVERSATIONS WITH FILMMAKERS SERIES
PETER BRUNETTE, GENERAL EDITOR

Photo credit: Photofest

HOWARD HAWKS

INTERVIEWS

EDITED BY SCOTT BREIVOLD

UNIVERSITY PRESS OF MISSISSIPPI / JACKSON

www.upress.state.ms.us

The University Press of Mississippi is a member of the Association of American University Presses.

Manufactured in the United States of America

First edition 2006

∞

Library of Congress Cataloging-in-Publication Data

Hawks, Howard, 1896–
    Howard Hawks : interviews / edited by Scott Breivold.— 1st ed.
        p. cm.—(Conversations with filmmakers series)
    Includes filmography and index.
    ISBN 1-57806-832-0 (cloth : alk. paper)—ISBN 1-57806-833-9
(pbk. : alk. paper)
    1. Hawks, Howard, 1896—Interviews. 2. Motion picture producers
and directors—United States—Interviews. I. Breivold, Scott. II. Title.
III. Series.

PN1998.3.H38A3 2006
791.4302'33'092—dc22   2005042427

British Library Cataloging-in-Publication Data available

CONTENTS

INTRODUCTION

HOWARD HAWKS, WHOSE CAREER in filmmaking spanned nearly fifty years and whose oeuvre includes over forty films in virtually every genre, is now widely regarded as one of the great American filmmakers of the twentieth century. However, his recognition as a true artist and auteur came late in life—toward the latter half of his prolific career.

As late as 1967, just ten years before the director's death, Robin Wood published an article entitled "Who the Hell Is Howard Hawks?" While his title may have been tongue-in-cheek, it illustrated the degree to which Hawks was largely overlooked by the critics, the Motion Picture Academy, and the public. Even today, his name is less familiar than contemporaries like Alfred Hitchcock, John Ford, Orson Welles, and Frank Capra, to name a few. On the surface, one might see how they eclipsed Hawks: Hitchcock, working primarily in one genre, earned the title "master of suspense"; Ford brought the western genre to new heights; Welles was the highly stylized and often controversial "boy genius"; and Capra captured America's heart with his unique brand of sentimentality.

Hawks, on the other hand, created such a diverse body of work—which included films in the gangster, action/adventure, screwball comedy, film noir, musical, and science fiction genres—that it is hard to clearly identify his artistic stamp unless his work is viewed retrospectively. And, as Joseph McBride put it in the introduction to the book *Focus on Howard Hawks*, "The reason Howard Hawks has been so underrated for so many years is that he has always been more concerned with the tangible elements of film-making—actors, mood, action, audience enjoyment—than in courting prestige by making self-consciously important 'statements.' "

The "discovery" of Howard Hawks began in the 1950s (ironically not in America but in France) with the publication of Jacques Rivette's 1953 essay. "The Genius of Howard Hawks" in the journal *Cahiers du Cinema.* A year later, François Truffaut published his seminal article on the auteur theory, placing Hawks and Hitchcock at the forefront of this new critical movement that acknowledged the director as the guiding artistic force (the "author") of a film. Hawks, through his financial independence, connections, and powerful personality, certainly managed to maintain a remarkable degree of control over his films. Though he worked during the era of the studio system, he might be considered one of America's first independent filmmakers—rarely committing to long-term contracts or answering to anyone but the studio heads.

In 1956, some of the French critics conducted what is regarded as the first important interview with Howard Hawks, which is where this collection begins. In it Hawks explains, "I have no desire to make a picture for my own pleasure. Fortunately, I have found that what I like, most people also like, so I only have to let myself go and do what interests me." When asked his opinion about one of the then "young" directors (Nicholas Ray), Hawks replies, "He is one of those directors of whom it is said, 'I will go see everything he does because he is a good story-teller.' " The desire to "tell a good story" is central to Hawks's philosophy of filmmaking, as he will reiterate many times. The interview medium seemed the perfect venue for Hawks to tell his story the way he wanted it told. A natural-born storyteller (reportedly a trait he inherited from his grandfather), Hawks missed no opportunity to regale his admirers with what became known as "Hawksian anecdotes."

As a filmmaker, Hawks's emphasis on storytelling was evident by his choice of writers and the amount of work he put into his scenarios. He collaborated with many of the best in the business, including Seton I. Miller, Ben Hecht, Charles MacArthur, Jules Furthman, John Huston, Charles Brackett, Billy Wilder, Charles Lederer, and Leigh Brackett. He also called upon literary heavyweights/friends like William Faulkner and Ernest Hemingway.

When asked if he always worked on his scripts, Hawks replies, "From the beginning and for all my films." Hawks was keenly aware of the kinds of stories and themes that he wanted to bring to the screen, and they invariably reflected his own background, interests, and somewhat cynical and unsentimental view of the world. If a producer approached him with a script that was "too corny" or just didn't interest him, he would simply say, "Look, I don't know how to tell that story." Yet Hawks was able to tell over forty stories in virtually every genre and learned how to brilliantly interweave dramatic and comedic elements. As Hawks explains it, ". . . a comedy is virtually the same as an adventure story. The difference is the situation—dangerous in an adventure story, embarrassing in a comedy. . . . The only difference between comedy and tragedy is the point of view." In a 1963 interview in *Cinema* Hawks says, "I work with the writers, and though the story becomes not so much an invention of mine, the decision as to the character is mine. Characters are very often invented by the writers, but they're interpreted by the director. The decision is my final decision as to the best way to tell the story."

In the later interviews, Hawks reveals that he focused on characterizations, dialogue, and making "good scenes." While having a good, well-structured story continued to be important to him, he eventually lost interest in plots. When discussing the complex (and often confusing) plot of *The Big Sleep* with an audience of film students at an American Film Institute (AFI) seminar he remarks, "And after people liked the picture and everything I thought, 'Why worry about plot and everything?' just worry about making good scenes. . . ."

As Hawks expounds about the making of his films, we get the sense that unlike Hitchcock (who felt the fun of making a film ended with the creation of the script and storyboards) the real joy of filmmaking for Hawks took place on the set—shooting scenes, perfecting characterizations, and working with his carefully chosen actors. He somewhat downplays the notion that he was highly improvisational on the set, but acknowledges, "I never follow a script literally and I don't hesitate to change a script completely if I see a chance to do something interesting." His approach to making a movie was a highly collaborative one, and he would often listen to suggestions from his crew, cameramen, editors, and actors if they had an idea for improving a scene.

Many of the interviews explore Hawks's discovery and relationship with his actors and his approach to characterization. The way that men and women are depicted in his films and the frequency with which Hawks played with male/female roles are often cited as distinguishing characteristics of his work. His male characters were (like Hawks) adventurous, independent, and highly professional. He found actors that personified the male image he was looking for, whether it was for a drama, comedy, or action film. Humphrey Bogart, Cary Grant, and John Wayne were among his favorites. Cary Grant appreciated Hawks's directorial style and once commented that he was among the directors who "permitted . . . the release of improvisation during the rehearsing of each scene . . . [and] . . . permitted me to discover how far out I could go with confidence, while guided by . . . quiet, sensitive directorial approval." Grant was masterful at maintaining the rapid pace, overlapping dialogue, and perfect timing that a Hawks comedy demanded. His female characters (like the women Hawks admired) were strong-willed, honest, and in control. He seldom cast the same actress twice and would often model his female leads after his first great discovery, Lauren Bacall (whose character Slim in *To Have and Have Not* was based on his first wife).

Hawks's cinematic technique is, by his own admission, simple and straightforward. He explains his approach early on saying, "I once made a film . . . with a great many camera effects, but I have never used such trickery since that time. . . . I try to tell a story as simply as possible with the camera at eye level." He believed in a basically subjective approach and rarely resorted to any type of "trickery" like slow motion, flashbacks, or highly stylized camera angles. Even something as fundamental as a close-up is used very sparingly in a Hawks film. When asked about whether he preferred working on the script, shooting, or editing, he declares, "I hate the editing," but later explains that he preferred to cut his films "simultaneously with the shooting, if possible." He would shoot his scenes with multiple cameras, but left very little room for interpretive cutting of the material. As he revealed to the AFI seminar audience, Hawks also preferred to shoot his scenes in continuity as much as possible, believing that it was the best way to see a growth of feeling in the characters. When asked if he was influenced by the work of other directors, he cited F. W. Murnau, John Ford, Ernst Lubitsch, and Leo McCarey—all of whom (like Hawks) were highly skilled cinematic craftsmen.

In his detailed biography, *Howard Hawks: The Grey Fox of Hollywood*, Todd McCarthy writes, "Howard Hawks was not a man of letters. . . .

For the most part, Hawks's legacy exists in the form of the interviews he so readily granted late in life, in which he expounded to acolytes about his career and accomplishments." McCarthy goes on to say (as his research often substantiates) that the interviews "go beyond ego in their self-aggrandizement into an advanced realm of imagination and fantasy." He later writes, "That Hawks was a natural storyteller may be a handicap to objectifying his life but a linchpin to defining his character."

The 1956 *Cahiers* interview is a good foundation for discovery of Hawks, exploring his choice of subjects, genres, techniques, and early influences. Peter Bogdanovich, who counted Hawks among his friends and mentors, was one of the writers and critics who brought Hawks the recognition he enjoyed late in life. His interview (actually a condensed version of a much longer series of interviews he conducted with Hawks) provides us with a chronological overview of his entire body of work to that date. Here Hawks gives insights into the genesis of many of the projects, discusses his perceived successes and failures, and talks about his approach to story, character, and theme. The AFI seminar offered a unique opportunity for young film students to hear the director discuss in some detail the making of one of his films. In the context of his western *Rio Lobo*, Hawks paints for his captive audience a wonderful picture of his filmmaking process, including his approach to story development, the staging of action, the shooting of scenes, the editing process, and his work with actors.

At the 1971 Chicago Film Festival, Joseph McBride and Michael Wilmington also had the opportunity to interview Hawks before an audience. In their introduction, they acknowledge Hawks's inclusion of some of his favorite anecdotes and point out that although they were familiar, he "embellished them with new twists and flourishes, just as his heroes repeat the same tasks in an endless but volatile routine until they achieve an almost effortless mastery." Hawks discusses his westerns and comments on how *Rio Bravo* was his reaction against *High Noon*. The interviewers probe his cinematic techniques—the shooting of action scenes, editing, his use of color, and the importance of structure. Hawks also talks about working with actors, the influence of John Ford on his work, the role of women in his films, and his reaction to the critical acclaim he had received from the French. In "Hawks Talks," recorded four years later, Joseph McBride and Gerald Peary cover topics not previously explored in earlier interviews. They explore Hawks's childhood and family, his experiences during the war, his early days in Hollywood, and his friendship with Ernest Hemingway. There is a wonderful moment in the interview where they read comments made about Hawks by one of his writers, Bordon Chase. Hawks wastes no time in telling what he thought about Chase and goes on at some length to give his side of the story. He also speaks about some of his collaborations with other writers and unrealized projects.

One of the most unusual and fascinating encounters with the director is the 1975 interview, "Hawks on Film, Politics, and Childrearing." Here, for the first time, the interviewers convince Hawks (who "considers himself an apolitical artist") to talk about the politics of the day—including the Vietnam War, the kidnapping of Patty Hearst, and the SLA. The ever conservative Hawks, no doubt aware of the liberal leanings of his interviewers, seems to have a great deal of fun with them in the process. He discusses whether films should affect people or make political statements and shares his views about the social responsibilities of film versus television and the elements of good and bad drama. In the wide-ranging interview, he discusses the new independent filmmakers, male and female relationships in film, young people and politics, and his feelings about Richard Nixon and other politicians. He even tells a story about his relationship with his son. Penley, Salyer, and Shedlin certainly succeed in their goal to get beyond the anecdotes and to explore Hawks's personal philosophy. Hawks no doubt gets the biggest laugh though. Near the end of the interview, he remarks, "This is the first discussion of politics that I've had, and I might say it's going to be my last."

In Tony Macklin's interview with Hawks, conducted that same year, he approaches Hawks in a much more respectful and traditional way. As a result, Hawks launches into his favorite anecdotes with unparalleled gusto, often circumventing the original question. All of Hawks's favorite stories seem to be featured here, with greater elaboration and detail than we have seen in earlier interviews. But some new ground is still explored amidst all the stories, including a discussion of directorial style, his contributions to *Macon County Line*, and his feelings about the Motion Picture Academy and his honorary Oscar.

In "Howard Hawks: A Private Interview," Peter Lehman and staff talk with the director when he is eighty years old. Many of the familiar anecdotes are here, but he also discusses the ninety-minute standard length of most Hollywood films, comedy on television, the unionization of Hollywood, star vehicles, the use of songs and music in his films, and the help he gave John Wayne with the making of *Alamo*. The final interview in this collection was conducted by Kathleen Murphy and Richard T. Jameson on July 12, 1976. This is probably the last recorded in-depth discussion with the director before his death in December 1977. As they indicate in their introduction, "We heard some of the anecdotes that previous Hawks interviews have included, and some of them are reproduced here yet again—partly because they will be new to some readers, partly because they're wrapped around other material, partly because even many months later they still seem different to us because we heard them from Howard Hawks himself and watched him while he told them." Here Hawks discusses his collaborations with various writers, the unrealized *Sun Also Rises* project, and the making of *Only Angels Have Wings* and *The Dawn Patrol*. He talks about his experiences working with John Wayne, Frances Farmer, Joan Crawford, and other actors, and he reveals his thoughts about the new Hollywood actors and industry.

The interviews that follow have been presented chronologically and reproduced in their entirety, with very little editing. Hawks's tendency (as McBride/Peary put it) to "slip in most of his favorite, and by now maddening, anecdotes" results in a healthy dose of repetition. But as you will discover, many of the fine interviewers featured here were able to insert their own astute observations and to probe deeper than mere anecdote, effectively peeling away the layers of Hawks's carefully crafted image to reveal much about the man behind the legend.

I would like to thank the following for their help, support, and encouragement with this project: Peter Brunette, Seetha Srinivasan, Anne Stascavage, Walter Biggins, Chris Kurtnaker, and my library colleagues at California State University, Los Angeles. This book is dedicated to the memory of Theodore M. Larson, my college film professor, mentor, and friend, who introduced me to the great directors and films of the classic American cinema.

SB

CHRONOLOGY

1896   Born May 30, 1896 in Goshen, Indiana, to Frank and Helen Hawks.
1908–1913   Attends Pasadena High School, Pasadena, California.
1914–1916   Attends Phillips Exeter Academy in New Hampshire.
1916–1917   Works in property department of Famous Players-Lasky (later Paramount) during his summer vacations from college.
1917   Graduates from Cornell University, New York, with a degree in mechanical engineering.
1918–1922   Serves in U.S. Army Air Corps as a flight instructor during World War I.
1919–1922   Works in airplane factory as a designer.
1922–1924   Works as independent producer, editor, writer, and assistant director of two-reel comedies, for such directors as Marshall Neilan, Allan Dwan, and Joseph Von Sternberg.
1924–1925   Employed in the story department at MGM.
1925   Signs a directing contract with William Fox Studios (now Twentieth Century Fox)
1926   Directs his first feature films, *The Road to Glory*, and *Fig Leaves*.
1927   *The Cradle Snatchers* is released in April; *Paid to Love* appears in May.
1928   Three Hawks films are released, including: *A Girl in Every Port* (February); *Fazil* (September); and *The Air Circus* (September).
1929   *Trent's Last Case* is released in March.
1930   Directs his first talking film, *The Dawn Patrol*, released in August; *Scarface* is filmed but withheld from distribution until 1932.

1931   *The Criminal Code* is released in January.

1932   *The Crowd Roars* and Hawks's landmark gangster film
        Scarface are released in April; *Tiger Shark* appears in
        September.

1933   *Today We Live,* based on an original story by William
        Faulkner, is released in March.

1934   Directs his first screwball comedy, *Twentieth Century,* star-
        ring John Barrymore and Carole Lombard.

1935   *Barbary Coast* appears in January; *Ceiling Zero* is completed
        and released in January of 1936.

1936   *The Road to Glory* appears in June; *Come and Get It* is
        released in October; assists with the writing of James Cruz's
        Sutter's Gold.

1937   Assists Victor Fleming with the script for *Captain's
        Courageous.*

1938   *Bringing Up Baby,* with Cary Grant and Katharine Hepburn,
        is released in February; Hawks assists Victor Fleming with
        the script for *Test Pilot.*

1939   *Only Angels Have Wings,* considered by many to be Hawks's
        finest work, is released in May; assists with screenplays for
        Victor Fleming's *Gone With the Wind* and George Stevens's
        Gunga Din.

1940   One of the fastest and funniest screwball comedies ever
        made, *His Girl Friday,* appears on January 18; Hawks works
        with Jules Furthman on the script for *The Outlaw* and begins
        shooting the film. Ten days into production, producer
        Howard Hughes decides to take over direction of the film.

1941   Gary Cooper is awarded the best actor Academy Award in
        the title role of Hawks's *Sergeant York,* which premieres on
        September 9.

1942   *Ball of Fire,* a comedy based loosely on the story of "Snow
        White and the Seven Dwarfs," is released.

1943   *Air Force,* one of the finest American propaganda films of
        WWII, appears on March 20.

1944   *To Have and Have Not,* noted for the first screen pairing of
        Humphrey Bogart and Lauren Bacall, premieres on
        January 20.

1946	The film noir classic *The Big Sleep* is released on August 31.
1948	*Red River*, regarded by many as one of the best films of the western genre, premieres on August 20, and *A Song Is Born* (a musical remake of the Hawks comedy *Ball of Fire*) premieres on November 6. Hawks receives the Quarterly Award from The Director's Guild of America, for *Red River*.
1949	*I Was a Male War Bride*, a zany farce with Cary Grant, premieres in September.
1951	Hawks serves as producer (and may have assisted with the direction) of *The Thing*, directed by Christian Nyby.
1952	*The Big Sky* premieres in August, and *Monkey Business* appears in September. Hawks also directs "The Ransom of Red Chief" episode for the film *O Henry's House*, released in September.
1953	Hawks directs the musical *Gentlemen Prefer Blondes*, starring Marilyn Monroe and Jane Russell, which premieres in August.
1955	*Land of the Pharaohs*, an epic filmed in Cinemascope, premieres on July 2.
1959	As a kind of rebuttal to what Hawks felt was a weak story in the popular Fred Zinnemann western *High Noon*, he directs *Rio Bravo*, which appears on April 4.
1961–1962	*Hatari!* premieres on December 31, 1961, and is released on June 20, 1962.
1964	*Man's Favorite Sport?*, a return to the screwball formula reminiscent of *Bringing Up Baby*, premieres on January 29.
1965	*Red Line 7000*, one of Hawks's weaker films, most notable for the exciting racing sequences, premieres on November 10.
1966–1967	*El Dorado* premieres on December 31, 1966, and is released on June 7, 1967.
1970	*Rio Lobo*, Hawks's last film, and his final western with John Wayne, premieres on November 6 and is released on December 16.
1974	Receives an honorary Academy Award for "A master American filmmaker whose creative efforts hold a distinguished place in world cinema."
1977	Howard Hawks dies on December 26, in Palm Springs, California.

FILMOGRAPHY

1926
THE ROAD TO GLORY
20th Century Fox
Director: **Howard Hawks**
Screenplay: Professor L. G. Rigby (from a story by **Hawks**)
Cinematography: Joseph August
Cast: May McAvoy (Judith Allen), Rockliffe Fellows (Del Cole), Leslie
Fenton (David Hale), Ford Sterling (James Allen)
93 minutes

FIG LEAVES
20th Century Fox
Director: **Howard Hawks**
Screenplay: Hope Loring, Louis D. Lighton (from a story by **Hawks**)
Cinematography: Joseph August
Cast: George O'Brien (Adam Smith), Olive Borden (Eve Smith), André
de Be ranger (Josef André), Phyllis Haver (Alice Atkins), Heine Conklin
(Eddie McSwiggen), William Austin (André's assistant)
109 minutes

1927
THE CRADLE SNATCHERS
20th Century Fox
Director: **Howard Hawks**
Screenplay: Sarah Y. Mason, (from a play by Russell Medcraft and
Norma Mitchell)

Cinematography: L. William O'Connell
Cast: Arthur Lake, Nick Stuart, Sally Eilers, Louise Fazenda, Ethel Wales, Joseph Striker, Dorothy Phillips
103 minutes

PAID TO LOVE
20th Century Fox
Director: **Howard Hawks**
Screenplay: William M. Conselman, Seton I. Miller (from a story by Harry Carr)
Cinematography: L. William O'Connell
Cast: Virginia Valli (Gaby), George O'Brien (Crown Prince Michael), William Powell (Prince Etic), J. Farrell MacDonald (Peter Roberts), Thomas Jefferson (King)
113 minutes

1928
A GIRL IN EVERY PORT
20th Century Fox
Director: **Howard Hawks**
Screenplay: Seton I. Miller (from a story by **Hawks**)
Cinematography: L. William O'Connell, R. J. Bergquist
Editor: Ralph Dixon
Cast: Victor McLaglen (Spike Madden), Robert Armstrong (Salami), Louise Brooks (Mademoiselle Godiva), Gretel Holtz (Other Girl in Holland), Natalie Joyce (Girl in Panama), Maria Casajuana (Chiquita)
97 minutes

FAZIL
20th Century Fox
Director: **Howard Hawks**
Screenplay: Seton I. Miller, Philip Klein (from play, *L'Insoumise*, by Pierre Frondaie, English adaptation, Prince Fazel)
Cinematography: L. William O'Connell
Editor: Ralph Dixon
Cast: Charles Farrell (Prince Fazil), Greta Nissen (Fabienne), John Boles (John Clavering), Mae Busch (Helen Debreuze), Tyler Brooke (Jacques

Debreuze), Eddie Sturgis (Rice), Vadim Uraneff (Ahmed), Hank Mann
(Ali), Josephine Borio (Aicha)
113 minutes

THE AIR CIRCUS
20th Century Fox
Director: **Howard Hawks** and Lewis B. Seiler
Screenplay: Seton I. Miller, Norman Z. McLeod (from a story by Graham
Baker and Andrew Bennison)
Cinematography: Daniel B. Clarke
Editor: Ralph Dixon
Cast: Arthur Lake (Speed Doolittle), Sue Carol (Sue Manning), David
Rollins (Buddy Blake), Charles Delaney (Charles Manning), Heinie Conklin
(Jerry McSwiggin), Louise Dresser, Earl Robinson (Lieutenant Blake)
118 minutes

1929
TRENT'S LAST CASE
20th Century Fox
Director: **Howard Hawks**
Screenplay: W. Scott Darling, Beulah Marie Dix (from a story by
E. C. Bentley)
Cinematography: Harold Rosson
Cast: Raymond Griffith (Phillip Trent), Marceline Day (Evelyn
Manderson), Raymond Hutton (Joshua Cupples), Lawrence Gray (Jack
Marlowe), Donald Crisp (Sigsbee Manderson), Edgar Kennedy
(Inspector Murch), Nicholas Soussanin (Marlin), Anita Garvin (Ottilie
Dunois)
96 minutes

1930
THE DAWN PATROL
First National-Warners
Director: **Howard Hawks**
Screenplay: **Howard Hawks**, Don Totheroh, Seton I. Miller (from the
story, "The Flight Commander," by John Monk Saunders)
Cinematography: Ernest Haller

Editor: Ray Curtiss
Special Effects: Fred Jackman
Music: Leo F. Forbstein
Cast: Richard Barthelmess (Dick Courtney), Douglas Fairbanks,
Jr. (Douglas "Scotto" Scott), Neil Hamilton (Major Brand), William Janey
(Gordon "Donny" Scott), James Finlayson (Field sergeant), Clyde Cook
(Bott), Gardner James (Ralph Hollister), Edmund Breon (Lieutenant
Phipps), Frank McHugh (Flaherty), Jack Ackroyd (Ackroyd, a mechanic),
Harry Allen (Allen, a mechanic)
95 minutes

1931
THE CRIMINAL CODE
Columbia
Producer: Harry Cohn
Director: **Howard Hawks**
Screenplay: Seton I. Miller, Fred Niblo, Jr. (from a story by Martin
Flavin)
Cinematography: James Wong Howe, Ted Tetzlaff
Editor: Edward Curtiss
Art Director: Edward Jewell
Sound: Glenn Rominger
Cast: Walter Huston (Warden Brady), Phillips Holmes (Robert Graham),
Constance Cummings (Mary Brady), Mary Doran (Gertrude Williams),
De Witt Jennings (Captain Gleason), John Sheeran (McManus), Boris
Karloff (Ned Galloway), Otto Hoffman (Jim Fales), Clark Marshall
(Runch), Arthur Hoyt (Leonard Nettleford), Ethel Wales (Katie Ryan),
Nicholas Soussanin (uncredited), Paul Porcasi (Tony Spelvin), James
Guilfoyle (Detective Doran), Lee Phelps (Detective Doherty), Lew
(Hugh Walker), Jack Vance (Reporter), John St. Polis (Dr. Rinewulf),
Andy Devine (Convict, kitchen worker), Russell Horton (State's Attornny),
Tetsu Komi (Convict), Al Hill (Gary)
97 minutes

1932
SCARFACE (aka: Scarface, the Shame of a Nation)
United Artists

Producer: Howard Hughes and **Howard Hawks**
Director: **Howard Hawks**
Screenplay: Ben Hecht, W. R. Burnett, John Lee Mahin, Seton I. Miller,
Fred Pasley (based on the novel by Armitage Trail)
Cinematography: Lee Garmes, L. W. O'Connell
Editor: Edward Curtiss
Production Designer: Harry Olivier
Music: Gus Arnheim, Adolph Tandler
Cast: Paul Muni (Antonio "Tony" Camonte), Ann Dvorak (Cesca
Camonte), Karen Morley (Poppy), Osgood Perkins (John "Johnny"
Loro), Boris Karloff (Gaffney), George Raft (Guino Rinaldo), Vince
Barnett (Angelo), C. Henry Gordon (Inspector Ben Guarino), Inez
Phalange (Mrs. Camonte), Edwin Maxwell (Chief of Detectives), Tully
Marshall (Managing editor), Harry Velar (Big Louis Costillo), Bert
Starkey (Epstein), Henry Arietta (Pietro), Maurice Black (Jim, head-
waiter), Purnell Pratt (Mr. Garston), Charles Sullivan (Costillo's hood),
Harry Ten brook (Costillo's hood), Hank Mann (Stag party janitor), Paul
Fix (Hood with Gaffney), **Howard Hawks** (man on bed), Dennis
O'Keefe (Dance extra)
90 minutes

THE CROWD ROARS
Warner Brothers
Director: **Howard Hawks**
Screenplay: John Bright, Niven Busch, Kubec Glasmon, Seaton I. Miller
(based on a story by **Hawks**)
Cinematography: Sidney Hickox
Editors: John Stumar, Thomas Pratt
Art Director: Jack Okey
Music: Leo F. Forbstein
Cast: James Cagey (Joe Greer), Joan Blondell (Anne Scott), Ann Dvorak
(Lee Merrick), Eric Linden (Edward "Eddie" Greer), Guy Kibbee (Pop
Greer), Frank McHugh (Spud Connors), William Arnold (Bill, himself),
Leo Nomis (Jim), Charlotte Merriam (Mrs. Ruth Connors), Harry Hartz
(Himself), Regis Toomey (Dick Wilbur), Ralph Hepburn (Himself), Fred
Guisso (Himself), Fred Frame (Himself)
85 minutes

TIGER SHARK
First National/Warner Brothers
Director: **Howard Hawks**
Screenplay: Wells Root (based on the story, "Tuna" by Houston Branch)
Cinematography: Tony Gaudio
Editor: Thomas Pratt
Art Director: Jack Okey
Costumes: Orry-Kelly
Music: Leo F. Forbstein
Cast: Edward G. Robinson (Mike Mascarenhas), Richard Arlen (Pipes
Boley), Zita Johann (Quita Silva), Leila Bennett (Muggsey), Vince
Barnett (Fishbone), J. Carrol Nash (Tony), William Ricciardi (Manuel
Silva), Edwin Maxwell (Doctor)
80 minutes

1933
TODAY WE LIVE
MGM
Producer: **Howard Hawks**
Director: **Howard Hawks**
Screenplay: Edith Fitzgerald, Dwight Taylor (based on the story "Turn
About" by William Faulkner)
Dialogue: William Faulkner
Cinematography: Oliver T. Marsh
Editor: Edward Curtiss
Art Director: Cedric Gibbons
Costumes: Adrian
Cast: Joan Crawford (Diana "Ann" Boyce-Smith), Gary Cooper
(Lieutenant Richard "Bogey" Bogard), Robert Young (Lieutenant Claude
Hope), Franchot Tone (Lieutenant Ronnie Boyce-Smith), Roscoe Karns
(Lieutenant "Mac" McGinnis), Louis Closser Hale (Applegate), Rollo
Lloyd (Major Robert B. Mosely), Hilda Vaughan (Eleanor)
113 minutes

1934
VIVA VILLA!
MGM
Producer: David O. Selznick

Director: Jack Conway (and, uncredited, **Howard Hawks**)
Screenplay: Ben Hecht, **Howard Hawks** (uncredited) (based on a story
by Edgecumb Pinchon and O. B. Stade)
Cinematography: James Wong Howe
Editor: Robert J. Kern
Art Director: Harry Oliver
Costumes: Dolly Tree
Sound: Douglas Shearer
Cast: Wallace Beery (Pancho Villa), Fay Wray (Teresa), Stuart Erwin
(Jonny Sykes), Leo Carrillo (Sierra), Donald Cook (Don Felipe de
Castillo), George E. Stone (Emilio Chavito), Joseph Schildkraut (General
Pascal), Henry B. Walthall (Francisco Madero), Katherine DeMille
(Rosita Morales), David Durand (Bugle boy), Phillip Cooper (Pancho
Villa as boy), Frank Puglia (Pancho Villa's father), John Merkel (Lopez),
Charles Stevens (Member of Pascal's staff), Steve Clemente (Member of
Pascal's staff), Pedro Regas (Tomás, Pancho's aide)
115 minutes

TWENTIETH CENTURY
Columbia
Producer: **Howard Hawks**
Director: **Howard Hawks**
Screenplay: Ben Hecht, Charles MacArthur (based on their play, adapted
from the play *Napoleon on Broadway* by Charles Bruce Millholland)
Cinematography: Joseph August, Joseph Walker
Editor: Gene Havlick
Cast: John Barrymore (Oscar "O. J." Jaffe), Carole Lombard (Lily
Garland, a.k.a. Mildred Plotka), Roscoe Karns (Owen O'Malley), Walter
Connolly (Oliver Webb), Ralph Forbes (George Smith), Dale Fuller
(Sadie), Etienne Girardot (Matthew J. Clark), Herman Bing (Beard #1),
Lee Kohlmar (Beard #2), James Curtis (Train Conductor), Billie Seward
(Anita, irate woman on train), Charles Levison (Max Jacobs), Edgar
Kennedy (Oscar McGonigle)
91 minutes

1935
BARBARY COAST
Goldwyn Productions/United Artists

Producer: Samuel Goldwyn
Director: **Howard Hawks**
Screenplay: Ben Hecht, Charles MacArthur, Edward Chodorov
Cinematography: Ray June
Editor: Edward Curtiss
Art Director: Richard Day
Costumes: Omar Kiam
Music: Alfred Newman
Cast: Miriam Hopkins (Mary "Swan" Rutledge), Edward G. Robinson (Luis Anamalis), Joel McCrea (Jim Carmichael), Walter Brennan (Old Atrocity), Frank Craven (Colonel Marcus Aurelius Cobb), Brian Donlevy (Knuckles Jacoby), Clyde Cook (Oakie), Harry Carey (Jed Slocum), Matt McHugh (Bronco), Otto Hoffman (Pebbles), Rollo Lloyd (Wigham), J. M. Kerrigan (Judge Harper), Donald Meek (Sawbuck McTavish), David Niven (Cockney sailor thrown out of saloon), Harry Holman (Mayor), Ethel Wales (Mayor's wife), Herman Bing (Fish Peddler), Kit Guard (Kibitzer), Jim Thorpe (Indian), Tom London (Ringsider with Bar girl)
91 minutes

CEILING ZERO
First National/Warner Brothers
Producer: Harry Joe Brown
Director: **Howard Hawks**
Screenplay: Frank Wead (based on the play by Frank Wead)
Cinematography: Arthur Edeson
Editor: William Holmes
Art Director: John Hughes
Special Effects: Fred Jackson
Costumes: Orry-Kelly
Music: Leo F. Forbstein
Cast: James Cagney (Dizzy Davis), Pat O'Brien (Jake L. Lee), June Travis (Tommy Thomas), Stuart Erwin (Texas Clarke), Henry Wadsworth (Tay Lawson), Isabel Jewell (Lou Clarke), Barton MacLane (Al Stone), Martha Tibbetts (Mary Miller Lee), Craig Reynold (Joe Allen), James Bush (Buzz Gordon), Robert Light (Les Bogan), Addison Richards (Fred Adams), Carlyle Moore, Jr. (Eddie Payson), Dick Purcell (Smiley), Bill Elliott (Transportation Agent)
95 minutes

1936
THE ROAD TO GLORY
20th Century Fox
Producer: Darryl F. Zanuck
Director: **Howard Hawks**
Screenplay: William Faulkner (based on the film, *Les Croix Des Bois*, directed by Raymond Bernard and the novel by Roland Dorgeles)
Cinematography: Gregg Toland
Editor: Edward Curtiss
Art Director: Hans Peters
Costumes: Gwen Wakeling
Music: Louis Silvers
Cast: Frederic March (Lieutenant Michel Denet), Warner Baxter (Captain Paul La Roche), Lionel Barrymore (Papa La Roche, aka Private Moran), June Lange (Monique La Coste), Gregory Ratoff (Sergeant Bouffiou), Victor Kilian (Sergeant Regnier), Paul Stanton (Relief Captain), John Qualen (Duflous), Julius Tannen (Lieutenant Tannen), Theodore von Eltz (Major), Leonid Kinskey (Ledoux), Jacques Lory (Courier), Jacques Vanaire (Doctor), Edythe Raynore (Nurse), George Warrington (Jean Dulac, Old Soldier), Louis Mercier (Soldier wanting out of trench)
95 minutes

COME AND GET IT
Goldwyn Productions/United Artists
Producer: Samuel Goldwyn
Director: **Howard Hawks** and William Wyler
Screenplay: Jules Furthman, Jane Murfin (based on the novel by Edna Ferber)
Cinematography: Gregg Toland, Rudolph Mate
Editor: Edward Curtiss
Art Director: Richard Day
Costumes: Omar Kiam
Music: Alfred Newman
Cast: Edward Arnold (Bernard "Barney" Glasgow), Joel McCrea (Richard Glasgow), Frances Farmer (Lotta Morgan/Lotta Bostrom), Walter Brennan (Swan Bostrom), Andrea Leeds (Evvie Glasgow), Frank Shields (Tony Schwerke), Mady Christians (Karie, Swan's niece), Mary Nash

(Emma Louise Glasgow nee Newitt), Clem Bevans (Gunnar Gallagher), Edwin Maxwell (Sid LeMaire), Cecil Cunningham (Josie, Barney Glasgow's secretary), Harry C. Bradley (Thomas Gubbins, Glasgow Butler), Rollo Lloyd (Steward), Charles Halton (Mr. Hewitt), Phillip Cooper (Chore Boy), Al K. Hall (Goodnow)
105 minutes

1938
BRINGING UP BABY
RKO
Producer: **Howard Hawks**
Director: **Howard Hawks**
Screenplay: Dudley Nichols, Hagar Wilde (based on a story by Hagar Wilde)
Cinematography: Russell Metty
Editor: George Hively
Art Director: Perry Ferguson, Van Nest Polglase
Costumes: Howard Greer
Music: Roy Webb
Cast: Katharine Hepburn (Susan Vance), Cary Grant (Dr. David Huxley), Charles Ruggles (Major Horace Applegate), May Robson (Aunt Elizabeth Random), Barry Fitzgerald (Mr. Gogarty), Walter Catlett (Constable Slocum), Fritz Feld (Dr. Fritz Lehman), Leona Roberts (Mrs. Hannah Gogarty), George Irving (Dr. Alexander Peabody), Virginia Walker (Alice Swallow), Tala Birell (Mrs. Lehman), John Kelly (Elmer), Edward Gargan (Zoo official), Buck Mack (Zoo official), William "Billy" Benedict (David's caddy), Buster Slaven (Peabody's caddy), Geraldine Hall (Maid), Stanley Blystone (Doorman), Frank Marlowe (Joe), Pat West (Mac), Jack Carson (Roustabout), Ward Bond (Motorcycle cop at jail), Pat O'Malley (Deputy), Asta (George, the Dog), Nissa (Baby, the Leopard)
102 minutes

1939
ONLY ANGELS HAVE WINGS
Columbia
Producer: **Howard Hawks**
Director: **Howard Hawks**

Screenplay: Jules Furthman, Eleonore Griffin (uncredited), William
Rankin (uncredited), (based on a story by **Hawks**)
Cinematography: Elmer Dyer, Joseph Walker
Editor: Viola Lawrence
Art Director: Lionel Banks
Special Effects: Roy Davidson, Edwin C. Hahn
Costumes: Robert Kalloch
Music: Manuel Maciste, M. W. Stolloff, Dimitri Tiomkin
Cast: Cary Grant (Geoff Carter), Jean Arthur (Bonnie Lee), Richard
Barthelmess (Bat Kilgallen-MacPherson), Rita Hayworth (Judith "Judy"
MacPherson), Thomas Mitchell (Kid Dabb), Sig Ruman (John "Dutchy"
Van Reiter) , Victor Kilian (Sparks, radioman) John Carroll (Gent
Shelton), Allyn Joslyn (Les Peters), Don "Red" Barry (Tex Gordon),
Noah Beery, Jr. (Joe Souther), Milisa Sierra (Lily), Lucio Villegas (Dr.
Lagorio), Forbes Murray (Mr. Harkwright), Cecilia Callejo (Felice Torras),
Pat Flaherty (Mike), Pedro Regas (Pancho), Pat West (Baldy), Manuel
Álvarez Maciste (The singing guitarist), Sammee Tong (Sam), Candy
Candido (Bass player), Charles R. Moore (Charlie)
121 minutes

1940
HIS GIRL FRIDAY
Columbia
Producer: **Howard Hawks**
Director: **Howard Hawks**
Screenplay: Charles Lederer (based on the play *The Front Page* by Ben
Hecht, Charles MacArthur)
Cinematography: Joseph Walker
Editor: Gene Havlick
Art Director: Lionel Banks
Costumes: Robert Kalloch
Music: M. W. Stoloff
Cast: Cary Grant (Walter Burns), Rosalind Russell (Hildegaard "Hildy"
Johnson), Ralph Bellamy (Bruce Baldwin), Gene Lockhart (Sheriff Peter
B. "Pinky" Hartwell), Helen Mack (Molly Malloy), Porter Hall (Murphy,
reporter), Ernest Truex (Roy V. Bensinger, Tribune reporter), Cliff
Edwards (Endicott, reporter), Clarence Kolb (Fred, the Mayor), Roscoe

Karns (McCue, reporter), Frank Jenks (Wilson, reporter), Regis Toomey
(Sanders, reporter), Abner Biberman (Louis, small-time hood), Frank
Orth (Duffy, Morning Post copy editor) John Qualen (Earl Williams),
Alma Kruger (Mrs. Baldwin), Billy Gilbert (Joe Pettibone), Pat West
(Warden Cooley), Edwin Maxwell (Dr. Max J. Eggelhoffer), Irving Bacon
(Gus, waiter), Earl Dwire (Pete Davis, man mistaken for Bruce)
92 minutes

1941
SERGEANT YORK
Warner Brothers
Producer: Jesse L. Lasky, Hal B. Wallis
Director: **Howard Hawks**
Screenplay: Harry Chandlee, Abem Finkel, John Huston (based on *War
Diary of Sergeant York* by Sam K. Cowan, *Sergeant York and His People by*
Cowan, and *Sergeant York—Last of the Long Hunters* by Tom Skeyhill)
Cinematography: Arthur Edeson, Sol Polito
Editor: William Holmes
Art Director: John Hughes
Music: Leo F. Forbstein
Cast: Gary Cooper (Alvin C. York), Walter Brennan (Pastor Rosier Pile),
Joan Leslie (Gracie Williams), George Tobias ("Pusher" Ross), Stanley
Ridges (Major Buxton), Margaret Wycherly (Mother York), Ward Bond
(Ike Botkin), Noah Beery, Jr. (Buck Lipscomb), June Lockhart (Rosie
York), Dickie Moore (George York), Clem Bevans (Zeke), Howard Da
Silva (Lem), Charles Trowbridge (Cordell Hull), Harvey Stephens
(Captain Danforth), Tully Marshall (Uncle Lige), Elisha Cook, Jr. (Piano
player), Gig Young (Marching soldier)
134 minutes

BALL OF FIRE
RKO
Producer: Samuel Goldwyn
Director: **Howard Hawks**
Screenplay: Charles Brackett, Billy Wilder (based on the story "From
A to Z" by Thomas Moore, Billy Wilder)
Cinematography: Gregg Toland

Editor: Daniel Mandell
Art Director: Perry Ferguson
Costumes: Edith Head
Music: Alfred Newman
Cast: Gary Cooper (Professor Bertram Potts), Barbara Stanwyck (Katherine "Sugarpuss" O'Shea), Oskar Homolka (Professor Gurkakoff, Mathematics), Henry Travers (Professor Jerome, History), S. Z. Sakall (Professor Magenbruch), Tully Marshall (Professor Robinson, Law), Leonid Kinskey (Professor Quintana), Richard Haydn (Professor Oddly, Botany), Aubrey Mather (Professor Peagram, Literature), Allen Jenkins (Garbageman), Dana Andrews (Joe Lilac), Dan Duryea (Duke Pastrami), Ralph Peters (Asthma Anderson), Kathleen Howard (Miss Bragg), Mary Field (Miss Totten), Charles Lane (Larsen, Miss Totten's assistant), Charles Arnt (McNeary, Lilac's lawyer), Elisha Cook, Jr. (Nightclub waiter), Eddie Foster (Pinstripe), Gene Krupa (Orchestra leader)
111 minutes

1943
AIR FORCE
Warner Brothers
Producer: Hal B. Wallis
Director: **Howard Hawks**
Screenplay: Dudley Nichols
Cinematography: James Wong Howe
Aerial Photography: Elmer Dyer, Charles Marshall
Editor: George Amy
Art Director: John Hughes
Music: Franz Waxman
Cast: John Garfield (Sergeant Joe Winocki, aerial gunner on Mary-Ann), John Ridgely (Captain Mike "Irish" Quincannon, pilot of Mary-Ann), Gig Young (Lieutenant Bill Williams, co-pilot of Mary-Ann), Arthur Kennedy (Lieutenant Tommy McMartin, bombardier of Mary-Ann), Charles Drake (Lieutenant "Monk" Munchauser, navigator of Mary-Ann), Harry Carey (Sergeant Robbie White, crew chief on Mary-Ann), George Tobias (Corporal Weinberg, assistant crew chief of Mary-Ann), Robert Wood (Corporal Peterson, radio operator of Mary-Ann), Ray Montgomery (Private Chester, assistant radio operator of Mary-Ann),

James Brown (Lieutenant Tex Rader, pursuit pilot), Stanley Ridges (Major Mallory, Clark Field), Willard Robertson (Colonel at Hickam Field), Moroni Olsen (Colonal Blake), Edward Brophy (Sergeant J. J. Callahan USMC), Richard Lane (Major W. G. Roberts, B-17 flight leader)
124 minutes

1944
TO HAVE AND HAVE NOT
Warner Brothers
Producer: **Howard Hawks**
Director: **Howard Hawks**
Screenplay: Jules Furthman, William Faulkner (based on the novel by Ernest Hemingway)
Cinematography: Sidney Hickox
Editor: Christian Nyby
Art Director: Charles Novi
Music: Leo F. Forbstein, Franz Waxman (uncredited)
Costumes: Milo Anderson
Cast: Humphrey Bogart (Harry "Steve" Morgan), Walter Brennan (Eddie), Lauren Bacall (Marie "Slim" Browning), Dolores Moran (Madame Hellene de Bursac), Hoagy Carmichael (Cricket), Walter Molnar (Paul de Bursac), Sheldon Leonard (Lieutenant Coyo), Walter Sande (Johnson, fishing customer), Dan Seymour (Captain M. Renard), Aldo Nadi (Renard's bodyguard), Paul Marion (Beauclere, Gaulist), Pat West (Bartender)
100 minutes

1946
THE BIG SLEEP
Warner Brothers
Producer: **Howard Hawks**
Director: **Howard Hawks**
Screenplay: William Faulkner, Jules Furthman, Leigh Brackett (based on the novel by Raymond Chandler)
Cinematography: Sid Hickox
Editor: Christian Nyby
Art Director: Carl Jules Weyl
Music: Max Steiner

Costumes: Leah Rhodes
Cast: Humphrey Bogart (Philip Marlowe), Lauren Bacall (Vivian Sternwood Rutledge), John Ridgely (Eddie Mars), Louis Jean Heydt (Joe Brody), Elisha Cook, Jr. (Harry Jones), Regis Toomey (Chief Insp. Bernie Ohls, District Attorney's Office), Sonia Darrin (Agnes Lowzier, salesgirl at A. J. Geiger bookstore), Bob Steele (Lash Canino), Martha Vickers (Carmen Sternwood), Tommy Rafferty (Carol Lundgren), Dorothy Malone (Acme Bookstore proprietress), Charles Waldron (General Sternwood), Charles D. Brown (Norris, Sternwood's butler), Tom Fadden (Sidney, Mars' flunky), Ben Welden (Pete, Mars' flunky), Trevor Bardette (Art Huck), James Flavin (Captain Cronjager), Joy Barlow (Taxi driver)
114 minutes

1948
RED RIVER
United Artists
Producer: **Howard Hawks**
Director: **Howard Hawks**
Screenplay: Borden Chase, Charles Schnee (based on the novel
The Chisholm Trail by Borden Chase)
Cinematography: Russell Harlan
Editor: Christian Nyby
Art Director: John Datu Arensma
Music: Dimitri Tiomkin
Special Effects: Donald Steward
Cast: John Wayne (Thomas "Tom" Dunson), Montgomery Clift (Matthew "Matt" Garth), Joanne Dru (Tess Millay), Walter Brennan ("Groot" Nadine), Coleen Gray (Fen), John Ireland (Cherry Valance), Noah Beery, Jr. (Buster McGee), Harry Carey (Mr. Melville), Harry Carey, Jr. (Dan Latimer), Paul Fix (Teeler Yacey), Hank Worden (Simms Reeves), Paul Fierro (Fernandez), William Self (Wounded Wrangler), Glenn Strange (Naylor), Shelley Winters (Dance Hall Girl in Wagon Train)
125 minutes

A SONG IS BORN
RKO
Producer: Samuel Goldwyn

Director: **Howard Hawks**
Screenplay: Harry Tugend (based on the story "From A to Z" by Thomas Monroe and Billy Wilder)
Cinematography: Gregg Toland
Editor: Daniel Mandell
Art Director: Perry Ferguson, George Jenkins
Music: Hugo Friedhofer, Emil Newman
Special Effects: John P. Fulton
Costumes: Irene Sharaff
Cast: Danny Kaye (Professor Hobart Frisbee), Virginia Mayo (Honey Swanson), Benny Goodman (Professor Magenbruch), Hugh Herbert (Professor Twingle), Steve Cochran (Tony Crow), J. Edward Bromberg (Dr. Elfini), Felix Bressart (Professor Gerkikoff), Ludwig Stössel (Professor Traumer), O. Z. Whitehead (Professor Oddly), Esther Dale (Miss Bragg), Mary Field (Miss Totten), Howland Chamberlain (Mr. Setter), Paul Langton (Joe), Sidney Blackmer (Adams), Ben Welden (Monte), Ben Chasen (Ben), Peter Virgo (Louis)
113 minutes

1949
I WAS A MALE WAR BRIDE
20th Century Fox
Producer: Sol C. Siegel
Director: **Howard Hawks**
Screenplay: Charles Lederer, Leonard Spigelgass, Hagar Wilde (based on a story by Henri Rochard)
Cinematography: Osmond Borradaile, Norbert Brodine
Editor: James B. Clark
Art Director: Albert Hogsett, Lyle Wheeler
Music: Cyril J. Mockridge
Special Effects: Fred Sersen
Cast: Cary Grant (Captain Henri Rochard), Ann Sheridan (Lieutenant Catherine Gates), William Neff (Captain Jack Ramsey), Marion Marshall (Lieutenant Kitty Lawrence), Randy Stuart (Lieutenant Eloise Billings), Eugene Gericke (Tony Jowitt), Ruben Wendorf (Innkeeper's Assistant), John Whitney (Bill Trumble), Kenneth Tobey (Red), Joe Haworth (Shore Patrolman), John Zilly (Shore Patrolman),

William Pullen (Sergeant), William Self (Sergeant), William Murphy
(Sergeant)
105 minutes

1952
THE BIG SKY
RKO
Producer: **Howard Hawks**
Director: **Howard Hawks**
Screenplay: Dudley Nichols (based on the novel by A. B. Guthrie, Jr.)
Cinematography: Russell Harlan
Editor: Christian Nyby
Art Director: Albert S. D'Agostino, Perry Ferguson
Music: Dimitri Tiomkin
Costumes: Dorothy Jeakins
Cast: Kirk Douglas (Jim Deakins), Dewey Martin (Boone Cardell),
Elizabeth Threatt (Teal Eye, Blackfoot princess), Arthur Hunnicutt (Zeb
Calloway/Narrator), Buddy Baer (Romaine), Steven Geray ("Frenchy"
Jourdonnais, riverboat captain), Hank Worden (Poordevil), Jim Davis
(Streak), Henri Letondal (La Badie), Robert Hunter (Chouquette), Booth
Colman (Pascal), Paul Frees (Louis MacMasters), Frank DeKova
(Moleface), Guy Wilkerson (Longface)
140 minutes

O'HENRY'S FULL HOUSE
20th Century Fox
Producer: Andre Hakim
Directors: **Howard Hawks** ("The Ransom of Red Chief" episode); Henry
Hathaway; Henry King; Henry Koster; Jean Negulesco
Screenplay: Richard Breen, Walter Bullock, Ivan Goff, Nunnally
Johnson, Ben Roberts, Lamar Trotti (based on the stories by O. Henry)
Cinematography: Lloyd Ahern, Lucien Ballard, Milton Krasner, Joseph
MacDonald
Editor: William B. Murphy, Nick DeMaggio, Barbara McLean
Art Director: Chester Gore, Addison Hehr, Richard Irvine, Lyle Wheeler,
Joseph C. Wright
Music: Alfred Newman

Cast: Jeanne Crain (Della, The Gift of the Magi), Farley Granger (Jim, The Gift of the Magi), Anne Baxter (Joanna, The Last Leaf), Jean Peters (Susan, The Last Leaf), Charles Laughton (Soapy, The Cop and the Anthem), Fred Allen (Sam, The Ransom of Red Chief), Oscar Levant (Bill, The Ransom of Red Chief), Dale Robertson (Barney Woods, The Clarion Call), Sig Ruman (Menkie, The Gift of the Magi), Harry Hayden (Mr. Crump, The Gift of the Magi), Fred Kelsey (Santa Claus, The Gift of the Magi)
117 minutes (**Hawks** segment, 25 minutes)

MONKEY BUSINESS
20th Century Fox
Producer: Sol C. Siegel
Director: **Howard Hawks**
Screenplay: I. A. L. Diamond, Ben Hecht, Charles Lederer (based on a story by Harry Segall)
Cinematography: Milton Krasner
Editor: William B. Murphy
Art Director: George Patrick
Music: Leigh Harline
Special Effects: Ray Kellogg
Costumes: Travilla
Cast: Cary Grant (Dr. Barnaby Fulton), Ginger Rogers (Mrs. Edwina Fulton), Charles Coburn (Mr. Oliver Oxley), Marilyn Monroe (Miss Lois Laurel), Hugh Marlowe (Hank Entwhistle), Henri Letondal (Dr. Jerome Kitzel), Robert Cornthwaite (Dr. Zoldeck), Larry Keating (G. J. Culverly), Douglas Spencer (Dr. Brunner), Esther Dale (Mrs. Rhinelander), George "Foghorn" Winslow (Little Indian), Emmett Lynn (Gus, the Janitor), Joseph Mell (The Barber), Harry Carey, Jr. (Reporter), Roger Moore (Bit Man)
97 minutes

1953
GENTLEMEN PREFER BLONDES
20th Century Fox
Producer: Sol C. Siegel
Director: **Howard Hawks**

Screenplay: Charles Lederer (based on the play by Anita Loos, Joseph Fields)
Cinematography: Harry Wild
Editor: Hugh S. Fowler
Art Director: Lyle Wheeler, Joseph C. Wright
Musical Director: Lionel Newman
Songs: Jule Styne, Leo Robin, Hoagy Carmichael, Harold Adamson
Costumes: Travilla
Special Effects: Ray Kellogg
Cast: Jane Russell (Dorothy Shaw), Marilyn Monroe (Lorelei Lee), Charles Coburn (Sir Francis "Piggy" Beekman), Elliott Reid (Ernie Malone), Tommy Noonan (Gus Esmond), George "Foghorn" Winslow (Henry Spofford III), Marcel Dalio (Magistrate), Taylor Holmes (Mr. Esmond, Sr.), Norma Varden (Lady Beekman), Howard Wendell (Watson), Steven Geray (Hotel Manager), Henri Letondal (Grotier, the Prosecutor), Leo Mostovoy (Ship's Captain), Alex Frazer (Pritchard), Harry CareyHarry Carey, Jr. (Sims), George Davis (Cab Driver Pierre)
91 minutes

1955
LAND OF THE PHARAOHS
Warner Brothers
Producer: **Howard Hawks**
Director: **Howard Hawks**
Screenplay: Harold Jack Bloom, William Faulkner, Harry Kurnitz
Cinematography: Lee Garmes, Russell Harlan
Editor: Rudi Fehr, V. Sagovsky
Art Director: Alexander Trauner
Music: Dimitri Tiomkin
Costumes: Mayo
Special Effects: Don Steward
Cast: Jack Hawkins (Pharaoh Cheops), Joan Collins (Princess Nellifer), Dewey Martin (Senta), Alexis Minotis (Hamar), James Robertson Justice (Vashtar), Luisa Boni (Kyra), Sydney Chaplin (Treneh), James Hayter (Vashtar's servant), Kerima (Nailla), Piero Giagnoni (Xenon, Pharaoh's Son)
103 minutes

1959
RIO BRAVO
Warner Brothers
Producer: **Howard Hawks**
Director: **Howard Hawks**
Screenplay: Leigh Brackett, Jules Furthman (based on a story by Barbara
Hawks McCampbell)
Cinematography: Russell Harlan
Editor: Folmar Blangsted
Art Director: Leo K. Kuter
Music: Dimitri Tiomkin
Costumes: Marjorie Best
Cast: John Wayne (Sheriff John T. Chance), Dean Martin (Dude,
"Borachón"), Ricky Nelson (Colorado Ryan), Angie Dickinson
(Feathers), Walter Brennan (Stumpy), Ward Bond (Pat Wheeler),
John Russell (Nathan Burdette), Pedro Gonzales-Gonzales (Carlos
Robante), Estelita Rodriguez (Consuela Robante), Claude Akins
(Joe Burdette), Harry Carey, Jr. (Harold, scenes deleted), Malcolm
Atterbury (Jake, stage driver), Bob Steele (Matt Harris, Burdette
gunman), Bing Russell (Cowboy murdered in saloon), Myron
Healey (Barfly), Eugene Iglesias (1st Burdette man in shootout),
Fred Graham (2nd Burdette man in shootout), Tom Monroe
(Henchman)
141 minutes

1962
HATARI
Paramount
Producer: **Howard Hawks**
Director: **Howard Hawks**
Screenplay: Leigh Brackett (based on a story by Harry Kurnitz)
Cinematography: Russell Harlan, Joseph Brun
Editor: Stuart Gilmore
Art Director: Carl Anderson, Hal Pereira
Music: Henry Mancini
Costumes: Edith Head
Special Effects: John P. Fulton, Richard Parker

Cast: John Wayne (Sean Mercer), Elsa Martinelli (Anna Maria "Dallas" D'Allesandro), Hardy Kruger (Kurt Muller), Gerard Blain (Charles "Chips" Maurey), Red Buttons (Pockets), Michele Girardon (Brandy de la Court), Bruce Cabot (Little Wolf, a.k.a. The Indian), Valentin de Vargas (Luis Francisco Garcia Lopez), Eduard Franz (Dr. Sanderson), Eric Rungren (uncredited), Queenie Leonard (Nurse, scenes deleted), Jon Chevron (Joseph), Henry Scott (Sikh clerk), Major Sam Harris (Man in store), Jack Williams (Man)
159 minutes

1964
MAN'S FAVORITE SPORT?
Universal
Producer: **Howard Hawks**
Director: **Howard Hawks**
Screenplay: Steve McNeil, John Fenton, Murray (based on the story, "The Girl Who Almost Got Away" by Pat Frank)
Cinematography: Russell Harlan
Editor: Stuart Gilmore
Art Director: Alexander Golitzen, Tambi Larsen
Music: Henry Mancini
Costumes: Edith Head
Special Effects: Ben McMahan
Cast: Rock Hudson (Roger Willoughby), Paula Prentiss (Abigail Page), Maria Perschy (Isolde "Easy" Mueller), Charlene Holt (Tex Connors), John McGiver (William Cadwalader), Roscoe Karns (Major Phipps), Forrest Lewis (Skaggs), Regis Toomey (Bagley), Norman Alden (John Screaming Eagle), Tom Allen (Bit Part), James Westerfield (Policeman), Tyler McVey (Customer Bush), Kathie Browne (Marcia), Joan Tewkesbury (Woman in Elevator), Betty Hanna (Woman in Elevator), Dianne Simpson (Elevator Operator)
120 minutes

1965
RED LINE 7000
Paramount
Producer: **Howard Hawks**

Director: **Howard Hawks**
Screenplay: George Kirgo (based on a story by **Hawks**)
Cinematography: Haskell Boggs, Milton Krasner
Editor: Bill Brame, Stuart Gilmore
Art Director: Arthur Lonergan, Hal Pereira
Music: Nelson Riddle
Costumes: Edith Head
Special Effects: Farciot Edouart, Paul K. Lerpae
Cast: James Caan (Mike), Laura Devon (Julie), Gail Hire (Holly), Charlene
Holt (Lindy), John Robert Crawford (Ned), Marianna Hill (Gabrielle),
James Ward (Dan), Norman Alden (Pat), George Takei (Kato), Carol
Connors (Waitress), Idell James (uncredited), Robert Donner (Leroy Agers)
110 minutes

1967
EL DORADO
Paramount
Producer: **Howard Hawks**
Director: **Howard Hawks**
Screenplay: Leigh Brackett (based on the novel, *The Stars in Their
Courses* by Harry Brown)
Cinematography: Harold Rosson
Editor: John Woodcock
Art Director: Carl Anderson, Hal Pereira
Music: Nelson Riddle
Costumes: Edith Head
Special Effects: David Koehler, Paul K. Lerpae
Cast: John Wayne (Cole Thornton), Robert Mitchum (El Dorado Sheriff
J. P. Harrah), James Caan (Alan Bourdillion Traherne, "Mississippi"),
Charlene Holt (Maudie), Michele Carey (Josephine "Joey" MacDonald),
Arthur Hunnicutt (Bull Harris), R. G. Armstrong (Kevin MacDonald),
Edward Asner (Bart Jason), Paul Fix (Dr. Miller), Christopher George
(Nelse McLeod), Johnny Crawford (Luke MacDonald), Robert Donner
(Milt, McLeod gang), John Gabriel (Pedro, McLeod gang), Marina
Ghane (Maria), Robert Rothwell (Saul MacDonald), Adam Roarke (Matt
MacDonald), Chuck Courtney (Jared MacDonald), Ann Newman-
Mantee (Sam MacDonald's wife, as Anne Newman), Diane Strom

(Matt's wife), Victoria George (Jared's wife), Olaf Wieghorst (Swede Larsen), Anthony Rogers (Dr. Charles Donovan), Dean Smith (Charlie Hagan, McLeod gang), William Henry (Sheriff Dodd Draper), Don Collier (Deputy Joe Braddock), Jim Davis (Jim Purvis), Nacho Galindo (Mexican saloon keeper), John Mitchum (Elmer, Jason's bartender)
125 minutes

1970
RIO LOBO
National General
Producer: **Howard Hawks**
Director: **Howard Hawks**
Screenplay: Leigh Brackett, Burton Wohl (based on a story by Burton Wohl)
Cinematography: William Clothier
Editor: John Woodcock
Art Director: William R. Kiernan
Music: Jerry Goldsmith
Costumes: Luster Bayless, Ted Parvin
Special Effects: A. D. Flowers, Cliff Wenger
Cast: John Wayne (Colonel Cord McNally), Jorge Rivero (Captain Pierre Cordona a.k.a. Frenchy), Jennifer O'Neill (Shasta Delaney), Jack Elam (Phillips), Victor French (Ketcham, boss of Rio Lobo), Susana Dosamantes (Maria Carmen, Tuscarora's girlfriend), Christopher Mitchum (Sergeant Tuscarora Phillips), Mike Henry (Rio Lobo Sheriff "Blue Tom" Hendricks), David Huddleston (Dr. Ivor Jones), Bill Williams (Blackthorne Sheriff Pat Cronin), Edward Faulkner (Lieutenant Harris), Sherry Lansing (Amelita), Dean Smith (Bide, Rio Lobo rancher), Robert Donner (Whitey Carter, Rio Lobo deputy), Jim Davis (Rio Lobo deputy), Peter Jason (Lieutenant Forsythe, gold train detail officer), Robert Rothwell (Gunman #3), Chuck Courtney (Chuck), George Plimpton (Gunman #4), Bob Steele (Rio Lobo deputy), Boyd "Red" Morgan (Train engineer), Hank Worden (Hank, hotel clerk), Chuck Roberson (Corporal in baggage car), William Byrne (Machinist)
114 minutes

HOWARD HAWKS

INTERVIEWS

Howard Hawks Interview

JACQUES BECKER, JACQUES RIVETTE, AND FRANÇOIS TRUFFAUT/1956

"THE EVIDENCE ON THE SCREEN is the proof of Hawks's genius," we had recently written. It would have been an exaggeration to pretend that this evidence was accessible to everyone; and critical unanimity is happily far from being settled on the genius of one of the great American cineastes: it is clear enough that our own evaluation has not changed.

It was not a question of interrogating Hawks on his "genius"; no metaphysical speculations; nothing that could distress the champions of clarity or common sense; at least, let us hope that each will find here his own account, and that includes the "Hitchcocko-Hawksians" of pure obedience.

When we arrived for our interview, we found Hawks conversing with whom? Jacques Becker, one of our old friends. The auteur of *Casque d'Or* courteously took his leave of the auteur of *Sergeant York* when we protested his departure: since Jacques Becker was a friend of Howard Hawks, the interview could only gain in interest. Furthermore, Becker's fluency in the language of Griffith made him more than an interpreter, a valuable collaborator.

Since our interview transpired a few days before the release of *The Land of the Pharaohs*, our first questions quite naturally dealt with that film.

From *Cahiers du Cinema*, No. 56, Vol. X, February 1956. English translation by Andrew Sarris. Reprinted by permission.

HOWARD HAWKS: I made this film for one simple reason: CinemaScope. At the time I was approached to direct a film in this new screen size, I was considering as a project the story of an astonishing feat of construction in China during the war. The American Army wanted an airfield which the engineers estimated would take eight months to construct. The Chinese supplied twenty thousand men and women, who carried stone in little baskets on their heads, and this huge airfield was completed in three weeks. I was about to abandon this project because the political situation made cooperation with Red China impossible; the producers then considered shooting the film in Thailand. It then occurred to me that the building of the pyramids was the same kind of story—it too demonstrated what man is able to create with his bare hands from sand to stone. This kind of story appeals to me tremendously. We thus wrote our script on this one theme: the construction of a pyramid.

CAHIERS: *What part did William Faulkner play in the development of the scenario?*
HAWKS: He collaborated with Harry Kurnitz in the writing of both story and screenplay. As always, he contributed enormously. He's a great writer; we are very old friends and work easily together. We understand each other very well, and any time I need any sort of help, I call on Faulkner. He has done three or four scenarios for me, but he has also helped me on many others. The story of *The Land of the Pharaohs* because his imagination was challenged by these men, their conversations, the reasons for their belief in a second life, how they happened to achieve these tasks for beliefs we would find it difficult to understand today, such as the slight importance attached to the present life in comparison with the future life, the rest that was to be assured to the Pharaoh in a place where his body would be secure . . .

CAHIERS: *For ages, or even . . .*
HAWKS: For eternity, for eternity. For all these reasons, Faulkner was the man for the assignment: he has an affinity for these ideas. They are what he is made for.

CAHIERS: *We would like to know how you transported your imagination back to an age so remote as the ancient Egyptian.*

HAWKS: We were assisted by several historians in Egypt's Department of Antiquities, and above all by a Frenchman who has lived and written numerous books on Egyptian history in a little house in the shadow of the great Pyramid—the exact spot on which we shot the picture. He and the other authorities instructed us in the ways and customs of the Egyptians. I'm afraid we paid attention only to what best suited our picture. It is possible to reconstruct the furniture and dress, and even some of the ritual, of the Pharaohs from the hieroglyphics and drawings on the tombs. We know what the soldiers' uniforms looked like, what musical instruments were played, and what utensils were used. As for the architecture, Trauner did a great piece of work. He is, without doubt, one of the greatest scene designers in the world. We tried to reproduce Trauner's visual conceptions exactly.

CAHIERS: *Did that French Egyptologist see what you shot each day?*
HAWKS: He saw some of the rushes, I think. He was very much interested in some of the schemes we concocted for moving and transporting the blocks of stone. According to him, it was quite possible the Egyptians had thought of the same stratagems. For example, we were in agreement about the use of a ramp to get the stones to the summit, and the subsequent dismantling of the ramp once it was no longer needed. The method by which stones are raised from the ground and lowered onto the boat in the film is our invention. So is the way the pyramid is sealed after its construction. The scholars were quite intrigued. We employed a hydraulic process which is quite modern, but instead of water or oil, we used sand. Thus, we had a huge stone rest upon enormous wooden pilings. Each pile was sunk in a hole, and each hole was filled with sand. For each block of rock to fall into place it was necessary merely to open a small hole which allowed the sand to run out. As the sand did so, the huge block settled down slowly into its final position. This is probably the method the Egyptians used. We don't know for sure.

CAHIERS: *Then you have tried to make a realistic film?*
HAWKS: As realistic as possible, but that didn't stop us from using camels, even though very few camels were in Egypt at the time of our story. Our justification, shaky on purely historical grounds, was that

camels did seem integral to our image of Egypt. There were many other things we could only guess about. That's why we had the workers be free at the start of the pyramid and slaves at the end. We reasoned that the employment of 10,000 men on a pyramid for 30 years would drain the country economically and that after the first few years of exaltation, discontent would smolder into collective rage and the workers would have to be enslaved to make them continue. This thesis is an integral part of our film.

CAHIERS: *You ordinarily avoid stories with a long time span, and the notion of continuity plays a great role in almost all your films. Were you bothered by the fact that this story extended over thirty years?*
HAWKS: Bothered, no, but handicapped. It was difficult to devise a story that lasted thirty years while maintaining an acceptable continuity.

CAHIERS: *What have you concluded from your experience with CinemaScope?*
HAWKS: We have spent a lifetime learning how to compel the public to concentrate on one single thing. Now we have something that works in exactly the opposite way, and I don't like it very much. I like CinemaScope for a picture such as *The Land of the Pharaohs*, where it can show things impossible otherwise, but I don't like it at all for the average story. Contrary to what some think, it is easier to shoot in CinemaScope—you don't have to bother about what you should show—everything's on the screen. I find that a bit clumsy. Above all, in a motion picture, is the story. You cannot shoot a scene as quickly in CinemaScope, because if you develop a situation quickly, the characters jump all over the wide screen—which in a way makes them invisible. Thus you lose speed as a means of exciting or augmenting a scene's dramatic tension. You have to proceed differently. What you lose on the dramatic plane, however, you gain on the visual plane. The result can be very pleasing to the eye. You have to decide what seems best. Have you seen a film entitled *The Tall Men* with Gable?

CAHIERS: *No, not yet.*
HAWKS: My brother produced it. It's *Red River*, but in color and in CinemaScope, and it's a very pleasant film to watch. It's not a great film, but a good film. It made me regret not having CinemaScope when I

made *Red River*. John Ford and I made some anamorphic attempts around 1926, but we didn't care for the results. I always think that the artist who paints a scene in a certain manner must, in changing his manner, change his scene.

CAHIERS: *And Africa?*
HAWKS: For this film we must use portable cameras. For certain scenes even hand-held cameras; the Cinemascope gear would be too difficult.

CAHIERS: *Will this be your next film?*
HAWKS: I don't really know. We can start shooting, the scenario is finished, but I must make another film before; we won't go down into Africa before next September.

CAHIERS: *Could you tell us a little about this other film?*
HAWKS: It's difficult, we are only beginning to work on it. I can't tell you very much, because we haven't even decided on the main plot line. I don't know what form it is going to take. I don't even know what genre of film it will be. Its point of departure is a true incident that I've heard about, but it might never become a film. It depends.

CAHIERS: *All your films are based on events which tend to show man in action, his effort and struggle. Even considering the wide variety of your projects, these themes keep recurring in almost all your films. Do you think this is so?*
HAWKS: That may be true, but I am not really aware of it. I make movies on subjects that interest me: That could be automobile racing, airplanes, a western or a comedy, but the best drama for me is the one which shows a man in danger. There is no action when there is no danger. It follows that if you achieve real action, there must be danger. To live or to die! What drama is greater? Therefore I have probably chosen this direction because I have gradually come to believe that it matters more than anything else. It's very easy to make a movie knowing that everyone will love it, but that doesn't count for much. What one should do, what one must do, is try to anticipate what the public is going to like. I don't think that these people are producers; they make a

picture because somebody makes a picture that is successful, so they make one like it, you know?

CAHIERS: *Yes, too many films exist only as imitations of others.*
HAWKS: That's true. We made *Scarface* because the violence of this particular era was interesting. *Scarface* is still being copied—and hence still lives. There were fifteen murders in *Scarface*, and people said I was crazy to have so many. But I knew that was the story: violence made the story. Also, in practice, all the gangster movies that have followed *Scarface* only reiterated the same material. Similarly, when I made *Red River*, I thought an adult western could be made for mature audiences, and now everyone is making "intelligent" westerns. And a film like *Twentieth Century* . . . have you seen *Twentieth Century*?

CAHIERS: *Hélas non!*
HAWKS: It was the first time the dramatic leads, instead of secondary comics, played for laughs. I mean we got the fun out of John Barrymore and Carole Lombard. It was two or three years ahead of its time.

CAHIERS: *We think that a film like* Monkey Business *has renewed American comedy, and is undoubtedly more ambitious than it seems . . .*
HAWKS: Oh, probably, yes. Because of its general theme: the laughs are born out of the inhibitions that restrict each of us and are here abruptly removed by rejuvenation. It was a good story. Perhaps we pushed the point a bit too far for the public. From this point of view, it is less amusing than *Male War Bride* or *Bringing Up Baby*. *Monkey Business* went too far, became too fanciful and not funny enough: this is my opinion.

CAHIERS: *And* Gentlemen Prefer Blondes?
HAWKS: Oh, that was just . . . fun! In other movies, you have two men who go out looking for pretty girls to have fun with. We pulled a switch by taking two girls who went out looking for men to amuse them: a perfectly modern story. It delighted me. It was funny. The two girls, Jane Russell and Marilyn Monroe, were so good together that any time I had trouble figuring out any business, I simply had them walk back

and forth, and the audiences adored it. I had a staircase built so that they could go up and down, and since they are well built . . . This type of movie lets you sleep at night without a care in the world; five or six weeks were all we needed to shoot the musical numbers, the dances and the rest.

CAHIERS: *What period of work do you prefer? Script, shooting, editing?*
HAWKS: I hate the editing.

CAHIERS: *But you do the editing of your films?*
HAWKS: Oh, yes! Simultaneously with the shooting, if possible. When I started out in this profession, the producers were all afraid that I made a film too short because I didn't give them enough film for editing. And I said: "I don't want you to make the movie in the cutting room, I want to make it myself on the set, and if that doesn't suit you, too bad." That's not to say that editing isn't a chore, particularly when you haven't done a good job with the shooting. Editing is a horror for me because I look at my work for a second time and say that's pretty bad, and that, and also that— The difficult work is the preparation: finding the story, deciding how to tell it, what to show and what not to show. Once you begin shooting you see everything in the best light, develop certain details, and improve the whole. I never follow a script literally and I don't hesitate to change a script completely if I see a chance to do something interesting. I like to work on the scenarios. Some of my best movies were written in very little time. *Scarface* took only eleven days, story and scenario.

CAHIERS: *Does that include the dialogues?*
HAWKS: Everything. The whole thing took eleven days. I know because I paid the writers who worked for me by the day.

CAHIERS: *Who gave you the material, the basic facts?*
HAWKS: The facts came from several reporters in Chicago, many books, and magazine articles. The outline was done by Ben Hecht. He didn't have to do any research. All he had to do was ask me about this or that detail, and I would rattle off the information because I had read a lot on the subject. For example, I don't know if you recall George Raft flipping a

"nickel" in his hand? There had actually been a large number of murders in Chicago, where, as a mark of disrespect, the killer stuck a nickel into the hand of the corpse. Raft's character being that of a killer, he always had a coin in his hand. We also exploited another little known fact: The papers that published the photos of a murder indicated "X marks the spot where the body was found." So we designed fifteen or twenty scenes around the X, finding all sorts of ways to use the X when a murder occurred.

CAHIERS: *Each time someone was killed, there was an X?*
HAWKS: Yes. X.

CAHIERS: *Did that have something to do with the scar on Muni's face?*
HAWKS: Yes. Once you start off on that path, why not go all the way? Do you remember the scene in which Boris Karloff is bowling? As he lets the ball go, he's hit; the pins all go down. An X for a strike is marked on the scorecard.

CAHIERS: *And the cloud in* Red River, *was it intentional or accidental?*
HAWKS: We saw it coming just as Wayne began reading the prayer over the grave. We told him to hurry his reading so that we could catch it at the right moment. This was a case of seizing an opportunity as it presented itself. I don't think we would have held up the scene to wait for a cloud.

CAHIERS: *You were the producer of* The Thing *without getting credit as a director, but you undoubtedly supervised the production very closely.*
HAWKS: Oh, yes. The direction was handled by my editor, but I was on the set for all the important scenes. It was a very pleasant assignment. We wrote the script in four and a half days. I had read the story in Germany, in Heidelberg, where we shot *Male War Bride*. We only used four pages from it. I bought the rights and hired two good screenwriters. The story interested me because I thought it was an adult treatment of an often infantile subject.

CAHIERS: *Many critics have complained about the big differences that existed between the Hemingway story* To Have and Have Not *and the film you shot from it. Why did you change it so much?*

HAWKS: Hemingway and I are good friends, but whenever I tried to per-
suade Hemingway to write for the movies, Hemingway insisted that he
could be a good writer of books, but he didn't know whether he could
be a good writer of movies. Once when Hemingway and I were hunting
together, I told him that I could take his worst story and make a movie
out of it. Hemingway asked me what was his worst story. *"To Have and
Have Not,"* I said. Hemingway explained that he had written the story in
one sitting when he needed money, and that I couldn't make a movie
out of it. I said I'd try, and while we hunted, we discussed it. We decided
that the best way to tell the story was not to show the hero growing old,
but show how he had met the girl, and, in short, show everything that
had happened before the beginning of the novel. After four or five days
of discussion I left. Faulkner and Jules Furthman then wrote a script
incorporating the ideas Hemingway and I had evolved on our hunting
trip. In fact, there was enough material left over for another movie
(Michael Curtiz' *The Breaking Point*) which was pretty good.

CAHIERS: *Your career has been divided equally between adventure films
and comedies. The adventure films seemed optimistic and the comedies
pessimistic, but there always seemed a lesson to be drawn from the humor
in both genres. Are you more interested in the mixture of genres within your
subject or in the clash of genres?*
HAWKS: Perhaps I can best answer in the following manner. Life is
very simple for most people. It becomes so routine that everybody
wants to escape his environment. Adventure stories reveal how people
behave in the face of death—what they do, say, feel, and even think. I
have always liked the scene in *Only Angels Have Wings* in which a man
says "I feel funny," and his best friend says "your neck is broken," and
the injured man then says "I have always wondered how I would die if
I knew I was going to die. I would rather you didn't watch me." And the
friend goes out and stands in the rain. I have personally encountered this
experience, and the public found it very convincing.

But a comedy is virtually the same as an adventure story. The difference is in the situation—dangerous in an adventure story, embarrassing
in a comedy. But in both we observe our fellow beings in unusual situations. You merely emphasize the dramatic or the comical aspects of the
hero's reactions. Sometimes you can mix them up a bit. My serious

pictures usually have their comic sides. You've seen *The Big Sky*? You remember the scene where they amputate Kirk Douglas' finger; it was really funny. I had already wanted to do that scene in *Red River*, but John Wayne had said that I was crazy to want such a scene played for comedy. I said okay, I would do it in my next picture instead. When Wayne saw it, he phoned me and said he'd do whatever I wanted to in our next picture together.

It's possible to do comedy scenes even at very tragic moments. I once told a Spaniard I was thinking of doing Don Quixote with Cary Grant and Cantinflas, and the Spaniard said it was impossible to make a comedy out of a tragedy. I asked the Spaniard to tell me the story of *Don Quixote*, and after the Spaniard had done so, I said, "You've just told me the story of three of Chaplin's best pictures." He looked at me and said, "You're right. Let's go make a comedy." And that's pretty much the way I see it. The only difference between comedy and tragedy is the point of view. That's the only way I know how to answer your question.

CAHIERS: *The question has been answered.*

HAWKS: You know the story of *The African Queen*? I turned down an invitation to direct it because I couldn't see any humor in the situation. It pleased me to see how they made it a comedy. There were some silly things in it, but it went. Whenever I hear a story my first thought is how to make it into a comedy, and I think of how to make it into a drama only as a last resort. Do you remember the story about the man who wanted to commit suicide and stayed on a window ledge—*Fourteen Hours*? They wanted me to do it, and I said no. "Why not?" they asked me. "It's a great story." I told them I didn't like suicides, and I told my friend Henry Hathaway that I didn't like the film he had directed. The public didn't like it either, and Zanuck told me I had been right. I told Zanuck: "I might have done it if it had been Cary Grant getting from the bedroom of a woman whose husband had come back unexpectedly and after he was found on the ledge he pretended he was contemplating suicide." Zanuck asked me if I wanted to start on that one the next day.

CAHIERS: *You're not interested in abnormal characters?*

HAWKS: Sometimes I get interested in the encounter of a normal person and an abnormal person. Almost all my caprices, my manias (like the way I am playing with key chain while I talk to you), I like to think that these are abnormal things. To see the difference in the way of thinking makes good scenes, but to tell a long story about a nut isn't easy. Besides, I don't like theoretical situations. I like stories like *Viva Villa!* which I wrote and half of which I directed. The Villa in that film, like the Villa in real life, was a quite bizarre man. So was Scarface. Ben Hecht agreed to write *Scarface* only after I told him that I wanted to make the Capone-like character a Caesar Borgia and Capone's sister like Lucretia Borgia. This analogy permeates that script, and every intelligent person senses something unusual, something that can't be brought out into the open, but affects all the scenes.

Pancho Villa had a very complex personality—that's what made him interesting—but these subjects are rare. Fox wanted me to do Zapata, but the script was all wrong about the character. Zapata was the worst murderer Mexico had ever seen. Had Fox been willing to tell the true story of Zapata, I would have been interested. But they made a sort of Santa Claus of him and had him riding around the country giving presents to poor peons.

CAHIERS: *In short, you're guided in your work by an intentional reaction to what is going on around you.*
HAWKS: Exactly. I've already said that it's easy, when one sees crowds rushing off to see a movie, to make another movie almost exactly like it. What is more fun is trying something new, and hoping it will work. That's how I hit upon the tempo of my movies. I made a film called *His Girl Friday* in which the characters spoke so fast that the characters kept stepping on each other's lines. The public liked it. Moreover, the tempo in *Scarface* was faster than usual in that period. I generally work with a faster tempo than that of most of my colleagues. It seems more natural to me, less forced. I personally speak slowly, but people generally talk, talk, talk without even waiting for other people to finish. Also, if a scene is a bit weak, the more rapidly you shoot it, the better it will be on the screen. Moreover, if the tempo is fast you can emphasize a point by slowing the rhythm. Similarly, when you have a scene with two characters, don't always use a close-up. When you use close-ups sparingly, the public realizes that they are important. I hate movies which, without any reason, are composed completely of close-ups. I don't like them. I don't want to say that they're necessarily bad movies, but I don't like that particular style of film-making.

CAHIERS: *Have any particular directors influenced you?*

HAWKS: In the beginning, I was very much impressed by Murnau's *Sunrise*, particularly for its camera movements. I once made a film in this style—*Paid to Love*—with a great many camera effects, but I have never used such trickery since that time. I try to tell a story as simply as possible with the camera at eye level. Since I had directed *Paid to Love* at a time when the public was easy to impress, the result was well-received. But I don't believe the future is in that direction. The other directors who have most impressed me are John Ford, Ernst Lubitsch, and Leo McCarey; these are the men who, in my opinion, have been the best.

CAHIERS: *What do you think of the young directors: Nicholas Ray, for example.*

HAWKS: I've seen several of Ray's films, and find them very promising. He is one of those directors of whom it is said: "I will go see everything he does because he is a good story-teller." But the actual situation in Hollywood is hard for young directors. They don't get the freedom we older directors enjoy. Young directors are told what to direct, where to shoot it, on what day to be finished. It's hard. However, the more successful a young director's movies, the more freedom he will be given.

CAHIERS: *What would be your ideal film, that which you would make for yourself alone?*

HAWKS: I have no desire to make a picture for myself. There has never been a picture so good the public didn't care to see it. I like to make comedies because I like to go into a theater and hear people laughing—the more laughter the better I feel. I have no desire to make a picture for my own pleasure. Fortunately, I have found that what I like, most people also like, so I only have to let myself go and do what interests me.

I am actually thinking about a subject for a movie. For four-fifths of the picture there is only one person on the screen. A girl, cut off from all contact with humanity by avalanches and melting ice, bears a child and cares for it for three months before she is found.

CAHIERS: *Do you always work on your scripts?*

HAWKS: From the beginning and for all my films.

CAHIERS: *If you had to choose three or four of your films to be saved, which ones would they be?*

HAWKS: For sentimental reasons, my first talking film, *Dawn Patrol*, then *Scarface* and probably *Twentieth Century*; but . . . there are many others I would like to save. *Dawn Patrol* was very interesting because it was my first experience with sound. I had not worked since the coming of sound because the producers didn't know if I could work with dialogue. I had never had any theatrical experience. I myself wrote almost the entire scenario, and during the shooting, everyone kept telling me: "It's not good dialogue, it's not dramatic. Everything is flat. Everything you're doing is going to be flat." No one liked the film because none of the characters cried or screamed. When the editing was finished, the studio had so little confidence in the movie, they dispensed with the premiere. They preferred to release it discreetly, and then it turned out to be the best film of the year, and then they got into the habit of screening it for other directors and saying: "That's what good dialogue is like."

Interview with Howard Hawks

PETER BOGDANOVICH/1962

1926 The Road to Glory

HH: I was not in a very good frame of mind and wrote a complete tragedy. I was told it is not what people like to see, so I switched with my next picture.

1926 Fig Leaves

PB: *This opened in the Garden of Eden and moved into a modern story of an Adam and an Eve.*

HH: I just tried to say people haven't changed much and that they're the same today.

1927 Paid to Love

PB: *A comi-tragic love story, set in a mythical country, about a Parisian night-club performer and a Prince who falls in love with her.*

HH: It has no relation to my work. That happened to be a story that I didn't work on and had no sympathy with. I didn't care to do it but was forced to under contract.

PB: Paid to Love *had a lot of trick work.*

HH: It was made right after Murnau's *Sunrise*, which introduced German camera trick-work to Hollywood. I was beginning to direct and

From *Movie*, 5 November 1962. Reprinted by permission of *Movie* and Peter Bogdanovich. Originally published as "The Cinema of Howard Hawks," by Peter Bogdanovich, Museum of Modern Art—Doubleday, 1962. The unabridged interview appears in *Who the Devil Made It*, by Peter Bogdanovich, Alfred A. Knopf, 1997; Ballantine, 1998.

was feeling around. They liked it; I didn't. I don't like tricks. I only tried that one time. I've always been rather mechanically minded so I tried a whole lot of mechanical things, and then gave them up completely— most of the time my camera stays on eye level now. Once in a while, I'll move the camera as if a man were walking and seeing something. And it pulls back or it moves in for emphasis when you don't want to make a cut. But, outside of that, I just use the simplest camera in the world.

1928 A Girl in Every Port
HH: This was the beginning of a relationship I have used in a number of pictures. It's really a love story between two men.

1928 Fazil
HH: I' m not very fond of the picture. It was a story about a sheik and a modern French girl. It was a contractual thing, someone else's story, and I just shot it.

1928 The Air Circus
HH: Very little story to it. It was just about how a boy learns to fly. I directed it alone and then they wanted to incorporate some talking sequences and they brought a man out who they said was an authority on dialogue and he turned out to be a burlesque comedian. I read the stuff he wrote and said, "But nobody talks that way." I said, if you want to do it go ahead, but I won't have anything to do with it. So Lew Seiler came in and did the mawkish dialogue stuff. And they generally botched up the picture.

1930 The Dawn Patrol
HH: It was all for real, even the forced landings. There were a number of scenes where I piloted the air plane with the camera up front. That airplane footage has been used in a number of other pictures: *The Last Flight*, for instance, and the remake of *The Dawn Patrol* with Errol Flynn.

PB: *In* Dawn Patrol, Road to Glory *and* Twentieth Century, *you end the picture as it began.*
HH: Yes, it's a form of story telling that I think is very fine. You create a character who has a problem and another man comes along and takes

over his problem and in the finish he's spent himself and then another man has the problem and it keeps on going. It's like a great mechanic who builds racing cars and one man is killed and then another man is killed and you keep on going—you're not going to stop because of that.

1931 The Criminal Code

PB: *Could you say something about the making of* The Criminal Code?

HH: *The Criminal Code* was a play that had merit but had failed on Broadway because of the ending. I got together with ten convicts and said, "How should this end?" and they told me in no uncertain terms. They had a great deal to do with the formation of many scenes because it was built more or less on the convicts' code of not squealing. I used ex-convicts as extra men all through the picture to give it authenticity. Of course, Huston was one of the greatest actors we've ever had. His character was based on a district attorney we had here in California who was finally tried and sentenced to prison, and they put him in the prison hospital to protect him because the place was full of men he had sent there. Finally, he said, "I can't take this any longer. I want to go out into the yard." He went out into the yard, and the scene we did in the picture was just what he did. Things like his being shaved by a man he had sent up for cutting somebody's throat were all true. It was the first time that I discovered almost any tragedy can also be very amusing. In *The Big Sky* we made a comedy scene of Kirk Douglas getting his finger cut off and cauterized and it was very funny.

PB: *How did the scene in which Phillips Holmes learns of his mother's death evolve. Was it in the script originally?*

HH: I don't think so. It's just that when I reach a scene that is too sentimental, I try to turn it and keep it from being sentimental. In *Only Angels Have Wings*, I had a man talking to his friend who's been in an airplane wreck just say to him, "Your neck is broken, kid." Just a flat statement; just try to keep things from becoming mawkish. Play against it completely.

1932 The Crowd Roars

PB: *The racers in* The Crowd Roars *seem to have a total disregard for the dangers of their profession.*

HH: They fall into the same category as the men in *Hatari!* catching wild animals in Africa. Every day is dangerous, terribly exciting, and they exist on that. They enjoy it and also they greatly understate their feats. After we left Africa, one of the men had a fight with a lion; he was terribly clawed and his reporting of it to me was the greatest piece of understatement I have ever known. He simply told me about the black boy who came up and took his gun and held it against the lion and killed the lion. And he said he was glad that he had trained him well.

1932 Scarface (Shame of the Nation)
PB: *How did* Scarface *come to be made?*
HH: *Scarface* was really the story of Al Capone. When I asked Ben Hecht to write it, he said, "Oh, we don't want to do a gangster picture." And I said, "Well, this is a little different. I would like to do the Capone family as if they were the Borgias set down in Chicago." And he said, "We'll start tomorrow." We took eleven days to write the story and dialogue. We were influenced a good deal by the incestuous elements in the story of the Borgias. We made the brother–sister relationship clearly incestuous. But the censors misunderstood our intention and objected to it because they thought the relationship between them was too beautiful to be attributed to a gangster. We had a scene in which Muni told his sister that he loved her, and we couldn't play it in full light. We wound up playing it in silhouette against a curtain with the light coming from outside. It was a little bit too intimate to show faces—you wouldn't dare take a chance.

PB: *How did Raft's coin flipping originate?*
HH: There were two or three killings in Chicago where in the fist of the victim they found a nickel. That was a mark of contempt. When we cast Raft in this picture, a coin seemed to be a good thing to use as a mark for the man. It was his first picture and it also helped him fill in things. It became his trade mark.

1932 Tiger Shark
PB: *In* Tiger Shark *you use the idea of a man not being admitted to heaven unless he is whole, and you use it again in* The Big Sky. *How did this develop?*

HH: I knew a man who believed that. He had lost a couple of fingers and he had saved the fingers because he believed that when he died he would have to go to heaven whole. It amused me and I used it several times.

PB: *How did the Robinson character develop?*
HH: The character was written as a very sedate, solid citizen. It was duller than hell so I stopped on the first day and said to Robinson, "We're really going to make a horrible thing here." And I told him about a man I knew that talked a great deal and very fast, and covered up his shyness by doing it. I said, "If you have enough nerve to try it I'll give you as much help as I can." So we changed a morose, silent, single-minded man into a very volatile character, who could also be pretty tough.

1933 Today We Live

HH: The picture was written just as it had appeared in the *Post*. It was the story of some men in England during the First World War. It was again our little love theme about two boys who get together. Well, Metro didn't have a picture for Joan Crawford, so a week before we started they announced to me that she was in the picture. We had to change it considerably from what we had started with; to make it worse, she tried to talk like the men. It didn't come out the same.

1934 Twentieth Century

PB: *The extremely fast pace of your comedies, like* Twentieth Century, *is not achieved through cutting, is it?*
HH: No, it isn't done with cutting. It's done by deliberately writing dialogue like real conversation—you're liable to interrupt me and I'm liable to interrupt you—so you write in such a way that you can overlap the dialogue but not lose anything. It's just a trick. It's a trick getting people to do it too—it takes about two or three days to get them accustomed to it and then they're off. You must allow for it in your dialogue with just the addition of a few little words in front. "Well, I think—" that's all you need, and then say what you have to say. All you want to do is to hear the essential things; if you don't hear those in a scene, you're lost. You have to tell the sound man what lines he must hear

and he must let you know if he does. This also allows you to do throw-aways—it keeps an actor from hitting a line too hard. Actually we started to use speed in *Scarface* and that had probably a twenty percent faster tempo than anything that had been made to date. And, of course, if I have a scene today that I don't think is very interesting the quicker I can play it the better off I am.

PB: *How did you arrive at your techniques of pacing?*

HH: As far as speed is concerned, I was trained in the old two-reel comedy school where all we were after was speed. People seemed to like it, so I thought why not play all comedy fast. The only other picture that was supposed to be fast was *The Front Page*; I said it had a false sense of speed. In *Dawn Patrol* we underplayed, dispensing with the emoting and ham-acting which was habitual up until then. Conse-quently I had one communication after another from the front office telling me I was not taking advantages of my scenes, but I was simply playing them a different way, you see.

PB: *The scene in the train compartment, when she tried to kick him, looks particularly impromptu. Was it?*

HH: That was the first scene we shot in the picture. Lombard had never done that kind of comedy before, but I cast her because I'd seen her at a party with a couple of drinks in her and she was hilarious and uninhibited and just what the part needed. But when she came on the set she was emoting all over the place. She was trying very hard, but it was just dreadful. Barrymore was very patient and we tried it a few times but she was so stilted and stiff. Then I said to her, "Come on, let's take a walk," and we went outside, and I asked her how much money she was getting for the picture. She told me and I said, "What would you say if I told you that you'd earned your whole salary this morning and didn't have to act any more?" And she was stunned. So I said, "Now forget about the scene; what would you do if someone said such and such to you?" And she said, "I'd kick him in the stomach." And I said, "Well, he said something like that to you, why don't you kick him?" And she said, "Are you kidding?" And I said, "No." So we went back on the set and I gave her some time to think it over and then we tried that scene and we did one take and that was it. And afterwards,

Barrymore said, "That was fabulous!" And she burst into tears and ran off the set. She never began a picture that she didn't send me a telegram saying, "I'm gonna start kicking him."

1935 Barbary Coast

HH: I don't remember the story too well except it was about a girl who arrived in the San Francisco Bay, in a ship that came round the Horn, only to discover that the man she was going to marry had been shot in a gambling game. I didn't like the picture much. I thought it was a contrived thing, more or less done to order, and a lot of trouble. As Ben Hecht said, "Miriam Hopkins came to the Barbary Coast and wandered around like a confused Goldwyn Girl."

1936 The Road to Glory

PB: *The men in your war and adventure films never question the impossible conditions under which they work.*

HH: They know there's nothing to be gained by it. It's part of the game. They take planes up and test them; they take cars out and test them. And having been schooled to the Army, they accept commands, no matter what the command. And that's what makes an army function. It's just a calm acceptance of a fact. In *Only Angels Have Wings*, after Joe dies, Cary Grant says, "He just wasn't good enough." Well, that's the only thing that keeps people going. They just have to say, "Joe wasn't good enough, and I'm better than Joe, so I go ahead and do it." And they find out they're not any better than Joe, but then it's too late, you see.

1938 Bringing Up Baby

PB: *In* Bringing Up Baby *and several of your other comedies, aren't you expressing your annoyance with scientists and academicians?*

HH: No, if you're going to do a picture, the fun of it is to do a characterization, something very close to caricature. And the moment you caricature it, you're accused of disliking it. But really you're just picking things that make a caricature—the attitude of newspapermen, the attitude of scientists—and it's bound to make people think you're poking fun at them. That's why a scientist or inventor or a man who's in a location that's interesting is fun to do. But it's a form of caricature work

that you're doing and we do it with Westerns, we do it with every picture. If you don't do a caricature, you don't have a character.

PB: *By the end of* Bringing Up Baby, *hasn't Grant abandoned his scientific
life?*
HH: Well, let's say he's mixed it. He had an awfully good time and if
you had to choose between the two girls, you'd certainly choose
Hepburn. You see, you start off, as I say, with a complete caricature of
the man and then reduce it to give him a feeling of normality because
he certainly wouldn't have had fun going through life the other way,
would he? He becomes more normal as the picture goes along, just by
his association with the girl. Grant said, "I'm kind of dropping my characterization." I said, "No, she's having some influence on you. You're
getting a little normal."

PB: *Is Hepburn then the normal one in the picture?*
HH: I think the picture had a great fault and I learned an awful lot
from it. There were no normal people in it. Everyone you met was a
screwball. Since that time I have learned my lesson and I don't intend
ever again to make everybody crazy. If the gardener had been normal, if
the sheriff had been just a perplexed man from the country—but as it
was they were all way off centre. And it was a mistake that I realized
after I made it and I haven't made it since. Harold Lloyd told me
though that it was the best constructed comedy he had ever seen and
that to him it was a classic.

PB: *It is much darker in terms of lighting than most comedies.*
HH: They're inclined to start a comedy with a very funny main title
and animated stuff that seems to say, "Now we're gonna be funny." In
Hatari! we started almost with tragedy and not until they discovered
the man was going to live did it become funny. It crept up on people;
they weren't told to laugh. And the more dangerous and the more
exciting, the easier it is to get a laugh.

PB: *There seems to be a very dark, though nonetheless hilarious,
quality to the night scenes when Grant and Hepburn are looking for the
bone.*

HH: Well, it was a complete tragedy to Cary, wasn't it? You see, you get a certain dignity with a scientist. Now if he gets down on all fours and scrambles for something, he becomes funny. And that's the thing Chaplin was always so good at. And it goes way back to the scene in *A Girl in Every Port* where they push policemen into the water. They didn't like cops. They weren't vicious or mean about it, but policemen interfered with their fun and so they disposed of them. The more dignified somebody is—Katie Hepburn in *Bringing Up Baby*—losing the back of her dress became funny because she was dressed up and superior to the whole situation and she became ridiculous.

1939 Only Angels Have Wings

PB: *In* Only Angels Have Wings *you established for the first time the theme for your love scene, variations of which you use in* To Have and Have Not, Red River, The Big Sleep, Rio Bravo, *and* Hatari! *You rather like a relationship where the woman is the aggressive one.*

HH: Yes, it was first used in *Only Angels Have Wings*, and it was in *To Have and Have Not* and *The Big Sleep,* and very definitely in *Rio Bravo* and *Hatari!* I do that on purpose every once in a while because it amuses people, especially the people I like. How many times are you going to use that? Just as often as they'll laugh at it. It's just a method of thinking and it becomes attractive because they don't act like a heroine or a hero. They're just kind of normal people. I call it honesty and it allows you to make a scene that's a little different. Hitchcock tried it in *North by Northwest.*

PB: *Were a lot of the incidents in* Only Angels Have Wings *things that you had heard about or experienced?*

HH: Yes, every character was taken from life. Barthelmess was a man I saw jump out of an airplane, leaving another behind. The linking of those incidents was done fictionally but actually the character of Jean Arthur and her relation to Cary Grant was a true story, based on fact. The bird coming through the windshield was a fact, and the place was real—a little Grace Line port in South America.

PB: *The characters in your films make a point of ignoring tragedy, as in* Only Angels *where Grant says "Who's Joe—" after Joe is killed.*

HH: Well, that's a simple thing. You take two viewpoints. One is Josef von Sternberg's. Somebody had a bright idea that if the two of us made a picture together we could make a super-picture, but I said it's utterly ridiculous. You can start the two of us off on the same story and you'd never recognize it as we'd change the characters. He blows up a little bit of a thing (and at that time he was one of the greatest directors we had) into a great big situation, and I take a great big situation and play it way down. So we'd have exactly opposite viewpoints. And I think you get a sigh of relief from an audience when they see a familiar old situation come up and you don't bore them with it—just hit it and go on. But, anyway, the men that I show and choose to show, they don't dramatize those things, they underplay them, which is normal with that type of man. The average movie talks too much; you have to make your scenes and plant them and then let the audience do a little work so they become part of it. Any script that *reads* well is no good. If you have to read it three times to understand it, you've got a chance of getting a movie out of it. But if it starts out saying, "He looks at her and the yearning of ten years shows in his eyes . . ." I've never found an actor who can do that.

PB: *Also in* Only Angels, *as in many of your films, there is the theme of professionalism. You have strong feelings about this, don't you?*
HH: And the men in it have too. It's their job, they're supposed to do it. You get a stunt team in acrobatics in the air—if one of them is no good, then they're all in trouble. If someone loses his nerve catching animals, then the whole bunch can be in trouble. I have a complete tape of all the sound of the British bombing the three dams that really changed the course of the war. And they got out there early in the morning and the leader said, "You fellows stick around and I'll take a run through and see if they've got any cables stretched." And then one of them said, "I'll buy you a beer when you get back." And the man says, "There's no cable, you can go right on through." He says, "I'll go a little off to one side and a little ahead of you and maybe I can draw their fire." And they got every other one through—first, third, fifth— but second, fourth and sixth were shot down. I was going to film that. They had a complete record of the entire conversation; Mr Churchill sent it to me. And these were kids—twenty-one was the oldest—but

they were fifty or sixty in their training. And that's the attitude they have. It isn't anything I've invented. It's just something I've seen and it interests me and so I use it.

1940 His Girl Friday

HH: I was going to prove to somebody one night that *The Front Page* had the finest modern dialogue that had been written, and I asked a girl to read Hildy's part and I read the editor and I stopped and I said, "Hell, it's better between a girl and a man than between two men," and I called Ben Hecht and I said, "What would you think of changing it so that Hildy is a girl?" And he said, "I think it's a great idea," and he came out and we did it.

1940 The Outlaw

HH: The original story I heard in New Mexico was that Pat Garrett had blown the face off somebody and buried him as Billy the Kid and let Billy the Kid go—so we started from that and we wrote a story. I found Jane Russell and Jack Buetel and I thought it was just a little Western and I had my fun with it. But I had a chance to do *Sergeant York*, and I wanted to do that, and Hughes wanted to direct, so I said, "You go ahead and direct and finish it." I made the introduction of Billy the Kid and Doc Holliday on location, and then Hughes messed up the rest. I directed a couple of weeks of it. Probably a thousand or fifteen hundred feet of what I did remained in it.

1941 Sergeant York

HH: Huston and I wrote the script. We just kept ahead of shooting. We threw away the written script and did what Jesse Lasky told us about the real Sergeant York. Huston and I were very much in accord and it became very easy to tell the story simply.

PB: *You particularly enjoyed making this film?*
HH: Especially because Lasky gave me my first good job and he was broke at the time and after I talked to him, I called up Gary Cooper and I said, "Coop, didn't Lasky give you your first job?" and he said, "Yes," and I said, "Well, he's broke and he needs a shave and he's got a story and I think we could do it and I don't think he would hurt us." So

Coop came over and we talked about everything but the story—he talked about a new gun and finally I said, "Let's talk about the story," and he said, "What's the use of talking about it, we're going to do the damn thing, you know that." And I said, "Well, let's go over to Warners and make a deal, and if I say 'Isn't that right, Mr Cooper?' you say yes." So I said, "We'll do it if you let us alone—isn't that right, Mr Cooper?" "Yes." "If you come in, if you butt in on us, we'll be really hard to handle. Isn't that right, Mr Cooper?" He'd say, "Yes." So we made the deal and we made the film. And Lasky made two million out of it and we were terribly pleased to have helped somebody. And the funny thing about it was that it turned out to be a hell of a picture and Cooper got an Academy Award and we had no idea it was going to be anything like that. (*Hawks was nominated for an Oscar for his direction; it was the first and last time to date.*)

PB: *The ending of* Sergeant York *is actually quite tragic, in that a very religious man is rewarded for going against his beliefs. Did you want it to appear that way?*

HH: Well, it was based on the theory you are talking about. It was based on a man who actually was very religious; and so they told him to go out and do everything his religion said not to do, and he became a great hero doing it. So there was bound to be a good deal of confusion in his mind and actually it *was* a form of tragedy. I asked him hundreds of questions, as you are asking me questions, and he answered them. I asked him how he got religion. "I got it in the middle of the road," he said. So my visualization of that was a mule, getting hit by lightning in the middle of the road. They wrote a remarkable scene of how he got religion and I didn't believe it. I said if anyone talked to me like that, I wouldn't get religion. So we got some real people from Tennessee to sing, they got excited, and we brought him to a little meeting house, and while they were singing he got religion. But if you will notice, again, it's underplaying. If they want to believe it, fine, but you don't cram it down their throats. I went back down there after the picture was made to see how good a job I had done and I heard some people talking and one of them said, "I saw me a picture last night—it was about hill people and the fellow certainly knew what he was doing when he made that picture. He's got them to look just like hill people—they talk just like hill people." Well, I had some of those people to help me, and they would say a line and then the actors would say the line, and things changed, you see. One of the best things in the picture was the mother who didn't do much talking. The writers had given her a lot of great lines and I kept taking them away from her and finally I said, "I know what we're after—I want somebody who doesn't talk." "That I can understand," she said. But they're very childlike, those people, they're extremely backward—the little scenes in the store indicated that—so you are not treating a sophisticated man—he was bewildered. And we tried to show a bewildered man. I don't attempt to preach or prove anything—I just figure out what I think was in the man and tell it. His comment was interesting. He said, "I supplied the tree and Hawks put the leaves on it." I thought it was kind of a nice comment.

1944 To Have and Have Not

PB: *How did the Bacall character in* To Have and Have Not *develop?*

HH: We discovered that she was a little girl who, when she became insolent, became rather attractive. That was the only way you noticed her, because she could do it with a grin. So I said to Bogey, "We are going to try an interesting thing. You are about the most insolent man on the screen and I'm going to make a girl a little more insolent than you are." "Well," he said, "you're going to have a fat time doing that." And I said, "No, I've got a great advantage because I'm the director. I'll tell you just one thing: she's going to walk out on you in every scene." "You've won already." So as every scene ended, she walked out on him. It was a sex antagonism, that's what it was, and it made the scenes easy. But it wouldn't be any good with John Wayne, because he is not the insolent type. There's a place in *Hatari!* where the girl says, "I was chased by a bull once," and he says, "Are you sure it wasn't the other way around?" That's more like Bogey.

PB: To Have and Have Not *and* The Big Sleep *seem to me the two most perfect elaborations of the Bogart character, and the most complete. How do you feel about that?*

HH: Well, that's just taking advantage of what I think about Bogart. To me, they are rather like the same picture. He was extremely easy to work with, really underrated as an actor. My kind of actor, you know.

And the little queer things he did because he had a nerve cut in his upper lip—so his upper lip wouldn't smile—only his lower lip would smile. We seemed to understand one another and work very well together. Without his help I couldn't have done what I did with Bacall. The average leading man would have gotten sick and tired of the rehearsal and the fussing around. Not very many actors would sit around and wait while a girl steals a scene. But he fell in love with the girl and the girl with him, and that made it easy.

PB: To Have and Have Not *is basically a love story. You don't think much of the political intrigues in the picture, do you?*
HH: Oh, well, you notice how long it took us to fill in the other plot. As a matter of fact, the writer got terribly worried. He said, "I'm going to quit." I said, "Why?" He said, "Here we are four reels into the picture and you're afraid to tell the plot—will you go on and do these scenes!" I said, "I guess I've just been steering away from them because they're so dull." But we had to have a plot, you know, a secondary plot, but it was just an excuse for some scenes. Out of the wounded man we got a marvellous scene about one girl fainting, and the other girl fanning ether fumes on her. And lines of hers as when Bogart is carrying the fainted girl, she says, "You trying to guess her weight?" That goes way back to Dietrich—in *Morocco*, Sternberg made Dietrich come in and find Cooper with two native girls on his lap, and she kind of congratulated him— she didn't get angry at it. So Bacall is a warmer version of Dietrich. Dietrich knew it the moment she saw the picture. She said, "That's me, isn't it?" and I said, "Yeah."

1946 The Big Sleep
PB: *What does the title,* The Big Sleep, *refer to?*
HH: I don't know, probably death. It just sounds good. I never could figure the story out. I read it and was delighted by it. The scenario took eight days to write, and all we were trying to do was to make every scene entertain. We didn't know about the story. They asked me who killed such and such a man—I didn't know. They sent a wire to the author—he didn't know. They sent a wire to the scenario writer and he didn't know. But it didn't stop the picture from being very fast and very entertaining. Then, when the picture was getting ready to go to

New York, the publicity man said, "Howard, what will I tell them about this picture?" And I said, "Well, tell them it's kind of interesting because it's told from the point of view of the detective and there are no red herrings. And if anybody can follow the plot they have to follow what he is thinking." And I can't, and he can't, so an audience might be amused. The picture turned out to be very good from an audience standpoint. And it disarmed the critics because they were trying to be as smart as the fellow in the picture and they ended up being no smarter.

PB: *It is really kind of a parody of private eye pictures, isn't it, with all the girls falling for Bogart?*
HH: Oh, yeah, you're just having fun. The main idea was to try and make every scene fun to look at. A place where Bogey was to walk into a book store I said, "This is an awfully ordinary scene. Can't you think of something to do?" And he just pushed up his hat brim, put on glasses and got a little effeminate. The moment he did that, I said, "O.K. come on, we're off, I'll write some new dialogue when we're inside." But just going in that way made it fun. It was just two people a little bit bored. About eight months after we had finished it, they asked me to make some more scenes between Bogart and Bacall—they said they didn't have enough scenes of them together. It was during the racing season at Santa Anita and I had some horses out there and so I made them talk about riding a horse, and it ended with "It depends on who's in the saddle." And it was just that I was thinking about racing and I thought, well, I'll do a scene about a little love argument about racing.

PB: *So, again, the plot mattered very little to you.*
HH: It didn't matter at all. As I say, neither the author, the writer, nor myself knew who had killed whom. It was all what made a good scene. I can't follow it. I saw some of it on television last night, and it had me thoroughly confused, because I hadn't seen it in twenty years.

1948 Red River
PB: *In* Red River, *as well as in* The Big Sky, Hatari!, *and even in* A Girl in Every Port, *you have two strangers meet, have a fight, and then become the best of friends. How did you come upon this idea?*

HH: Oh, I don't know. Probably the best friend I ever had I ran off a race track through a fence before I met him, and then we met and became friends. And you are always more interested in an antagonist than somebody who's terribly nice to you. In *Red River*, Wayne admired Clift's spirit. It was done to try and show why there is a relationship between people.

PB: *There is a certain ambiguity in Wayne's character, isn't there? What was your opinion of his character?*

HH: Well, Wayne is a man who made a big mistake and lost the girl he was really in love with because of ambition and the great desire to have land of his own. Having made a mistake, it would make him all the more anxious to go through with his plans. Because a man who has made a great mistake to get somewhere is not going to stop at small things. He built up an empire, and it was falling to pieces. He warned them about what they were getting into and said there would be no quitting. And they quit on him. We were walking a tightrope in telling a story like that. Are you still going to like Wayne or not? Fortunately, we ended up with a good characterization and you did like Wayne. Let's say his motive was entirely self-centered. In contrast, Cary Grant in *Only Angels Have Wings* had no selfish motivation at all. He was doing a job for a man he liked—a man who was unable to do it himself—so it was pure friendship. He could look at the Dutchman and say, "I can't let this fellow get away with this;" so he said, "You're fired, you're through, because you want to quit."

PB: *You were criticized for not ending* Red River *with someone getting killed—either Wayne or Clift—but that would not have fitted in with your point of view, would it?*

HH: No, the premise of the scene, I think, is logical. If we overdid it a little bit or went too far, well, I didn't know any other way to end it. I certainly would have hated to kill one of them. It frustrates me to start killing people off for no reason at all. I did it in *Dawn Patrol*, but when I finished, I realized how close I'd come to messing the thing up, and I didn't want to monkey with that again. I'm interested in having people go and see the picture, and enjoy it.

1949 I Was a Male War Bride (You Can't Sleep Here)

PB: *What would you say* I Was a Male War Bride *was really about?*

HH: Oh, I don't know. Two people get married and red tape keeps them from sleeping together. There's a Polish version of the same story done dramatically, *The Eighth Day of the Week*, with one funny sequence in it, but basically it's a complete tragedy. Like that picture about the suicide, *Fourteen Hours*. I said the only way I would have done that was if the man had been Cary Grant and he'd been making love to this woman and her husband came in so he jumped onto the window ledge and pretended to be attempting suicide. After *War Bride*, Zanuck said, "I've got a great idea—you and Grant do *Charley's Aunt*" and I said, "We just did it." One of the good scenes in *War Bride* is where the brides marrying GIs had to say if they had any woman trouble or had they ever been pregnant, and it was a beautifully written scene, and Grant, being a man, was supposed to be embarrassed. And I said, "Try it the opposite way. Let the sergeant be embarrassed at having to ask you these things. Say, 'Oh, many times, Sergeant. Oh, I have a great deal of trouble.'" Then it became funny, and the other way, it wasn't. And that's the good thing about Grant. You say, "Cary, let's try it the opposite way. It will change your dialogue, but don't let it worry you. Say anything you think, and if you can't think of the right thing, I'll write it down for you." But he thinks of the right thing and we go ahead and do it. We have a scene in *Bringing Up Baby* where he's angry. I said, "Pretty dull. You get angry like Joe Doaks next door. Can't you think of somebody who gets angry and it's funny?" And then I remembered a man who practically whinnies like a horse when he's angry—so he did it.

1951 The Thing (From Another World)

PB: *Were you purposely criticizing scientists in* The Thing?

HH: Oh, no, it just worked out that way. You see we had to make it plausible—why they let the thing live. In order to make it plausible we turned them into heavies—it had to be an honest sort of dedication on their part. That was fun to do, taking a stab at science fiction. I bought the story; it was just four pages long, and we took about a week to write it. We had trouble the first two days finding a way of telling the story. Finally we got the idea of the reporter and we told it through his eyes.

1952 The Big Sky

PB: *Wasn't the end of* The Big Sky *intended to be tragic, in that Martin stays behind with the girl, not because he loves her, but because if he doesn't stay with her he will lose the friendship of Douglas, who actually does love her?*

HH: Yes, that's very much what we were trying to do there, but I don't think I did a good job of it. Oddly enough, I don't think there was any warmth in the relationship of those two people. I had planned it but it just didn't come off. And I think it is very much of a failure on my part in telling the story of friendship between two men. I look on Kirk as being one of our great heavies—every time he's played that kind of thing he's been awfully good. And when he attempts to be too pleasant or show friendship, it doesn't come off. I think he was the wrong person to put into that picture to make it really come off as I had planned.

1952 O. Henry's Full House

PB: *This episode was cut on some parts of its release.*

HH: I imagine it was cut because it wasn't really O. Henry. I started out just to make a comedy and got a long way from O. Henry. They probably didn't think it fit with the other episodes that had been made for the picture.

1952 Monkey Business

PB: *What are your feelings about* Monkey Business?

HH: I don't believe the premise of *Monkey Business* was really believable and for that reason the film was not as funny as it should have been. The episodes that directly concerned the monkey were unbelievable. The other episodes seemed to work out very well where you could accept the premise. But I think we got the audience started on the wrong foot. I don't think they believed a monkey could put those things together, so it became a little too much of a farce. Also the great trouble with the scenes where Ginger Rogers becomes adolescent was that they were completely repetitive. Cary Grant had already done it and he had the best of it because he had done it first—and his part was written better.

1953 Gentlemen Prefer Blondes

PB: *Don't you find it ironic that some people found Monroe and Russell sexy in* Gentlemen Prefer Blondes, *when you actually intended the opposite?*

HH: It's ironic. Actually to me they were very amusing and it was a complete caricature, a travesty on sex. It didn't have normal sex. Jane Russell was supposed to represent sanity and Marilyn played a girl who was solely concerned with marrying for money. She had her own little odd code and she lived by it. The child was the most mature one on board the ship, and I think he was a lot of fun. We purposely made the picture as loud and bright as we could, and completely vulgar in costumes and everything. No attempt at reality. We were doing a musical comedy, pure and simple.

1955 Land of the Pharaohs

PB: *Why do you like this least of your own films?*

HH: I don't know how a Pharaoh talks. And Faulkner didn't know. None of us knew. We thought it'd be an interesting story, the building of a pyramid, but then we had to have a plot, and we didn't really feel close to any of it.

PB: *Is the last line, "We have a long way to go," your comment on humanity?*

HH: Yes, on that phase of humanity. You see, the Pharaoh was a little too narrow, too one-sided a character. He had one belief and he stuck to it and you heard it too many times. I got a feeling we were doing repetitive scenes and it was awfully hard to deepen them because we didn't know how those Egyptians thought or what they said. All we knew about them was this strange desire to amass a fortune to be used in their second life, as they called it. So you don't know what to try for at all. You don't know whether to make the girl a little more evil or the Pharaoh a little more dominating. You kind of lose all sense of values. You don't know who somebody's for and if you don't have a rooting interest and you're not for somebody then you haven't got a picture.

PB: Land of the Pharaohs *is the only film you've made in CinemaScope. What do you think of the process?*

HH: I don't think that CinemaScope is a good medium. It's good only for showing great masses of movement. For other things, it's distracting, it's hard to focus attention, and it's very difficult to cut. Some people just go ahead and cut it and let people's eyes jump around and find what they want to find. It's very hard for an audience to focus—they have too much to look at—they can't see the whole thing. If you are going to cut to a close-up, you should have a man speaking in the same relative position on the screen. It's hard to form those compositions. I like the 1.85 to 1 ratio better than any other—the one we used for *Rio Bravo* and *Hatari!*—it gives you just a little more space on the sides. If the CinemaScope size had been any good, painters would have used it many years ago—and they've been at it a lot longer than we have.

1959 Rio Bravo

PB: *After* Pharaohs, *you waited three years before making* Rio Bravo. *Why?*

HH: Well, I just got to thinking of how we used to make pictures and how we were making them now, and I reviewed the making of a lot of pictures that I had liked. Today they want you to stick to a script and the easiest, simplest way for the physical facilities of a studio is the best way to do it. So I determined to go back and try to get a little of the spirit we used to make pictures with. We used to use comedy whenever we could and then we got too serious about it. So, in *Rio Bravo* I imagine there are almost as many laughs as if we had started out to make a comedy. I also decided that audiences were getting tired of plots and, as you know, *Rio Bravo* and *Hatari!* have little plot and more characterization. And so far it has worked out very well. People seem to like it better. I don't mean that if a story comes along you shouldn't do it, but I think the average plot is pretty time-worn. Television has come in and they have used so many thousands of plots that people are getting tired of them. They're a little too inclined—if you lay a plot down—to say, "Oh, I've seen this before." But if you can keep them from knowing what the plot is you have a chance of holding their interest. And it leads to characters—so that you may write what the character might think and the character motivates your story and the situations—and it's when a character believes in something that a situation happens, not because you write it to happen.

PB: *But haven't most of your pictures dealt with characters rather than situations?*

HH: Well, sometimes it takes you a little while to realize what you did unconsciously, and then you can begin to do it purposely, and then it makes working very much simpler. But harder, too, because it is easy to follow a plot but without one it's pretty hard sometimes to tell what to do.

PB: *Was* Rio Bravo *made up as you went along?*

HH: No, it was just an elaboration of the characters. We'd say, now here we have a scene; let's put a little character in it. What do you think this man would do? And, no, he wouldn't do that, he'd do this. And you can't do it in an office. With a play the writer sits and watches dozens of rehearsals and things change. We can't change. Once we've got a scene in the can, as it were, it's going to be there on the screen, so we have to feel our way as we go along and we can add to a character or get a piece of business between two people and start some relationship going and then further it. In *Rio Bravo*, Dean Martin had a bit in which he was required to roll a cigarette. His fingers weren't equal to it and Wayne kept passing him cigarettes. All of a sudden you realize that they are awfully good friends or he wouldn't be doing it. That grew out of Martin's asking me one day "Well, if my fingers are shaky, how can I roll this thing?" So Wayne said, "Here, I'll hand you one," and suddenly we had something going. Or like the baby elephants in *Hatari!* and what they did. You can't just start out to do a thing like that. I don't think the average studio would be pleased to spend six or seven million dollars on a picture of that sort without any story. But it isn't as odd as it sounds. You may have a perfectly good scene, but as the character develops in the story, as he becomes clearer to you, you realize that the scene you are doing has little or no characterization; so you begin to add character to the man. You're actually doing the same scene but you're giving him a few different words and you're getting new attitudes into it. The crux of *Rio Bravo* is not Wayne—it is Dean Martin's story. As a matter of fact, Wayne said, "What do I do while he's playing all these good scenes?" "Well," I said, "you look at him as a friend." And he said, "OK. I know what to do." Actually it becomes a great part for Wayne because he's going through all these things because of friendship. He's wondering how good this man is, whether he's been ruined or whether he's going to come out all right. You watch a man develop and end up well and the friend is glad for it.

PB: *How did you come to make* Rio Bravo?

HH: It started with some scenes in a picture called *High Noon*, in which Gary Cooper ran around trying to get help and no one would give him any. And that's rather a silly thing for a man to do, especially since at the end of the picture he is able to do the job by himself. So I said, we'll do just the opposite, and take a real professional viewpoint: as Wayne says when he's offered help, "If they're really good, I'll take them. If not, I'll just have to take care of them." We did everything that way, the exact opposite. It annoyed me in *High Noon* so I tried the opposite and it worked, and people liked it. And then, of course, we had a lot of fun in the picture. I mean crazy reactions—I don't think they're crazy, I think they're normal—but according to bad habits we've fallen into, they seemed crazy. Everyone was urged and egged on to find new things. Things like the explosion of dynamite at the end—that was the art director's creation. He overdid it one time and in our big explosion he put in red and yellow and green paper and when it went up the whole house looked like a big Chinese firecracker. We all started to laugh and I said, "What did you do?" And he said, "Well, I figured that that building would have invoices of different colours, but," he said, "it's the most horrible looking thing I've ever seen." He rebuilt it and we did it normally, but it looked like some huge marvelous bomb going off at Monte Carlo—it was very funny.

1962 Hatari!

PB: Hatari! *was largely improvised while on location, wasn't it?*

HH: Well, you can't sit in an office and write what a rhino or any other animal is going to do. From the time we saw one of them to the time we either caught it or failed to, it wouldn't be more than four minutes. So we had to make up scenes in an awful hurry; we couldn't write them. We threw out many good scenes—maybe we can use them in another picture sometime. But the whole story was outlined when we started. We were lucky enough to catch every kind of animal in Africa—everything we'd hoped for—usually if you get one-third you're lucky.

PB: *Then you really caught those animals yourselves?*

HH: Oh, yes, there was no doubling at all—the actors caught the animals. We chased sixteen rhinos and caught four with ropes. You know, there is a lot of excitement when you get hold of one of those things. They caught a number of animals not shown in the film—you can't keep going forever. I've got enough footage for another hour.

PB: *The picture is really a series of vignettes, isn't it?*

HH: I'd rather say that the form of the picture is a hunting season, from beginning to end. It's what happens when a bunch of fellows get together and hunt during a season. Elsa Martinelli is the famous girl photographer, Ylla, who was so damned attractive that men would put her in the places where she could get the best pictures in the world. She fell off a truck and got killed in South Africa. I heard about some of her romances and that's where that character started. The character of the younger French girl was based on a true story of a girl with a famous father who was killed by a rhino and these men used his farm, and the girl grew up with these men around her. Instead of getting a little, frail girl, I got a big, lusty kid who's just growing up, you know, who kind of lumbered around, and had fun with it.

PB: *How did the scene of Buttons repeatedly asking them to tell him about the rocket develop?*

HH: Have you ever seen *Of Mice and Men*?

PB: *You mean where Lennie asks George to tell him about the rabbits. Was that scene your take-off on it?*

HH: Yes. I brought down a copy of the book and let Red read it, and wrote some dialogue and said, "Go ahead and make it." First take and we made it.

PB: *Which of your pictures do you like best?*

HH: Oh, I imagine I like *Scarface*, and I like *Male War Bride*, and I like the last one, *Hatari!*

Interview recorded in Hawks's office in Paramount Studios, Hollywood, April 9 and 10, 1962.

American Film Institute Seminar

JAMES SILKE/1970

JAMES SILKE: *I am obliged to start it off since I had the opportunity to come on your set while you were making* Rio Lobo. *I was just fascinated. I don't think anybody else makes a motion picture quite like that. I am referring to the way which you used the script and worked the dialogue and actors. Well, that's the on-set procedure, and if you could just maybe outline your procedure.*

HOWARD HAWKS: Well, we had a lot of good actors and you watch them as you go along. One of them is particularly good doing something—then you kind of stress that. The girl (Jennifer O'Neill) was a new one. I didn't know quite how she worked when we started and it became kind of fun as we, got further along. (John) Wayne I know pretty well. The Mexican boy (Jorge Rivero) did a good job. He got more confidence as the picture went along. Mitchum's son (Chris Mitchum), I think is going to be a real good man one of these days.

JAMES SILKE: *Did that part kind of grow?*

HOWARD HAWKS: Yes. He was good, and people seemed to like him. I don't want to make a speech. Ask some questions, maybe I can answer them.

QUESTION: *Some of the scenes, the interiors, where you had most of the cast and they weren't shooting, had a real improvisational quality to them.*

From the American Film Institute Seminar with Howard Hawks, held November 19, 1970, moderated by James Silke. © 1978 American Film Institute.

I mean, one had the feeling of watching through the keyhole while people were horsing around.

HOWARD HAWKS: Well, it wasn't really an improvisation. It is just trying to get them to act natural, you know. We kind of want people to break over the other person and the actors have fun doing it. They all wanted to break over somebody. And so they finally got a chance to do it. I think that it gives it rather a natural feeling.

JAMES SILKE: *I guess you didn't have any—you had dialogue, you had the scene, but Wayne kind of—when he walked into the door, I think the script called for a weapon. And I watched Wayne; he just kind of looked at the actor and said, "I can handle it without a gun." So he immediately improvised.*

HOWARD HAWKS: Well, the first thing we want is the action, you know, and we don't worry too much about what the script says about that, and if somebody gets an idea we try it that way. If it hadn't worked out we try it another way because you can always do it as many times as you feel you want to. But Wayne gives it a lot of thought and I say, "If you've got any ideas about how to come into this room—" He said, "Well, let me just take after him." Well, he did. He said, "That's what I would be doing if I'd chased a man that long."

JAMES SILKE: *That came from him at that point?*
HOWARD HAWKS: Yes.

JAMES SILKE: *The geography of that room—we're a bunch of young film-makers here and I don't think you really established the whole room as such in any way that we would normally call an establishing shot, and yet somehow it's all very clear where everybody is and what they're doing, and it is just from making films?*

HOWARD HAWKS: On a long shot and establishing shot, it's only good if you've got something particular that you want to show them. It's just a room, there is no reason to do it. Pretty soon you should get your geography out of it. If you got a long shot, like when they come up to Phillips's ranch and look it over, you want to see what's there. But I don't believe there was anything in the other ranch we wanted to see particularly. We saw through the window, we saw where he was. Wayne went through the door, walked into another room, came back to—he would have liked to stay in there, but we didn't have any set in there, so we came back again.

QUESTION: *I was interested in the plot of the film—I guess it was about an hour and a half in when I realized where the story was. Does that worry you? Would you have commercial worries about that?*

HOWARD HAWKS: I don't think so. I don't think plot as a plot means much today. I'd say that everybody has seen every plot twenty times. What they haven't seen is characters and their relation to one another. I don't worry much about plot anymore. Quite a while ago I made a picture called *The Big Sleep*. Somebody said, "Who killed such and such a man?" I said, "I don't know." Somebody spoke up and said, "I think so and so killed him." And we said, "No, he couldn't have done it." So we sent Raymond Chandler a wire and said, "Who killed him?" And he sent a wire back: "Joe did it." And I sent him a wire saying, "Joe is out in the ocean; he couldn't have possibly done that." And after people liked the picture and everything I thought, "Why worry about plot and everything?" Just worry about making good scenes and just keep—so that's all that we tried to do, hook it together with something that keeps your interest. But I go to too many pictures and the first hundred feet come on and somebody behind me says, "Oh, this is that old story about such and such, let's go to another movie." And they walk out. We just' let it develop and try and keep you interested while it's developing.

QUESTION: *Could you elaborate more about your job—about acting and characterization. Jennifer O'Neill stumbled over a few lines.*

HOWARD HAWKS: Well, that stumbling over a few lines—I am very pleased with that, because people talk that way, and I don't attempt to change that. And as a matter of fact I tried to tell them to start one way and finish up another way because when you're trying to describe something that's the way you do it in normal conversation. The girl, she knew that she is quite talented as far as that goes—got a quality quite different from other people. I don't know whether that answers your question or not.

QUESTION: *Well, I saw her in one picture and she seemed like a growing star, and that sort of stopped it for me. So I wondered what you think about her acting?*
HOWARD HAWKS: I am not so interested in whether the acting—is whether their personality—or they do a little something different. And it will remain to be seen as to how well she does that. Whether she is different or whether she just falls into the mold of a lot of other people. That boy, (Chris) Mitchum, is a distinct personality. I think that most of you would agree to that. I think he only had one line in a picture before. Heads of the studio objected very much to the fact that we were going to give a good part to a boy that hadn't had any more experience. I saw him about three days working and signed him to a five-picture contract. Because he, in my opinion, has every quality of being quite a big figure.

QUESTION: *How do you cast someone like him? Can you just sense it by meeting him that he has that—?*
HOWARD HAWKS: Oh, I don't know. I went down to see Durango in Mexico as a possible place to make a picture. And Wayne was making a picture down there. And this boy, I think, had one line in it. And I met him and made a little test of him and put him in the part.

JAMES SILKE: *Jennifer got in kind of late. Normally you look around quite a bit, don't you, for the girls to get this kind of aggressive—and a strong female—*
HOWARD HAWKS: Well, we had a girl that was right and we couldn't get the permit to bring her over to this country and work. I thought it was a kind of a hard part to cast and I saw this Jennifer do a test where they didn't think she was any good and I thought she was great. So we used her.

QUESTION: *Did you see her other picture? It was called* The Glass House.
HOWARD HAWKS: No, I didn't see it.

QUESTION: *She's got kind of an independent streak in person, and you kind of magnify—is that a conscious effort on your part?*

HOWARD HAWKS: Oh, sure. You take the way the girl strikes you and then you work on that because that's an outstanding characteristic that she has.

JAMES SILKE: *The Lansing girl (Sherry Lansing), now you worked with her longer as I understood.*
HOWARD HAWKS: Oh, I don't think it was too long. It wasn't over a week or so. You know, just to make a test, and she did a good job and so—

JAMES SILKE: *Was that her first role?*
HOWARD HAWKS: Yes.

JAMES SILKE: *And the Mexican girl? (Susanna Dosamantes)*
HOWARD HAWKS: I think she has a history of some pictures in Mexico. That's her first American picture.

QUESTION: *Was it a conscious decision on your part to end this film the way you did?*
HOWARD HAWKS: Oh, I don't know. We didn't want Wayne to go running around in the usual shoot-out in the end, so we looked around for somebody else to kill the heavy and we decided on the girl doing it.

QUESTION: *There are three women in your film. You never have that many women, do you, in a Western? I am wondering if that was a conscious decision?*
HOWARD HAWKS: Well, I don't remember. I couldn't answer that. I'd have to do a lot of thinking back and see whether I think maybe that was a few more than we generally had. I don't know.

QUESTION: *One piece of action I saw and liked very much was the taking of the train.*
HOWARD HAWKS: Did you ever see an airplane land on the first flattops?

RESPONSE: *No.*
HOWARD HAWKS: Well, they have a hook underneath it and they used to pick up ropes that had a bag of sand on each side. And the more

they picked up the slower they went, and they stopped. So we thought we could try it with a train.

QUESTION: *Was this done all by you and the writers, or had the writers already written this scene and then you were transforming—?*
HOWARD HAWKS: Oh, we invented it and then the special effects man—it probably took him—Paul [Helmick, associate producer on *Rio Lobo*] how long did it take him? Three weeks or a month to get that thing ready? Quite a work to make the trees pull them out, you know, and he was a little worried as to whether the train was going to stop or keep on going down to Cuernavaca.

JAMES SILKE: *How many times did you do that?*
HOWARD HAWKS: Once. These fellows do remarkable things. In that picture *Hatari!*, we had a special effects man, and I said, "I want you to build a rocket that will take a net over a tree with 500 monkeys in it." He said, "Are you serious?" I said, "I am serious." I didn't see him again for weeks. I think Paul [Helmick] finally came in and said, "That fellow spent $40,000 experimenting out there and he says it will work." And we didn't know it would work until we got down to Africa and tried it. We scheduled it and he came up and he said, "Not today, there is too much wind blowing." Finally he said, "This is the day." He was really one of the most nervous men I've ever seen in all my life. [Laughter in the audience]

QUESTION: *Were the monkeys waiting in the tree all that time?*
HOWARD HAWKS: When we shot the rocket we had some prop monkeys up in the tree. When we ran over there to start making the scenes we had real monkeys. It was quite a lot of fun because I told the whole cast I don't know what a monkey would do, but I thought that they better protect themselves as well as they could, and they put on all kinds of armor; they all made their own coverings and went in there.

JAMES SILKE: *The cast actually built those?*
HOWARD HAWKS: I gave them a free hand to order what they wanted. There was a sudden demand for hockey chin guards, baseball catchers, and stuff—flower pots, everything.

JAMES SILKE: *On that train sequence I guess it is right to left. Do you have any real reasons for making it go that way rather than left to right?*

HOWARD HAWKS: A good shot at the station had the train go out left to right, and so we took everything left to right until we got to the top and then we turned it around and went right to left. If we had switched that you would have gotten all confused.

JAMES SILKE: *You maintain that in every shot? That's just something you do naturally?*

HOWARD HAWKS: Yes. Well, you send out a note. The train going to the destination goes left to right, coming back it goes right to left. Of course, if we do run into a good shot that works the other way, we flip the film over. And if you can't read the lettering on the side of the train it works fine. People's coats are buttoned on the wrong side, they're left-handed with guns, but nobody seems to notice that.

QUESTION: *In the structure of a movie like this do you have several key scenes, and the other scenes that you use are worked out? Or is it all thoroughly worked out from beginning to end when you begin to shoot?*

HOWARD HAWKS: I don't think any action picture is thoroughly worked out. You can't write an action picture; you have to get out and get ready to make it. The form of the picture and the sequence of the picture and everything is worked out. But if the writer puts in the fact that somebody says something coming into a room on a run, you can't do it. I mean, you've got to get your action first and then use your dialogue—put your dialogue in afterwards. At least, that's the way I work.

QUESTION: *What would you say about the staging of that very first gun scene when the four deputies come in. That scene takes ten seconds, not more than that. Have you storyboarded all the angles?*

HOWARD HAWKS: Well, you tell the art director what you want. You know which way the men are going to come in, and then you experiment and see where you're going to have Wayne sitting at a table, and you're going to see where the girl sits, and then in a few minutes you've got it all worked out and it's perfectly simple as far as I am concerned.

QUESTION: *Did you shoot it about one to one, or did you cover yourself with a cover shot?*

HOWARD HAWKS: Well, the only cover shots that you make is if you see—watching the action, if you see something that is a good bit of action you go in and get that. And then you use it if you wish to. You don't make just one shot of one of the things, but—because if you see something else it's silly not to do it while you're there, because you may want to be a little closer to somebody when they shoot a gun, or you may want to be further away. We put up a couple of cameras and shoot it and we use whichever angle we want to. But you plan the cutting of a scene before you shoot it.

JAMES SILKE: *You say, "plan." You don't have drawings?*

HOWARD HAWKS: Oh no, you visualize the thing, you know, and you get so that you know what you're going to do and the cutter comes—

JAMES SILKE: *Was it always like that?*

HOWARD HAWKS: Oh, I think so. I don't think there is any effort in using a camera if you're just telling a story. People get mixed up if they try to do fancy things with it. If they tell it from the viewpoint of—as though you're looking at a thing and then you're telling a story and you say, "And then she drew a gun." Well, you won't be able to see that she draws a gun, so you go up and make a shot of drawing a gun. And usually, a good cutter comes out on the set and you tell him how you shot it, and occasionally he'll say, "I got an idea for doing it a little different way." Well, that's fine, because you can always put it back the way that you did. Very often you're very pleasantly surprised he's got a much better way.

JAMES SILKE: *You don't hide anything from the audience in a sense. You make sure by this process that the audience knows exactly what's going on everyplace.*

HOWARD HAWKS: I don't like tricks in telling a story. I mean, I don't thing they're—

JAMES SILKE: *Surprises?*

HOWARD HAWKS: Oh, I don't mean surprises. You can do that in your cutting. But I mean tricks. I don't see any reason for shooting some of these shots that you see in pictures—the camera wanders all around and doesn't really show you anything. It's just an artificial movement. I don't like things like in *The Wild Bunch* where—you just said—how long did you say it took us to kill three or four people there. Ten seconds? I don't like it when they go into slow motion of somebody killed and prolong it. I can kill four or five while in *The Wild Bunch* they're doing one. He uses more red paint than I do.

QUESTION: *Wasn't Wayne's beating of Mitchum kind of prolonged?*
HOWARD HAWKS: Yes, but you find an audience today—they enjoy it. We made a distinct effort to let Wayne let himself go and just as near as he could, beat this fellow up, and I think he did it. I've seen it in front of a couple of big audiences; I think they begin to enjoy it.

QUESTION: *Do you think they might enjoy five minutes of (Sam) Peckinpah's violence as well?*
HOWARD HAWKS: I don't know. I don't think that's true violence. I think that's why they go into a slow motion shot all of a sudden.

JAMES SILKE: *There is something about the tempo in that scene too. You expressed to me at the time that you wanted to maintain the tempo in that scene because the situation edges on reality. They're busting in there, taking that guy out, nobody is going to get them. Am I retelling it correctly?*
HOWARD HAWKS: Yes, you're trying to crowd an awful lot of stuff into a thing. Wayne has been years following that man and his natural inclination is to take it out on him. We tried to set it up so it would be fairly real. I don't know—the whole situation of a hostage is always pretty good because people are slowed up. They don't know quite what to do. Of course, that's what they were after. They were after a hostage to work with and it was only possible when that happened. You ought to be familiar with that. You read about it every day in hijacking an airplane. I mean that's nothing, but it is the same situation.

JAMES SILKE: *Was it an idea you had when you made* Rio Bravo?
HOWARD HAWKS: Well, in working on *Rio Bravo* many times we found ourselves with a choice of two things we thought were pretty

good. So the one we didn't use we made a note of it. Very often in a story you run up against sometimes two, three, four situations—you don't know what one to use. Sometimes you even want to flip a coin to see which one to use. Sometimes there is no real reason why you picked one instead of the other.

QUESTION: *At what point do you make that decision? At the scripting point, or do you really make radical changes in the story once you get on the set?*

HOWARD HAWKS: Very often we have a story point and the writer says, "I think it would work." I'll say, "Well, write it there, but also write it in another place." And then the writer comes back and says, "I can think of another place," and they write the same story point. We don't shoot them all. Sometimes we shoot two of them, sometimes only one, because as you get to telling your story you begin to realize where the story point ought to come.

JAMES SILKE: *Did Leigh Brackett work on a Burton Wohl story?*

HOWARD HAWKS: Well, Burton did the first thing on it, yes.

JAMES SILKE: *He initiated it? There is a story about calling up Wayne and saying, "We're going to make* El Dorado *again." He says, "Do I get to play the drunk?" So it comes from you, but then what goes on? I know there was a very long script prepared.*

HOWARD HAWKS: Oh, I don't know. You get a writer, and Burton is an excellent dramatic writer, and he did a script and it was very good. But it was all extremely serious. And I thought it would be boring, so instead of asking him to turn it over and try to get—Leigh Brackett came in on it. I didn't think the thing would hold up as a completely serious picture. I thought it would be much better and more entertaining if there would be fun in it.

JAMES SILKE: *When I came out on the set and I asked for a script they said they'd get me one, but it was kind of useless to read it at that point. Does that bother your actors, when you come out with those little pieces of paper every morning and after lunch?*

HOWARD HAWKS: Well, if it does, they keep awful quiet about it. I don't know. Now, I don't think so. Occasionally they'll say—they'll make an excuse. They'll say, "I didn't have very much time to study these lines." I'd say, "You can do them," and they do it. As a matter of fact, I think a lot of them are a great deal better if they don't have too much rehearsal. A lot more natural. They make some mistakes in the lines, stumble a little bit, and I like it better.

JAMES SILKE: *You let them change it too, don't you? I mean if they say essentially what—*
HOWARD HAWKS: Sure. It seems to work pretty well.

JAMES SILKE: *[Jack] Elam I just think is terrific in this film. He doesn't seem to be used to that degree. Did a lot of this come from him?*
HOWARD HAWKS: Elam has been playing the heavy. But I always thought he was a comedian. So he came in and I said, "You want to do a funny part?" He said, "I'd love to." And we had a lot of fun doing it. He's a good actor. But those things, I don't know, they just come out. That's the only way I know how to use an actor—is to use the things that I think are the best. He would do the scene and I'd say, "Hey, bust out a little bit more." "O.K." And then he would do one of those crazy things that he does.

QUESTION: *Why were the costumes so newly washed and pressed and all the hair so neatly trimmed? I thought it tended to take away from the reality.*
HOWARD HAWKS: In what case? Whose hair?

RESPONSE: *In the beginning, the close-up of the dying soldier he looked like he just came from the barber because the* side-burns *were just so—every hair was in place. It took away from the reality of him coming back from the battle. John Wayne's shirt never had a wrinkle.*
HOWARD HAWKS: Well, I missed out on that probably. I thought that the dying fellow really looked like an unholy mess you know. We had an awful time getting the make-up for the wasp thing, you know—hornet thing—and I didn't notice it, to be frank with you.

RESPONSE: Maybe it's just the Italian Westerns I've seen recently were exceptionally dirty.

JAMES SILKE: *The Mitchum costume is different, more ragged in that sense. Did the actor help you at all in that?*
HOWARD HAWKS: Well, I don't know. All the descriptions that I read about the Civil War is towards the end of the war when the South was really starving for money. I wanted a ragtag bunch and I certainly got it. And you know where the Union Cavalry were far better set up than they were. But that was just part of the story as far as I was concerned.

QUESTION: *You were saying how Wayne contributed to a sequence by sort of projecting his own attitude: If I were chasing this guy I'd jump into this room. How does he contribute to scenes where women are involved? He had a lot of good lines in there and he also seemed to be giving her a lot of help because she was really warmer when they were together than when she was either doing a close-up or—*
HOWARD HAWKS: Well, it's very simple. A girl comes into the room and we didn't have anything written about where she turns around and says, "What have you got to do with this? Well, then stay out of it." And Wayne says, "Oh, that's good. Now I can look at her as a kind of a feisty little thing and I don't have to warm about it." On the other hand, he felt sorry for the girl with the scar on her face, you know. So he was a good deal warmer toward that girl. But there wasn't any feeling of a love story or anything.

RESPONSE: *I don't mean a love story in the script, but I mean Wayne's performance on the set, whether he was talking—*
HOWARD HAWKS: That's the thing that changes the most, you know, when you're making any scene—is the attitude, and an actor plays the thing. "We'll try it with a little more bite in it. Don't be so soft. Don't try to make the whole audience like you. Be kind of a stinker." So they play it a different way, you know. And then you say, "Well, don't be quite that much of a stinker," and start over. You want to remember that if you're doing a play you have five or six weeks rehearsal. You have a chance to see the whole damn thing up in front of you. Making a movie you go in the first day and by 10:00 there are some scenes of

the film in a can already and that's the way it's going to be. So you have to figure attitudes very carefully, especially when you start. It usually takes about two or three weeks to really find the attitude of Wayne and the sergeant. He would say, "Yes, Sergeant," and you know he surely liked the boy afterwards. He and the captain got along well together without any real reason to become strong friends. But Wayne is awfully easy to work with that way, because all I want to do is to tell him about his attitude. Say: "I think you've got the wrong attitude," or "I think this is the right one."

QUESTION: *Don't you feel it necessary to have them know each other in the scene in the cave where they come through that hole, retelling their past? Did they develop a liking for each other at that time?*
HOWARD HAWKS: Oh, I don't know. You're starting a new boy and you want to give him some type of introduction, and that was the reason for that scene. I don't think there was any other thing.

JAMES SILKE: *You say it takes two or three weeks to really get those attitudes out. Do you design your production schedule in such a way that you can do other things that are not going to be as crucial?*
HOWARD HAWKS: Oh, no. We try to start at the beginning of a picture and go right through. You can't do that when you start on location, because you can't do your interiors. But you run over the interior that comes in-between so that they know what the attitude is going to be and then you keep on going. I try to shoot as much in so-called continuity as possible, because you can get into horrible mistakes if you don't. It's very hard sometimes to get out of continuity.

JAMES SILKE: *Is that partly due to the way in which you shoot, the way you change things so much that you want to maintain that continuity, or is it—*
HOWARD HAWKS: No. I think it's almost all the people that I would say are good directors use that. I don't know. They're telling a story and how are they going to tell it when they start in with the finish and then jump around and everything—then they're not story tellers. They're reading a script and say, "It says here that they come in here," and so you come in there and you come in here and they play a scene—there is no growth of

any feeling. And I think that's what makes good scenes; that's what makes a picture more interesting. I've done a play a couple of times. Then it wasn't hard at all, because I knew what the play was like and I knew what the attitudes—and we were able to shoot in any kind of order. But it is a very very difficult thing to jump way ahead and commit yourself to the attitude of somebody who has finished a really good scene and all of a sudden you realize that you made a scene that follows and you can't make the scene that you want beforehand because you can't follow it.

JAMES SILKE: *Is that what gives your film the structure—this kind of developing attitudes between the characters, that they finally more or less find themselves when you're shooting?*
HOWARD HAWKS: Well, I've always worked that way and I wouldn't know any other way. I find myself too, in doing it.

JAMES SILKE: *While you're shooting it?*
HOWARD HAWKS: Yes.

JAMES SILKE: *You actually find the film?*
HOWARD HAWKS: Sometimes you find it in a hurry. I was making a picture at one time with Edward G. Robinson and about 4:00 in the afternoon I stopped the thing. I didn't know him very well and I said, "Mr. Robinson, this is going to be one of the dullest pictures that's ever been made. You are sour and the scenes are flat and it's really going to—I don't think it's going to be any good at all." And he said, "What can we do?" And I said, "Well, can you play a very talkative man who laughs and jokes and is fun?" "Yes," he said, "If you help me with what I say." I said, "I'll help you, but you're going to have to do a lot of it yourself." And we made a picture called *Tiger Shark*. He played a good character and every day we had fun changing this whole thing around. I hate to think of what the picture would have been if he'd stayed in that sour character.

JAMES SILKE: *So it's kind of a mutual discovery between you and the actors?*
HOWARD HAWKS: Well, that's what you can do when you've got a good man.

JAMES SILKE: *How did it work with Bogart?*

HOWARD HAWKS: Oh, he was a joy to work with. He is one of the finest actors we've ever had. He is capable of doing any kind of scene that you can think of and he was really awfully good to work with. I had a lot of fun with him because we were working on a story and we got an idea—we were talking about Bogart's influence, because no matter what you wrote he was insolent. So he said, "Well, let's make a girl insolent." We started to work and we worked out the part. And I said to Bogart, "As long as it doesn't come as a surprise to you, we're going to make the girl more insolent than you are." Well, he said, "You've got a fat chance in doing that." I said, "I don't know, I think we've got a pretty good chance. I'll tell you one thing, every scene that we make with her she is going to walk out and leave you with egg on your face." He just looked at me and I said, "After all, I'm the director." He said, "Yeah, and you have a pretty good chance of getting away with what you're going to try too." And we did it. Actually, we had an awful lot of fun with the insolence of the two people in their relation to each other. That's another thing about attitude. Mitchum, for instance, I liked him when he smiled. So we made scenes that he could, you know, have a good sense of humor. (Jorge) Rivero was good, but his English wasn't so good. So we made capital of that in the scenes with the girl, where he just didn't know what to say to her. I can give you a pretty good example. We were doing *Male War Bride* [*I was a Male War Bride*] with Cary Grant. We had a scene where Cary as a French captain had to answer questions from an American sergeant that would usually be asked of a little French girl who is marrying a GI; such questions as, "You ever had female trouble?" and "Have you ever been pregnant?" and all kinds of ridiculous questions. We looked forward to making the scene. We got up to making it and it wasn't funny at all. We didn't know what was the matter. And Cary said, "It's falling flat, isn't it?" And I said, "It certainly is." I don't know where the suggestion came from that a man like Cary Grant would be amused at the sergeant having to ask him these silly questions: "Oh, sergeant, female troubles? I've had them all." All of a sudden, "We can do that, we can do that," and he got over in the corner with the sergeant who was asking and in two or three minutes the scene became very, very funny because the sergeant was embarrassed and Cary was having fun with him. We had started an entirely different scene. I remember making a scene with him one time where he said, "How is that?" And I said, "Pretty dull." "Why does it go wrong?" And I said, "The way you're getting mad, you're getting mad like an ordinary person. Let's find some different way of getting mad." And we started trying different ways. And then somebody said, "I know a fellow who when he got mad used to whinny like a horse." Cary said, That's fine. I'll do that." And we did that. That's attitude. That's what I call an attitude, you know, toward a scene.

COMMENT: *The girl in this movie does most of the fighting with Wayne instead of with the dramatic lead.*
HOWARD HAWKS: Well, you got a star, Wayne, and I don't know—it is pretty hard to do romantic scenes, but we can do scenes of fighting and argument, so we do them. And he is tickled to death not to have any romance in the picture, but he doesn't mind a good fight with somebody, you know.

QUESTION: *How do you communicate with newcomers?*
HOWARD HAWKS: Well, I get a lot of help from the pros and Wayne has been that all the time. The first picture I made with him was *Red River*. We had a new boy, Montgomery Clift, and after the first scene Wayne said, "This kid is all right," and he took an interest in him. He didn't mind working with him, he didn't mind my changing Clift around and trying it a different way. Wayne would do anything to make a better picture. He is one of the most helpful people that I know. Lots of times he doesn't know what's the matter, but when he starts kind of making faces to himself I say, "What's bothering you?" "Something is wrong with this scene." And then you find out what's wrong. He doesn't know how to help it, but he is awfully pleased when you do manage to find out what's wrong and help it out. Many years ago I told him, "You play two or three good scenes in a movie and don't annoy the audience the rest of the time and you'll be a star." He still keeps remembering this. "This is one of those things when you can annoy them, for goodness sake get it over in a hurry."

JAMES SILKE: *Do you work with your film editor, or do you just advise him?*

HOWARD HAWKS: Well, it's almost cut when we're finished. It's assembled in shots so it can be assembled. He comes down there and says, "What have you figured on doing to this?" He watches the film and he goes out and he puts it together and by the next day he is ready to show it. If he is particularly pleased with it you see it right away, and if he is still working on it I can tell what's happening because he doesn't show it to me for two or three days. Some pictures you get two days after you finished. Other pictures are hard. For instance, the cutting on that train coming downhill can't be done in a day or so—that has to be all assembled. (John) Woodcock is a very fine editor. He doesn't like to start on a sequence unless he's got all the material on hand. And naturally the things with the hornets and the men inside the car and everything was made way, way afterwards. We did nothing with that sequence until we got all the film.

JAMES SILKE: *As he assembles does he show you pieces, or the whole thing—what he's just put together?*
HOWARD HAWKS: We do it by sequences. When a sequence is finished we all see it so that you know what to expect. You know what somebody is doing, what to avoid, what they don't do well and what to press on if they do well.

JAMES SILKE: *It's part of the building process.*
HOWARD HAWKS: Yes.

QUESTION: *Do you try to cut a scene several times sometimes, or as long as it works you just leave it the same way? I mean, like the train sequence you mentioned. Did you try different ways, or you had it all set up more or less before the cutting so—*
HOWARD HAWKS: No, the only thing we did to the train sequence was to just take out a few scenes—a few shots that were repetitive or something like that. There are five or six cameras on that thing.

QUESTION: *So most of the time your cutting is already in your head, and once you shot it it's more or less the same way? It's not a question of too much cutting or recutting?*

HOWARD HAWKS: Oh, I don't think so, no. You know, there is just a steady progression of saying once you drop that scene it's no use in the picture—and just drop it. Or the end of a scene. For instance, after Wayne had captured the two Southerners and they wouldn't tell him about who the trader was, he called the Union cavalry over and we faded out and went right into the next scene. I think Wayne ended the scene with his hands up in the air. I made a scene where the Union captain that came up wondered why Wayne was in a Confederate uniform, why the other fellow—there was no sense in explaining it so we just cut it out of the picture.

QUESTION: *Do you spend a lot of time in the postproduction?*
HOWARD HAWKS: Oh, no. You go through every reel.

QUESTION: *I just wondered particularly in respect to some sound effects. The beginning seemed to me very emphasized and then it sort of slowed down, unless I got used to the picture, which I didn't seem to.*
HOWARD HAWKS: Well, I don't know what to answer because I can't really figure, I don't know where you thought it was.

RESPONSE: *In particular, I don't know what the name of it is—the beginning of the picture seemed to be very much—*
HOWARD HAWKS: Well, I don't know. I don't know how to answer it. I do know that—I don't think that this print that you see is the final balance print. I don't think the sound is all balanced. When we go out to a preview, we have a failure and we can control it. Here we couldn't control the sound so we noticed in some cases it went way up, and in some cases it dropped down. Does that answer at all?

COMMENT: *There was a sound no one seemed to notice. I thought it was just too loud. It was on a close-up of the gun.*
HOWARD HAWKS: Oh, something happened to the sound in there. Paul, you have any idea what that was?
PAUL HELMICK: That's the way a Derringer sounds, Mr. Hawks, as compared to the other guns—rifles and pistols. That's a Derringer shot that is in the sound track.

JAMES SILKE: *That's really the way it sounds, in other words. Did you bring that sound up because you're coming in close?*
HOWARD HAWKS: You have perspective to all sound—you hope you have.

JAMES SILKE: *You use sound very sparingly, normally, I mean, and use it for effect later. You don't make a big thing out of effects normally.*
HOWARD HAWKS: I try not to. Sometimes you can't help yourself.

JAMES SILKE: *This film is full of people in many instances. Even the city itself seems to be more full of people than say, for instance,* Rio Bravo, *which seemed to be a very empty city. Was there an idea in your mind?*
HOWARD HAWKS: No, nothing. Except that it was just the way we happened to see the town. The assistant asks you how do you see this, and you say, "It can be fairly busy." "How do you see this scene?" "Well, I prefer not to see too many people."

JAMES SILKE: *What do you say to [Jerry] Goldsmith [composer of the score on* Rio Lobo]
HOWARD HAWKS: Oh, I don't know. There is a whole lot of conversation. We go over a thing and talk in general, and he works on it. We're not always right. Sometimes after we finish we say, "Let's chop off the music here," you know. "Let's start it a little quicker." It just depends.

QUESTION: *What is your next project, Mr. Hawks?*
HOWARD HAWKS: Oh, we're going to do a crazy story about some young fellows who are geologists for the oil companies. I happened to run into a bunch of them. They go all over the world. Anywhere they smell oil, they show up. They have to get the rights to drill. Sometimes they start revolutions, sometimes they kidnap people, and sometimes they just get them drunk. They lead a marvelous existence. It goes over about five or six countries and I'd say it was kind of a modern comedy. We hope it's going to be funny, but it's just two fellows who started out. One of them is always behind the other. He gets about as far as a knee and he finds a garter somebody has given to this girl beforehand. When he finally catches up with the man they become friends. And then one

falls in love with a girl with an accent who is in a little circus and rides an elephant that doesn't like red. Later in the scene she sits in the back of the elephant holding a fishing pole with a piece of red flannel making the elephant run. But anyway, she's got an accent, she is getting a lot of information from this one man who falls in love with her, and then the other fellow comes back and it's his ex-wife. She doesn't have any accent at all. So the girl sticks around with the two men—her ex-husband and lover—and then she runs off with another man at the end of the story, leaving the two of them together, and it's really a crazy story, a good one.

JAMES SILKE: Thank you very much.

"Do I Get to Play the Drunk This Time?" An Encounter with Howard Hawks

JOSEPH McBRIDE AND MICHAEL WILMINGTON/1971

HE IS APPROACHING SEVENTY-FIVE, but Howard Hawks still fits the old Ben Hecht description of him as "a drawling fashion plate, apurr with melodrama." On the stage of the Carnegie Theater for the Chicago Film Festival last November, a month before the premiere of his *Rio Lobo,* he was the image of the consummate professional. He was wearing rimless dark glasses, and kept them on even when the audience, through an electrician's error, was left in darkness. As he sat there in the spotlight, asking for light, it seemed oddly appropriate—recalling Robin Wood's words about "the eternal darkness . . . against which the Hawksian stoicism shines."

The lights came on again, and Hawks stoically endured a long eulogy by Charles Flynn, editor of *Focus!* magazine. Flynn closed with, "Unless Mr. Hawks wants to say something at the end . . ." Hawks, visibly grimacing, replied, "I think you've said more than enough," and from that point on the audience was his. Hawks kept the talk going by quietly nodding at each new questioner, quickly asking for repetition if a question confused him, and beguiling the audience with a flow of anecdotes. Some were familiar, but he embellished them with new twists and flourishes, just as his heroes repeat the same tasks in an endless but volatile routine until they achieve an almost effortless mastery. When a

From *Sight and Sound,* Spring 1971. Reprinted by permission.

particularly obtuse question came up—such as one which criticized his direction of Henry Hathaway's *The Sons of Katie Elder*, or another which asked where to obtain a "Red River D Belt buckle"—he would field it gracefully, with a barely perceptible irritation. What follows is an edited transcript of his remarks, rearranged by topic.

HH: Well, when we came to a certain place in *Rio Bravo*, we had a choice between going in this direction and going in that direction. But we made notes to remember because we said, "That is so good we can use it again." So when we started on *El Dorado*, I said to the writer, the same one who worked on *Rio Bravo* [Leigh Brackett], "Now, look, we had a very good boy gunman in *Rio Bravo*, let's make it a boy who can't shoot at all." That wasn't the same, was it? I said, "John Wayne was the sheriff in *Rio Bravo*, so let's have Bob Mitchum the sheriff in *El Dorado*." You're right, there is a similarity, but it comes from style, it comes from writing, it comes from the fact that it's made in the same part of the country, because the costumes are very much the same . . . *Rio Lobo* is quite different because it starts in the war between the North and the South, so you don't quite think it's going to be a Western, then it changes to the Western. You can probably say that Western is a lot like the other two. Sure. You've got fellows with guns, and one of them's a sheriff . . . You know, there isn't much you can do.

Q: *What kind of working relationship do you have with John Wayne?*
HH: The last picture we made, I called him up and said, "Duke, I've got a story." He said, "I can't make it for a year, I'm all tied up." And I said, "Well, that's all right, it'll take me a year to get it finished." He said, "Good, I'll be all ready." And he came down on location and he said, "What's this about?" And I told him the story. He never even read it, he didn't know anything about it.

Q: *Didn't it sound familiar to him, though?*
HH: Yes, he said, "Do I get to play the drunk this time?"

Q: El Dorado *seems to start out in a very sombre vein and then loosen up toward the middle.*
HH: That's a particular theory of mine, that if people start a picture and they have a funny main title, a lot of funny things, it's as much as

to say, "We expect you to laugh." I think that's committing suicide. So I start out and try to get their attention with a good dramatic sequence, and then find a place to start getting some laughs. We did that with *Rio Bravo*, we did that with *El Dorado*, and we did it very much with the new picture. It starts off being *very* serious and then before the audience realizes it, you're starting in having some fun.

Q: *Could you explain how* Rio Bravo *was made as a reaction against* High Noon?
HH: I saw *High Noon* at about the same time I saw another Western picture, and we were talking about Western pictures and they asked me if I liked it and I said, "Not particularly." I didn't think a good sheriff was going to go running around town like a chicken with his head off asking for help. I said that a good sheriff would turn around and say, "How good are you? Are you good enough to take the best man they've got?" And the fellow would probably say "No" and he'd say, "Well, then I'd just have to take care of you." And that scene *was* in *Rio Bravo*. Then I saw another picture where the sheriff caught a prisoner and the prisoner taunted him and made him perspire and worry and everything by saying, "Wait till my friends catch up with you." And I said, "That's a lot of nonsense, the sheriff would say, 'You better hope your friends *don't* catch up with you, 'cause you'll be the first man to die'." While we were doing all this, they said, "Why don't you make a picture the other way?" And I said "O.K.", and we made *Rio Bravo* the exact opposite from *High Noon* and this other picture—I think it was called *3:10 to Yuma*.

Q: *What sort of stories would you like to do in the future?*
HH: Cary Grant and I were talking the other day, we'd always wanted to do *Don Quixote* and have Cantinflas do Sancho Panza. Before Cary gets too old or I get too old, we hope to do it. Outside of that, any story that I think's fun to do, I expect to do. Things are changing so rapidly now that I like to know what they're beginning to think. I talked to an exhibitor the other day and he said booking a picture today is like playing Russian roulette.

Q: *How would you attempt to do such a complex philosophical work as* Don Quixote?

HH: I think we could have a lot of fun with it. To me, *Don Quixote* is a great comedy. I think that Don Quixote is the basis really for the Chaplin character. I think we all found that funny, and I don't see why we can't make *Don Quixote* very funny.

Q: *Is there any chance of* Scarface *being redistributed?*
HH: We're working on it. We think we'll probably re-release it and send it out for television. I'm trying to get it ready and modernise it a little bit. The picture holds up very well, but some of the music and some of the stuff that the censors made us put in at that time I'd rather not leave in, so we're taking that out of it.

Q: *I have a very hard time convincing people that* Red Line 7000 *is a great film. How do you feel about it?*
HH: I don't like it. I was trying to do something, I tried an experiment. I had three good stories about the race track—I used to race, I know it pretty well—but none of them would make a picture, so I thought maybe I can put them together. And just when I got people interested in two people, I cut over and started to work with two more, and when the audience got interested in them, I went over to two others, and pretty soon the audience got disgusted and I got disgusted too. To be serious, I think there were some pretty good things in it, but as a piece of entertainment I don't think I did a good job. I think there were some individual scenes that were pretty good, and there were a lot of great race scenes. But I'm not proud of the picture as a whole.

Q: *On a movie such as* Hatari!, *it's obvious that you can't control much of what's going to happen. Could you explain how you prepared for the hunting scenes?*
HH: We had some marvelous camera cars—sixth months building, could do about eighty miles an hour over no roads—and a pretty well-trained crew. And we had airplanes spotting up above that had radio connection with the cars. We had around fifty jeeps of various kinds: little jeeps, station wagons, everything. I could talk to the airplanes, and I could talk to the cars. An airplane would say, "Car thirty-three is headed for a good bunch of rhinos." So I'd say, "Where's car thirty-three?" They put up a flag, and we'd find out where thirty-three was,

and we'd all head for thirty-three. And then we'd hear a voice say, "Be careful when you swing round that bunch of trees, they're right behind there and they look kinda mean." And then you'd hear, "Look out there!" and a big crash, and the boys in the airplane would say, "I told you they were mean." Then we'd make a scene—we only had three or four minutes to make a whole scene. We had to catch them and get 'em into a cage. Three or four minutes was a long time, because they weren't fun. I think we chased nine rhinos and caught four to get the scenes in this part of the picture.

Q: *How much control do you have over the editing of your films?*
HH: Oh, practically complete control. I've had a little trouble on a couple of pictures that they thought were too long. I made the mistake of making them too long and they made the mistake of trying to shorten them.

Q: *Is there one of your films that stands out as being particularly satisfying to you?*
HH: I don't think you can answer that question. You make a comedy—you take it out, if the people laugh, you're *immediately* pleased, you get an immediate reaction and the pleasure that you've done a good job. If you make a drama, it takes a little bit longer. You have to have people come up to you and say, "I enjoyed that," because they can give you no visible expression in a theatre. Oh, if they don't walk out, that's pretty good. I think probably the last picture that worked out well is your favourite for a while, and then you start thinking about it and you go back a little further. Not that you're trying to make every scene a great scene, but you try not to annoy the audience. If I can make about five good scenes and not annoy the audience, it's an awfully good pic-ture. I told John Wayne when we started to work together, "Duke, if you can make two good scenes and not annoy the audience for the rest of the film, you'll be a star." So he always comes up to me and says, "Is this one of those not-annoy-the-audience . . .?" And I say, "You better believe it." Or he says, "Is this one of our good ones?" And I say, "Well, this is *almost* that . . ." We work that way, and now he preaches that as though it's gospel, and he does a great job of not annoying the audience.

Q: *Would you say something about your use of colour?*
HH: When we were making *Red River*, we discussed whether to use colour or not. At that time colour wasn't very good. It had a kind of garish look to it. I didn't like it, and we were trying to get a feeling of the period, so we made *Red River* in black-and-white. Some things I think go well in black-and-white; they give you a feeling of being *older*. Now colour is better, and it'd be pretty hard for me to make a picture without colour. I think I enjoy it now. We've learned how to handle it, to control it, to print it. The colour is faster, so we can use it just as if we were using black-and-white; it doesn't jump at us. We can use all the fall colours, ambers and muted colours, and come out with a very good-looking picture. On *El Dorado*, I noticed that the Remington paintings always had a great slash of light across the street coming out of the saloon door. So I said to the cameraman, "How do we get that?" He said, "Use yellow light, but don't walk your people through it—they'll look like they had yellow jaundice or something." He used back light on them and it was a very mellow, pleasant look. We used it in the last picture.

Q: *What kind of relationship do you like to have with your cameraman?*
HH: There's a lot of cooperation with a good cameraman, and I've been fortunate in having good ones. Some of them get very tired of working in normal stuff, they relax and then you pep them up and get them to take chances. I tell them, "If you make two good scenes for me, you can make two mediocre ones and one bad one." All I'm interested in is the good one. So they go ahead and take chances, and their work shows it. Because you people pass up the bad scenes, but you really appreciate the good one.

Q: *Could you say something about the way you improvise with actors, how many liberties you're willing to take with a scene?*
HH: A lot of that has been overemphasised. We have a scene that we're going to do: I'm interested first in the action and next in the words they speak. If I can't make the action good, I don't try to use the words. If I want something to happen in a hurry, I can't have a man stop and read a line. I let him run on through yelling something. I must

change to fit the action because, after all, it's a motion picture. I don't change it so much—we end up with the same scene, except we just do it in a little different style.

Q: *I recently saw* Tiger Shark *and I was amazed by Edward G. Robinson's performance. It seems so much better than what he did in* Little Caesar.
HH: When we started that picture, it was written as a very dour, sour man. At the end of the first day I said to Eddie Robinson, "This is going to be the dullest picture that's ever been made." And he said, "What can we do?" I said, "Well, if you're willing to try it with me, why, let's make him a happy-go-lucky, talkative . . . you're going to have to keep talking all through the picture." He said, "Fine, let's do it." So every day I give him a sheet of yellow paper and say, "Here's your lines." He's a fine actor, and I thought he did a great job. But I hate to think of what the picture would have been if we'd done the dour, sour man instead of this rather gay, futile man, because the whole tenor of the picture changed.

Q: *Could you tell us something about the off-camera lives of people like Bogart and Cagney?*
HH: I had enough trouble with them on the set to worry about.

Q: *How do you handle difficult actors?*
HH: Look, if they're good, they're no trouble to handle. The only people that are hard to handle are bad actors. I had trouble the first day with Bogart. I think I grabbed him by the lapels and pushed his head up against the wall and said, "Look, Bogie, I tell you how to get tough, but don't get tough with me." He said, "I won't." Everything was fine from that time on.

Q: *Do you pick the scripts you work on?*
HH: I get complete opportunity to pick the script. There are only a few times that I've done a favour for somebody and made a picture, and usually it hasn't been good because I know the kind of a story I can tell and that I enjoy telling. Then it's fun.

Q: *Could you explain how the day-to-day writing goes on a script?*
HH: Well, when Hecht and MacArthur and I used to work on a script, we'd sit in a room and work for two hours and then we'd play backgammon for an hour. Then we'd start again and one of us would be one character and one would be another character. We'd read our lines of dialogue and the whole idea was to try to stump the other people, to see if they could think of something crazier than you could. And that is the kind of dialogue we used, and the kind that was fun. We could usually remember what we said, and put it right down and go on working. And sometimes you're so far in a picture, and you get an idea that you're going to change a character, so you just go back and change the lines that you've written for that character and start all over again.

Q: *One of the best known lines in American films is, "If you want any-thing, just whistle" in* To Have and Have Not. *Who was responsible— Faulkner, Furthman, Hawks, or was it improvised?*
HH: I was making a test of Bacall, so I wrote the scene just for the test and it went over so well we had an awful time trying to put it into the picture. Faulkner was the one who found a place to put it. He said, "If we put these people in a hotel corridor where nobody else is around, then I think we can make that scene work." So we did it. I wrote the line, but he wrote the stuff that led up to it. Bill and I were very good friends. We hunted and fished a lot. I bought the first story that he sold; he was working as a clerk in Macy's basement in New York. He worked with me on, oh, half a dozen pictures. I could call on him any time and ask him for a scene, and he always gave it to me.

Q: *Could you tell us something about* Land of the Pharaohs?
HH: We had a lot of fun, and we had a pretty good premise of a story. For writers we had Bill Faulkner and Harry Kurnitz, a very fine play-wright. We started to work on it, and Faulkner said, "I don't know how a pharaoh talks." I said, "Well, I don't know, I never talked to one." And he said, "Is it all right if I write him like a Kentucky colonel?" And Kurnitz said, "I can't do it like a Kentucky colonel, but I'm a student of Shakespeare—I think I could do it as though it were *King Lear*." So I said, "Well, you fellows go ahead and I'll rewrite your stuff." They did it, and I messed it up, and . . . we didn't know what a pharaoh *did*.

Q: *The dialogue in your films is very sophisticated. Have you ever found the Production Code restrictive?*

HH: Oh, no. We made one picture, *Big Sleep,* and they read the script and they didn't care for the end Chandler wrote. I said, "Why don't you suggest a better one?" And they did. It was a lot more violent, it was everything I wanted, and I made it and was very happy about it. I said, "I'll hire you fellows as writers."

Q: *What things do you think you have in common with John Ford?*

HH: A great deal. He was a good director when I started, and I copied him every time I could. I don't think I've done nearly as good a job as Ford on some things. I think he's got the greatest vision for a tableau, a long shot, of any man. One of my favourite pictures of all time is *The Quiet Man,* which I think was just a beautiful picture. Ford, oh, he has done some things that are just fabulous. And he was the first man to do them. Every time I run into a scene that I think Ford does very well, I stop and think, "What would he have done there?" And then I go ahead and do it, because he gets more use out of a bad sky . . . he goes right on shooting whether the weather's bad or good, and he gets fabulous effects. I was making a picture with Wayne, *Red River.* We had a burial scene, and the cameraman said, "We'd better hurry, there's a cloud coming across that mountain right behind." So I said to Wayne, "Now, look, you go out there—if you forget your lines, just say anything, keep talking until I tell you to come on in. We'll make the sound afterwards." And I waited until the cloud got near, thought of Ford, and started the scene. Then we started the burial service, and the cloud passed right over the whole scene. I told Ford. I said, "Hey, I've made one almost as good as you can do. You better go and see it."

Q: *Could you comment on your earliest films?*

HH: A very astute and wise man gave me a chance to direct, and I made a picture *[The Road to Glory, 1926]* that I don't think anybody enjoyed except a few critics. And he said, "Look, you've shown you can make a picture, but for God's sake go out and make entertainment." So I went home and wrote a story about Adam and Eve waking up in the Garden of Eden and called it *Fig Leaves.* It got its cost back in one theatre. And that taught me a very good lesson; from that time on, I've been following his advice about trying to make entertainment.

Q: *You're famous for taking a scene that has elements of pain and humiliation, such as the finger amputation in* The Big Sky *or the steak scene in* Only Angels Have Wings, *and either playing it lightly or for outright slapstick . . .*

HH: You're looking for something new to be funny. I told John Wayne (on *Red River*), "Look, I've got an idea for a funny scene. You get your finger caught between a saddle horn and a rope, and it's mangled, and they say, 'Well, that finger isn't going to be much use to you.' And they get you drunk and they heat up an iron in the fire and sharpen a knife and cut off your finger." He said, "What kind of a scene is that?" "Oh," I said, "It's supposed to be funny." He said, "That isn't funny." "Oh," I said, "if you're not good enough, then we won't do it. I'll do it with somebody else who's a better actor." So I did it with Kirk Douglas, and I told John, "You better go see that picture." And he came back and said, "If you say a funeral is funny, I'll do a funeral." Because I think that was a funny scene. I think that humour comes very close to being tragedy. In *Rio Bravo*, Wayne hit a fellow across the face the most horrible way. Dean Martin said, "Hey, take it easy." And Wayne said, "I'm not gonna hurt him." The audience thought it was funny. In *Rio Lobo*, we set a man on fire. He's burning and somebody goes to pick up a blanket to put the thing out, and Wayne says, "Let him burn." And the other fellow says, "Don't let him burn so much he can't sign the papers we want him to sign." And, I don't know, to me it was funny.

Q: *Pauline Kael attacked your films because she said they are examples of male chauvinism.*

HH: God, I don't know what that means.

Q: *That the role of women is seen to be subservient and auxiliary to the heroics of the men.*

HH: Well, I've seen so many pictures where the hero gets in the moonlight and says silly things to a girl. I'd reverse it and let the girl do the chasing around, you know, and it works out pretty well. Anyway, I know that a little better than I do that other stuff.

Q: *You say you are an entertainer, and the French critics in the last few*
years have been treating you as an entertainer and a philosopher . . .
HH: Oh, I listen to them, and I get open-mouthed and wonder where
they find some of the stuff that they say about me. All I'm doing is
telling a story. I'm very glad that they like it, and I'm very glad that a
lot of them are copying what I do, but they find things . . . I work on
the fact that if I like somebody and think they're attractive, I can make
them attractive. If I think a thing's funny, then people laugh at it.
They give me credit for an awful lot of things that I don't pay any
attention to.

Q: *Your films always have a solid structure. But in today's films it almost*
seems unfashionable to have one . . .
HH: If they let those fellows that are making them today go on with
no structure, when they make the second or third picture I think
they'll begin to learn that they better have a little structure. We made
a picture that worked pretty well called *Big Sleep*, and I never figured
out what was going on, but I thought that the basic thing had great
scenes in it and it was good entertainment. After that got by, I said,
"I'm never going to worry about being logical again." But I think that
in some of today's pictures you don't know where you are, who's talking, or anything, and that's why they have got motion pictures lying
around over in Hollywood that they can't make head or tail out of. I
think a director's a story-teller, and if he tells a story that people can't
understand, then he shouldn't be a director. You take the Western.
Every time a man I know is a first-rate director goes after a Western, you
come out with a pretty good picture, because a Western's good entertainment, it's dramatic . . . But you get somebody who's going to
make a Western about a psycho or a left-handed gun or something
like that, then it's no good, it doesn't live up to what people want in a
Western.

Q: *What did you think of* The Wild Bunch?
HH: Somebody asked me about it, and I said, "Well, he doesn't know
how to direct. I can kill four men and bury 'em before he gets through
using slow motion to make one die." All I saw was a lot of red paint and
blood running.

Q: *You're quite an inspiration for a lot of young European directors . . .?*
HH: A number of them have a great deal of talent, but they're telling pictures that are good for only France, Italy and Germany. When I go over there I talk to them about it. I say, "Why don't you fellows widen out, make a picture that is good for the world? You aren't going to get enough money to work with unless you get it out of universal entertainment." And I think they're beginning to work on that. A couple of the Frenchmen do beautiful jobs, and I admire their work. Peter Bogdanovich, who made *Targets*, I think is eventually going to turn out some very fine work. Of the older directors, I admire Carol Reed's work very much. I like Hitchcock's work, and Billy Wilder's. When I think I can learn something, I go to see any of their pictures, but if I think I can't learn, I don't go.

Hawks Talks: New Anecdotes from the Old Master

JOSEPH McBRIDE AND GERALD PEARY / 1974

HOWARD HAWKS, GOING ON seventy-nine, is full of ideas for movie projects, and he didn't say a word about retirement during an interview in February at his home in Palm Springs. Drawing on an amazing reserve of energy, Hawks kept talking for five hours, forgetting about a stew he was planning to cook for dinner. When we left, dazed with fatigue, Hawks immediately went into a story conference with the actor Max Baer, who had come to ask his help with a script. Hawks had already made some characteristic suggestions to Baer, advising him to cut out a flashback and giving him tips on how to make one scene more violent.

We began the interview by asking Hawks if we could discuss subjects which hadn't been covered in his previous interviews, and he seemed glad for the opportunity, talking at length about his early years in Hollywood and clearing up some mysteries about his career. On a few points, though, he remained intractable. We found it difficult, for example, to sustain a discussion of the sexual relationships in his films. As Molly Haskell pointed out in her article on Hawks in the last issue of *Film Comment*, Hawks is "at once the most knowing and naive" of directors, and much of the thematic complexity of his work springs from unconscious sources: witness his guileless response to our prodding questions about some unmistakable sexual imagery in *A Girl in Every Port*. Hawks also showed little interest in discussing his family, a subject which his interviewers (ardent Fordians) hoped would shed some light on the absence of nuclear family life in his work. The very fact that Hawks remained reticent on the subject is in itself very revealing.

Another Hawksian idiosyncrasy was the way he somehow managed, despite our stated intentions, to slip in most of his favorite, and by now maddening, anecdotes (discovering Jane Russell in a dentist's office, teaching Lauren Bacall how to talk, etc.). At the end he casually remarked, "Some of that stuff has been printed before, you know, but you can just cut it out." He also told us, off the record, about several amusing scenes he plans to use in a picture about world-traveling oil riggers, to be shot in Europe with a plot loosely reminiscent of *A Girl in Every Port*. And three weeks after the interview, appearing at the Los Angeles County Museum of Art to conclude a retrospective of his work, Hawks revealed yet another project—a Western with Cary Grant playing a consumptive dentist partially modeled on Doc Holliday.

Q: *Mr. Hawks, we'd like to begin by talking about your family and your early years in Indiana.*
HAWKS: We moved from Indiana to Neenah, Wisconsin, when I was about two years old. My father, my grandfather and my uncle all had paper mills. Then due to my mother's health we came to California when I was ten years old. We lived in Pasadena. My father was vice president of a hotel company that owned a bunch of the big hotels up in San Francisco. And then we had an orange grove in Glendora. I went to some high school in Glendora and to a fine school in Pasadena that taught woodworking and metalworking; it was where anybody went who was going to study engineering. I went to Exeter to prep school and then to Cornell University.

Q: *Is it true that* Come and Get It *was based on your grandfather?*
HAWKS: Yes, well, it was based on about four men. She [Edna Ferber] took parts from each man. They were all big lumber men. She was a clerk in a five-and-ten-cent store or something like that in Appleton, Wisconsin.

Q: *Have you ever put other members of your family into a movie?*
HAWKS: I put my grandmother in. Whenever she was happy she started to cry. She'd say "I'm so happy!" and start to cry. She was a marvelous characters. And I've used things about everybody. There are a lot of incidents that have happened or that I've seen happen that I've used in pictures. That's where you get them.

Q: *Could you tell us about your brother Kenneth?*
HAWKS: For brothers we got along very well. I was national junior champion in tennis and he was intercollegiate champion. Ken was awful good; he beat Tilden four weeks before Tilden won at Forest Hills. We used to play every day with two world's champions, Maurie McLaughlin and Tom Bundy. We were the only competition they could get in Santa Monica. I helped my brother get started as a director. He did a pretty good job with his first picture and then when he was doing his second picture he was killed [in the crash of an airplane doing an aerial scene in 1930].

Q: *What kind of director do you think he would have developed into?*
HAWKS: Well, he seemed to be developing into a fellow who was much warmer than I was—a little bit more like Frank Borzage was, that kind of picture.

Q: *How old were you when you were a race car driver?*
HAWKS: Oh, seventeen or eighteen, somewhere around there. I raced cars for about three years, did my own work on them, and built a car that won Indianapolis. I won quite a few races because I had a better car than the other fellow had. This was a Mercedes that my grandfather gave me. I had a sort of partner and he had a great big chain-driven Fiat. It had a great deal more power but it didn't handle as well. We raced on dirt tracks. It wasn't very polite racing. If you could shove somebody through a fence you did it.

Q: *Did you have any bad accidents?*
HAWKS: Oh no, just a broken leg.

Q: *Did your family ever try to steer you toward any kind of a profession?*
HAWKS: No, I wanted to be an engineer. I went to school where I wanted to; my whole family seems to do that. I went to Cornell, my brothers went to Yale, my son went to Princeton. In the summer, to make some money, I worked at Famous Players-Lasky Studio [later Paramount]. I was sort of an assistant property man. Douglas Fairbanks was making a picture, and he wanted a modern set, a modern apartment. Nobody knew what the hell a modern thing was, but I had studied about five or six years of architecture, and I knew, so I said, "Oh, I can do that." Doug said he liked it, and he and I became friends. He was courting Mary (Pickford) at the time, and so Mary made me her property man. I think principally because I could get them both to go to work when they were in their bungalow. [Laughs] Then she moved me up to assistant director. And one day [on *The Little Princess*, 1917, directed by Marshall Neilan] the director got drunk and Mary said, "I guess we can't work." I said, "Why don't we make some scenes?" She said, "Can you do it?" and I said, "Yeah." I made some and she liked it very much.

Q: *Do you remember what your first moment as a director was like?*
HAWKS: She played a dual role, and she said, "I wish I could follow myself into the room." We drew a blank after she entered the room, crossed the film behind her, then rewound it and let her come in. And it happened that they matched. The cameraman was just sweating because he said it's only one chance in ten that it'll match. But it worked beautifully, and she was so pleased. And I remember another scene where she wished that a doll could come into the room; it was a fantasy, you know, one would talk to her. "Well," I said, "we can do that." We put soft solder in the arms and legs of the doll and we made it so we could move it by stop motion a little ways at a time. You didn't really direct Mary. She was a very sure person in her own category. But I made the scenes. Then the war came along and I got quite a little bit of notoriety because she came up on a bond drive and said she would come out to where our squadron was training and I could take her around. So, holy smoke, officers and colonels, everybody like that was wondering what the devil the private was doing with Mary.

Q: *What kind of experiences did you have during the war?*

HAWKS: There wasn't very much. We went through what they called ground school. I was commander of a squadron. While I was waiting to be called I went out and got about an hour's experience flying. And then when we got down to flying school I think I got about an hour and three quarters flying and they made me an instructor. Nobody flew in those days; nobody knew how to. And it was awfully slow because there were two thousand cadets down there and only seven airplanes. I remember one time the colonel came out, we were all digging post-holes, and he said, "What are you doing, young men?" And one guy said, "Learning to fly, sir." They threw him in the brig for doing it. The chance of getting into combat was very futile, and I went into a course in big gun spotting, flying and spotting artillery shelters. Then the war was over.

Q: *How did you become a producer for Famous Players-Lasky?*

HAWKS: After the war my brother and I rented a house in Hollywood, and there was a little red-cheeked Jewish boy, very bright guy, I used to talk stories with him. I really didn't know what he did. And one day Jesse Lasky called me and asked me to come up and see him. He asked if I would like to take charge of making forty pictures for him. I said, "Why did you pick me?" He said, "Irving Thalberg"—that was the little fellow I knew—"said you know more about stories than anybody that he knows, so I'd like to have you." I said, "Just what do you want?" and he said, "I'd like to know in the next two months forty pictures that we're going to make. You have to get the stories. You think you can do it?" I said, "How much money do I have to do it with?" And he said, "All you want." I said, "Sure I can do it."

At that time all stories for pictures were written just for pictures, and the writers weren't too hot. But I bought two Rex Beaches and two Joseph Conrads and two Zane Greys. Anybody could buy 'em; nobody had ever sold anything. The forty pictures I made for Paramount, that was the most successful year Paramount ever had. I really had too much to do, because I was writing the titles—they were silent pictures—and reading the scripts and seeing the film. Forty pictures, that's just too much. So I hired some newspapermen to write titles. I started the horrible thing of associate producers. I produced about sixty pictures for Famous Players-Lasky and Thalberg wanted me to come down to Metro-Goldwyn, so I went down there. Then I quit.

Q: *You directed a couple of short comedies before you became a feature director. Do those still exist?*
HAWKS: Christ, I don't know.

Q: *How did you get to make them?*
HAWKS: I knew Jack Warner—he was just beginning, didn't have too much money in those days. And I think that I loaned Warner some money. So he said, "Would you like to make some comedies?" And I said sure. I made three or four of them, I don't remember how many, and then I got bored with doing them.

Q: *Who was in them?*
HAWKS: The star was Monty Banks. I named him—his name was Mario Bianchi—and Monty Banks married Gracie Fields and became a multimillionaire. He got fifty dollars a week. One time he got fresh, so I put a ladder up to the house and had him climb into the chimney. He got all covered with black and he got down on his knees and begged me to let him back. So we let him back but I always kept the ladder around. The girl was Alice Terry, who married Rex Ingram and became quite a big star.

Q: *Do you remember the titles of those pictures?*
HAWKS: God, no.

Q: *Could you tell us the stories?*
HAWKS: No.

Q: *Do you remember anything else about the shooting?*
HAWKS: Oh, I remember that I used to drive automobiles in stunts. Tipped over on the wheels, skidded, drove into poles. I did everything in the pictures. The budget was only three thousand dollars.

Q: *Were they successful?*
HAWKS: Yeah, very successful.

Q: *Were you doing them in the hope of becoming a feature director?*
HAWKS: I don't remember that. I didn't feel I knew enough about directing pictures. I finally got tired of other people directing and me writing, so I went to see a movie every night for six months. And if I thought the movie was worth studying I saw it twice that same night until I felt that I knew enough to direct. I learned right in the beginning from Jack Ford, and I learned what not to do by watching Cecil De Mille.

Q: *Your first feature,* The Road to Glory, *apparently doesn't exist. I read the plot synopsis and it seems a very solemn thing, quite unlike the films you did later.*
HAWKS: Well, I was working at Metro-Goldwyn for Thalberg and he promised to give me a chance to direct. I said, "A year ago you said I could direct. You fooled me." He said, "Howard, Christ, we can get all the directors we need. I can't get anybody to do your work." I said, "I just quit this morning." He and I were very good friends, and he said, "Nothing could change your mind?" I said, "Nothing can change it." "Well," he said, "I could let you direct." I said, "No, I don't want you to do that. You can let me direct some time after I show you what I can do." And I went off to play golf. I ran into the head of Fox Studios [William Fox]. He said, "What are you doing?" I said, "Playing golf." "No," he said, "I mean where are you working?" I said, "Playing golf." "Aren't you working for Metro?" I said no. He said, "When could you start to work for Fox?" I said, "No, I had enough of that job. I'm gonna direct." He said, "O.K., you start to direct." And I wrote the story.

It was taken from a little incident that happened once where a beautiful girl went blind from drinking bootleg liquor at my house. While we were waiting for the doctor, she said, "Just because I'm blind it doesn't mean I can't perform pretty good in bed." Nobody seemed interested in that kind of thing then. I loved the attitude that she had, and I wrote the story, which was a very dramatic, serious, downbeat story. It didn't have any fun in it.

Q: *What do you remember about some of your other silent pictures—* Fig Leaves, *for instance? Part of it was supposed to have been in color.*

HAWKS: I couldn't remember *Fig Leaves* until I saw it a couple of years ago in France. I thought it was amazingly modern. It's got two reels of color in it. I didn't know how to use color so I got this big set, had it done in black and silver, had all the color taken out of it. And if I remember right, I don't think the color showed up. I think they printed that part in black and white.

Q: *Most of your movies, even the oldest ones, look very fresh and modern today. Why do you think that is?*
HAWKS: Most of them were well written. That's why they last.

Q: *What was* Fazil *like?*
HAWKS: Christ almighty, can you imagine Charlie Farrell as an Arabian sheik? Charlie was such a shy, withdrawn guy, and we had a beautiful Swedish girl, Greta Nissen, in it. Their courtship ended by drawing back from a shot of the Eiffel Tower down to the two of them in bed under a sheet. I told the girl, "Now, Charlie's real shy, you're going to have to do something under those covers." And I told Charlie, "Now, this girl's real shy . . ." Well, they were two of the busiest beavers you've ever seen in all your life. At least I got fun out of *that*.

Q: The Air Circus?
HAWKS: *Air Circus* was a good picture. It was about two kids learning to fly, and they took off and flew in the picture; they actually soloed. The only trouble was at that time sound came in, and they asked me, "What do you know about dialogue?" And I said, "I just know how people speak." So they gave me a dialogue director [Lewis R. Seiler] who used to be a burlesque comic for Minsky's. He made the dialogue scenes because I wouldn't make them. I said, "Nobody talks like that." Seiler was a director who did anything they wanted him to do. And you have never *known* such bad dialogue. So I didn't make a picture for three years in a row. They wanted everybody to make a scene to show that they could use dialogue. And the production head, Winnie Sheehan, didn't like me because I made a picture called *A Girl in Every Port* where we threw a cop into the water. Sheehan used to be police commissioner in New York, and he didn't like to see that. When he came out of the preview, he said, "This is the worst picture that Fox

ever made." It got its cost back in one theater. So he didn't like me too well. And every time I got a story ready, he'd turn it down.

Q: *What is the reason for the running bit of business in* A Girl in Every Port *of one guy pulling the other guy's finger?*
HAWKS: You ever hit anybody hard? Your finger goes out of joint, and somebody takes it and pulls it back into joint. I hit Hemingway and I broke the whole back of my hand. I wish it had just gone out of joint.

Q: *Why did you hit Hemingway?*
HAWKS: He just said, "Can you hit?" I broke my whole hand. He laughed like hell and he sat up all night making a sling out of a tomato can so that I could go shooting with him the next morning. It didn't do my hand any good. It's an absolutely different shape.

Q: *Was the finger business supposed to be a gesture of friendship? You used it again with Kirk Douglas and Dewey Martin in* The Big Sky.
HAWKS: Oh, it's just like in *Rio Bravo* when Wayne rolled cigarettes for Dean Martin because his fingers were shaking. One thing you can do is to look at all the pictures I've ever made and you'll see that nobody pats another on the back. That's the goddamnedest inane thing I've ever known.

Q: *You were quoted in* Variety *a couple of years ago as saying you were going to direct a film about the friendship of Hemingway and Robert Capa, the famous news photographer. Are you still working on that?*
HAWKS: Well, I tell you, when you make a picture about real people and their names are used, you have more trouble. . . . In making *Sergeant York* we had to get twenty releases—every member of his squad in the army, his lieutenant, his captain, his major, anybody that we mentioned we had to get releases. I think the story of getting the releases, where we found the various people and how we paid them off, was almost better than *Sergeant York*. I'm too goddamn lazy, and I've got to have too much fun to run around getting releases. The head of one of the big companies, who wants me to make it, I told him I'd make the story if he'd get the releases. He said, "I didn't know it was that much trouble." You've got Hemingway's family to contend with,

his ex-wives. . . . Oh, Christ! So for the moment it's stymied, but I think we can probably do it.

Q: *That's an interesting period in Hemingway's life. From reading about it, it seems he was a little unbalanced. He was doing a lot of bizarre things, getting into the war even though he was a correspondent, blowing up pillboxes. . . .*

HAWKS: I wouldn't say it was in that period; he had done that all his life. What the hell, he was mixed up in the Spanish War long before that. I remember one funny thing—Capa went over with the first wave that went through the water at Anzio beachhead. He made those marvelous pictures of everything shaking. Ernest got over by flying over three or four days later. He got mixed up in some way and Capa found him shot in the leg or something. Capa left him for about three hours and went on to get his camera so he could get a picture of Ernest's leg. [Laughs] You see, the story of one man gets kind of boring but the story of a friendship is something that lets you make better scenes. I remember another time when he was throwing knives at Ernest; Ernest was standing like this [Hawks makes a crucifixion pose] in front of a door. And all kinds of crazy things they used to do. Nobody else can do 'em, they don't know the things, because I've seen them happen.

Q: *Would it be a comedy?*

HAWKS: Well, I don't know. Especially in the last ten or twelve years, every time I can get some comedy into a scene, I'll do it. You can call it a comedy if you want to. It isn't an outright comedy, but I would much rather tell these things than something serious. Hemingway was . . . we were good friends. He interested me. Strange guy.

Q: *Some people have said that the male characters in your films border on homosexuality. What do you think of that?*

HAWKS: I'd say it's a goddamn silly statement to make. It sounds like a homosexual speaking. [Smiles]

Q: *Well, a lot of your movies, such as* El Dorado, *end on a shot of two men together. You don't like to end a movie with a man and a woman together in the last shot.*

HAWKS: Do *you*? I'm not doing a love story, I'm doing a story of friendship. In a picture like *Love Story* it's great to end the thing like that. *That's* a love story. But it's a misnomer in *El Dorado*. The girl is sleeping with one man and Wayne comes to town and she starts sleeping with him. I'm just doing the way people really are. That's what happens in life.

Q: *Two men in love with the same woman is a situation which occurs in your movies over and over again. Does that come out of your experience?*
HAWKS: That's one of the simple rules of drama. It makes good scenes. If people that the audience like in a picture like somebody else, that's the best boost for a character that you can make. Now, if you've got a heavy liking someone, that's no boost for the person that they like. But when you've got a nice guy that likes someone, immediately that character is boosted.

Q: *What makes someone a villain in your movies? There are certain kinds of characters who seem to deserve getting killed.*
HAWKS: Oh, I don't know. I think Chris George in *El Dorado* was a pretty nice guy, wasn't he?

Q: *Yes, but why wouldn't you have him sent through the door to get shot as the Robert Donner character was? What's the difference? What kind of man do you consider a bad guy?*
HAWKS: Anybody who frames somebody, to kill him. How would you feel if you were in there, and there was some guy framing you? You'd say, "You son of a bitch, you're going to get what you were gonna do to me." But Chris George said, "You didn't give me a chance." And Wayne said, "You're too good to give a chance to." That's their theory, that's their code, their religion.

Q: *Why do you think scenes of violence are funny?*
HAWKS: I've seen so many people laugh at violence when it happens. Kind of hysterical laughter. It's the easiest time for you to get a laugh. I'm getting goddamn sick of these pictures, you know, nothing but violence. Peckinpah and I believe in exactly the opposite thing. I like it when it's so quick that you say, "My God, did it really happen?"

Q: *The ending of* Air Force, *the obliteration of the Japanese fleet, goes on so long that it seems like you were piling it on.*

HAWKS: That wasn't my fault. We took thousands of feet of film of miniatures and all those things. They just saw the first cut; they released the first assembly. Nothing I could do. Warner said, "Look, I'm not going to have it spoiled. This is the way it goes out." There was too much of it.

Q: *What was the scene you cut out of* RIO BRAVO *because you thought the film was getting excessively violent?*

HAWKS: It was the idea of a bunch of horsemen coming around a corner and one man throws himself on the ground. He said, "A man can't shoot you because a horse won't step on a man." Now, that is not strictly true; a horse will step on a man, but he'll *try* not to. I used that in *El Dorado.* I even thought about trying to use the same film because it was the same street. [Laughs] I took it out for a very good reason. It was too much of a good thing. If you get too much violence you lose the whole thing.

Q: *Is it true that you've never used a flashback?*

HAWKS: I can't remember.

Q: *What's wrong with flashbacks?*

HAWKS: What's good about 'em? If you're not good enough to tell a story without having flashbacks, why the hell do you try to tell them? Oh, I think some extraordinarily good writer can figure out some way of telling a story in flashbacks, but I hate them. Just like I hate screwed-up camera angles. I like to tell it with a simple scene. I don't want you to be conscious that this is dramatic, because it throws it all off. People ask me why I had the shot in *El Dorado* of the man falling into the camera. Well, they don't know that I didn't have any set to work with; I *had* to do it that way. I like the scene in *El Dorado* where Wayne and the girl said goodbye in the door and he rode off amongst the cactus as the sun was going down. When I got down there I said, "Build me a set with a big doorway." We watched the sun go down, picked out a spot, staked it in the ground, set up the camera, and waited for a good sunset. I went and made it in ten minutes and walked away. It looked beautiful on the screen.

Q: *What's the function of the old man character in your Westerns?*
HAWKS: I think it's a way of telling the story, telling the plot. They tell
it in an interesting way. You're not conscious that you're getting the
plot; you're being amused by him. I don't want to use a half-wit, and I
don't like psychiatric characters. I like people that they like. When I
couldn't get Walter Brennan I got somebody else. When I was casting
Barbary Coast, they brought in Walter Brennan and I looked at him and
laughed. I said, "Mr. Brennan, did they give you some lines?" And he
said, "Yeah." I said, "Do you know them?" "Uh-huh." "Do you want to
read them?" And he said, "With or without?" I said, "With or without
what?" He said, "Teeth." I laughed again and said, "Without." He
turned around and read the lines, and I said, "You're hired." When we
were going to do *Red River*, there was one line in the scenario, it said,
"The cook's name was Groot." He said, "What are we going to do?"
Didn't worry me. I said, "Remember how we met, that 'with or without
teeth'? Well, I got an idea that you're gonna lose your teeth in a poker
game with an Indian. And every night he makes you give them back."
"Oh," he said, "we can't do that." I said, "Yes, we can."

Q: *Do you plan to make another picture with John Wayne?*
HAWKS: I don't want Wayne anymore unless I get a story that's right
for him. Duke called me a while ago and said, "Howard, let's make a
picture. Everything I've been doing has been lousy." I said, "Well, I
haven't found a story." He said, "I found one. I'd play the part of an old
gunfighter. He's walking down the street and some guy calls him out,
but he's lost his glasses, and the man is hazy. Finally a girl comes running up and brings him some glasses, and he shoots the guy." I said,
"Duke, all your life you've stood for something. Why should you throw
it away for something like this?" He said, "Don't you think it's funny?"
I said, "No, I think it's pitiful."

"What about *True Grit*?," he said. I said, "*True Grit* was an
exaggerated thing and it got by because the director didn't know
whether he was making a comedy or a drama." Right now, when you
pay Wayne a million dollars, I wouldn't say he was worth it unless you
had the right story. And another thing, I'll tell you very frankly, I'm
not very interested in making pictures about old men. Like in *Rio
Lobo*—Wayne had a hard time getting on and off his horse; he can't

move like a big cat the way he used to. He has to hold his belly in; he's a different kind of person.

Q: *I thought in* El Dorado *especially you made use of Wayne's age in a very moving way, showing how he was slowing up.*
HAWKS: Oh, we made use of it, yeah. In *Red River* he wasn't sure whether he wanted to play an old man, and I said, "Duke, you're going to be old pretty soon, so you'd better get some practice." Wayne did a hell of a job, and Jack Ford said, "I never knew that big sonofabitch could act." So every time I made a picture with Wayne, Ford would come around and watch. But, you can't do a love story with him now, and he doesn't want love stories. Well, it makes it pretty hard to find a story. I could have made a good picture out of the ransom picture he did. *Big Jake*, was that the one? I could have done a good job on that. But I tell you, some of these fellows . . . Eastwood makes so much money now that you'd stand a better chance without him. You can't afford to pay him so much money because you're competing against pictures that don't cost so much. You're better off using someone who isn't so expensive.

I had a call last week from Eastwood; he said he'd like to make a picture with me. He wants to be a director and he wants to study the way I work. He said he's doing well enough now that he can afford to take a share of the picture. "Anything that I lose won't hurt me," he said. I don't know about it, but I'd like to try. He's a personality, and if you look at my career you'll find that I like actors less than I do personalities. Bogart was a great actor but he was also a hell of a personality. Muni was a great actor but not a real personality. Huston had a terrific personality. Eddie Robinson wasn't half as good an actor as he was supposed to be, but he was a hell of a personality.

Q: *We brought along a magazine,* Film Comment, *because we want to show you something Borden Chase said about you. They never gave you a chance to reply, so we thought in all fairness you should be given a chance to go on the record with a response. [Hawks spent about five minutes reading Chase's remarks on* Red River *from an interview with Jim Kitses in the "Hollywood Screenwriter" issue of* Film Comment, *Winter 1970–71. Briefly, Chase attacked Hawks for changing parts of his script; for historical inaccuracies; for shortening John Ireland's part because Ireland was "fooling around with Howard's girl"; and for allegedly stealing part of the ending from Howard Hughes's* The Outlaw. *Hawks chuckled occasionally as he read the interview.]*

HAWKS: He must have been drinking when he wrote this because he's so full of shit. That's funny. Borden Chase is the kind of a writer that imagines an awful lot of things; he does quite a bit of drinking. I bought the story from him and asked him to work on it. I'd been working on a story of the King Ranch. The fellow that asked me to make it owned the King Ranch; we were friends. I thought it was a good story. I chased down a Catholic priest down there, and the priest told me many, many things about the King Ranch. I talked to the fellow that owned the ranch and I said, "I'm not going to do a milk-and-water version," so I gave it up, but I had a lot of stuff left over. And every time I tried to change Borden Chase's story he objected to it.

He did not work on it at the same time [Charles] Schnee did and all that stuff he talked about. I got Schnee and we rewrote the story. We rewrote a whole bunch of things. He hadn't finished the story for the simple reason that when he finished it, *The Saturday Evening Post* didn't like it. They said they'd take it if he'd rewrite it. I thought the way he wrote it was pretty lousy. I never introduced Schnee as my secretary or any of that crap. He just got angry at the idea that we were going to change the story that he wrote. We were going to make a movie, not write a serial for *The Saturday Evening Post.*

Where he says he was telling Wayne how to make that walk through the cattle—he didn't even know that was going to be done. He never saw that until it was done; it was not in the script. You didn't have to tell Wayne anything about walking through cattle; Wayne knew. He took his horse right to the cattle and then he walked through 'em. They just accidentally got in his way and he just shoved 'em and kept on walking.

I never had any talk with [Chase] about [Hughes]. He was sucking around Hughes afterwards, trying to get some work, and actually he got it all wrong because Hughes went to him and offered him a job if he would testify so Hughes could say that I was stealing from him. For instance, the part where he says "The Brothers Warner stole *Hell's Angels* and changed it to *Only Angels Have Wings* and it was Howard Hawks then and by God now he's done it again." *Only Angels Have Wings* was not made for Warner Brothers; it was made for Columbia. And it was made from a story that I wrote. This is a lot of garbage, because *Only Angels Have Wings* was made about a true incident; it was told to me by a bush pilot down in Mexico. He told me a marvelous thing I couldn't put in the picture. He went to a dinner in Mexico where there was a very attractive girl who had been married for a year to a fellow with a burnt face and great eyes. A fellow was saying, "A year ago tonight we were celebrating the marriage. About one o'clock you shoved us all out. You went to bed about two minutes past. Then you got up at ten minutes past one, and then you had at it again a bit later." The girl said, "You son of a bitch, you were peeping." He said no, and brought out a graph that was made from a machine that you attach to your airplane. It shows when you started the motor, when you bounced while taking off, when you got up. And they hung it under the bed. The girl hung it up, she was so proud of it. This was exactly how they met in *Only Angels Have Wings*. So he couldn't have had anything to do with *Only Angels Have Wings*. [*Chase confused Only Angels Have Wings with the 1930 Dawn Patrol, produced and released in 1930; Hughes Hell's Angels was begun in 1927 and completed in 1930. Chase's mistake was corrected in the Film Comment book, The Hollywood Screenwriters—editor.*]

Then Chase goes on, "Duke said, 'We're dropping Cherry Valance.' I said, 'What do you mean?' 'Well,' he said, 'he's fooling around with Howard's girl.' I can't remember her name, she's married now." Actually what happened was that I got tired of this actor [John Ireland] getting drunk every night, losing his gun and his hat, smoking marijuana, and I just cut the hell out of his scenes and gave them to somebody else. We just couldn't take time from work for this man; one of the worst things for morale when you're making a picture is to stand a guy up in front of the camera. And he wasn't fooling around with my girl, he was fooling around with the girl who was playing in the picture [Joanne Dru]. I'd never been out to dinner with her or anything else. [Laughs.] So that's why we cut out his part. He sends me these wires saying, "You gave me one chance, please give me another, I won't blow it."

Chase says he was a big guy with horses. Well, I raised horses for fifteen years. I knew them goddamn well. And he said, "The phony parts of the picture, number one, are the guns. Everybody was carrying a six-shooter around. Well there weren't six of them in all of Texas and they were owned by the Rangers." I got a bunch of letters about using six-shooters, but I didn't want to stop a scene to have a guy reload his gun before he could fire. He says, "He talks about being a Western director. You know what that fool did? He had five thousand head out in the grass, they ate it all off and they had to hand-feed them. They had to hand-feed five thousand head, and they were white face because you can't get that many longhorn." You *can't* get that many longhorn, so we put the longhorn up front. But anyway we bought Mexican cattle, hand fed them, and made a hell of a lot of money selling them after the picture was over. [Laughs]

And as far as the end of the picture, I told Hughes years ago I didn't think he made the scene very good in *Hell's Angels* and I made it again. The only thing we cut out of it was one line, "Draw your gun." It played better without the line. I got some of the funniest telegrams from other directors—Billy Wilder sent me a telegram saying, "I got the rights to say 'They went that-a-way.'" And Frank Capra said, "I got the rights to say 'I love you.'" Hughes sent down a battery of lawyers; we'd have won if we'd wanted to defend it, but finally I cut it out and it was better. I had a hangover one Sunday morning and Hughes showed up at the house and said, "I'm making a picture called *Hell's Angels*. I'm making a scene of a flyer getting shot in the chest and the plane explodes. You've got the same scene in your picture [*The Dawn Patrol*]. I don't want you to do it." I said, "Howard, I make pictures for a living, you make them for fun. I got a hangover, I'm not interested in talking about it."

So he got his writer to go to my secretary and offer her two hundred dollars for a script. She told me about it, and I had a couple of detectives hiding in her closet. When the guy offered her the money, they said, "You're under arrest." Hughes called me and said, "Hey, you've got that writer of mine in jail." And I said, "You son of a bitch, he'll stay there." He said, "What did you do that for?" I said, "I don't like anybody corrupting a nice girl. If you had wanted the script why didn't you ask me for it?" He said, "Would you have given it to me?" I said, "Sure, I would have. You can't own a scene like that. A person that gets shot riding in an airplane almost always gets shot in the chest." So he was doing everything he could to keep our picture from coming out before his. People do strange things.

Like Borden Chase. He wasn't content with writing a story, he wanted to tell you how to do it. I wouldn't say that he was the greatest judge of how to do it. He never had another good picture. Look, I liked his story but I didn't care much for Chase. I thought he was a goddamn idiot. When he came down here to work, he brought a peroxide blonde with him, and he was a lot more interested in getting back in the box with her than he was in working on the story. I never had any luck in getting the writer of a thing to do the scenario except for Bill Faulkner.

Q: *Why was it that Faulkner occasionally contributed scenes for your movies without credit?*
HAWKS: Bill, like a lot of people, didn't make any money until paperbacks came in and until France and other countries found him. You know, he was too hard to read. So he needed money and very often he'd let me know, and I'd see that he'd do a scene. Like the death scene of the pilot in *Air Force*; he wrote it overnight. He worked on *The Big Sleep* with Leigh Brackett; they did the script in eight days. It's a *great* script.

Q: *Which of Faulkner's books do you like best?*
HAWKS: I was back in New York working with Hecht and MacArthur and they hung around with the intelligentsia, the literary crowd, and one day I said, "Have you fellows ever read anything by William Faulkner? I just read a book you should read, called *Soldier's Pay*." And they borrowed the book and discovered Faulkner.

Q: *What contribution do you think Faulkner made to your films?*
HAWKS: We seemed to talk the same language. He knew what I wanted. Bill drank too much, but when he wasn't drinking he was awful good. He wrote *Pylon* which wasn't an awful good book because he got drunk when he went down to an air show to see what it was like. He had kind of a hazy idea of it. [Laughs]

Q: *What writers do you admire besides Faulkner?*
HAWKS: I like the fellow who wrote *The Big Sleep*. I like Hemingway. I like Dashiell Hammett.

Q: *Did you ever think of doing a movie from a Hammett book?*
HAWKS: I got the movie for John Huston to do, *The Maltese Falcon,*
because the script he wrote for me [*Sergeant York*] was so good. I told
Warner, "You ought to make him a director." I told John, "Now, it's
fine to write and direct, but not on your first picture. It's hard enough
being a director. There's a story that Warners owns, *The Maltese Falcon.*"
Warner said, "Oh, we already did it," and I said, "It wasn't *The Maltese
Falcon.*" Then I told John, "Go and do it exactly the way Hammett
wrote it. Don't change a goddamn thing and you'll have a hell of a
picture."

Q: *Are there books you've wanted to make into movies but haven't been
able to buy?*
HAWKS: Oh, Lord, I've tried to buy lots of stories that I haven't gotten.
I wanted to do the Bond series. It was done by my former assistant
director Cubby Broccoli.

Q: *What was it about the Bond books that appealed to you?*
HAWKS: The great imagination that the writer had.

Q: *You were supposed to be planning a film of* The Sun Also Rises *at
one time.*
HAWKS: Yeah, I bought it fifteen years before I sold it to Zanuck.

Q: *It's said that the reason you didn't make it was that you couldn't decide
how to turn it into a comedy.*
HAWKS: Oh, no.

Q: *What was the reason?*
HAWKS: I thought it was hard to do. It was about a fellow who was
impotent. I never could figure it out.

Q: *Jules Furthman is sort of a mysterious figure. It's hard to know exactly
what he contributed to your work.*
HAWKS: Well, a kind of cynicism, an idea of doing different things.
For instance, when we were doing *To Have and Have Not*, he wrote an
introduction to Bacall: she was a stranger in a strange land, and her

purse was stolen. He said, "What do you think of it?" I said, "Jules, I don't like it at all—a girl who gets her purse stolen, that's. . ." "Jesus, that's a great scene, you sonofabitch," he said. And he went off and he wrote a scene where *she* stole the purse.

Well, that was Furthman. He had a great ability to think of new ways of doing things. Because, you see, everybody's done every story. There are only a few stories. All you can do is change the characters around. Von Sternberg could use Furthman because of the fact that he did things differently. And Fleming could use him; I could use him. We were about the only people who could put up with the son of a bitch. He was bright, and he was short. He'd say "You stupid guy" to somebody who wasn't as smart as him. Anyway, we made some good pictures, good entertainment.

Q: *A question about the script of* To Have and Have Not—*do you remember the reason you decided not to have Harry Morgan missing one arm, as he was in the book?*
HAWKS: A very simple reason: I don't know how to do a one-armed man. I could put a hook on him like I did with Eddie Robinson in *Tiger Shark*, but every time I got Eddie in a scene I had to arrange it so you can't see that it was an extension on his arm. The only good thing about the one-arm thing was that the girl made that one arm an asset. She received the one arm and got a physical kick out of it. He poked it in her. That was a great relationship—a girl that would do that. So that gave us a lot of ideas about some relationship.

Q: *How do you come up with names for characters?*
HAWKS: By just thinking of people. Wayne said to me, "Hey, that's a good name you've got for me—Chance." And I said, "Well, she was a damn good-looking girl." [Laughs.] In *His Girl Friday*, we had a fellow called Stairway Sam. He was always watching girls' legs go up and down a flight of stairs. That came after we finished the script. Another thing was when Cary Grant said to this gorilla. "There's a guy down in the car waiting," and he said, "What does he look like?" Well, they had a description of him. I said, "That's kind of dull." Ben Hecht said, "I know what he could say—'He looks like the actor, Ralph Bellamy.'" Now a line like *that* you could remember. That got a big laugh.

Hecht and MacArthur were just marvelous. The first picture we worked on they said, "Oh, we're all through now." I said, "No, tomorrow we start on something new." The fellows said, "What?" I said, "Different ways of saying things." And they had more fun, we had more fun, for about three days saying things in different ways. I'd say, "How do you say this—you've got a line, 'Oh, you're just in love.'" One of them came up with. "Oh, you're just broke out in monkey bites." The audience knows vaguely what you're saying, they like the method of saying it. We go through the entire script in sequence; one of us suggests something and what you suggest somebody else twists around. Noël Coward came to see me once, introduced himself, and said, "What do you call the kind of dialogue that you use?" And I said, "Well, Hemingway calls it oblique dialogue. I call it three-cushion. Because you hit it over here and over here and go over here to get the meaning. You don't state it right out."

Q: *How did Hecht get involved in helping you adapt* The Front Page? *He isn't given screen credit for the script.*
HAWKS: I phoned Ben and I said, "What do you think about changing Hildy Johnson and making her a girl?" He said, "I wish we'd thought of that." And he said, "I'm stuck on a story, if you'll help me I'll come out there and help you." So he came out and I helped him with his story and he helped me.

I went in to Harry Cohn and I said, "You said any time I wanted I could start a film that day by just telling you I'm ready to do a picture." He said, "That's right." And I said, "Well, I'm ready to make one." He said, "What?" I said, "A remake of *Front Page*." "Oh," he said, "you don't want to do that." I said, "O.K.," I got up, and he said, "Where are you going? Now, well, wait a minute, wait a minute. You must have a good idea." I said, "I think I have." He said, "Well, wouldn't Winchell be good as the editor and Cary Grant as the reporter?" "Well, you're half right," I said. "Cary Grant would make a good editor and a girl could be the reporter." And he said, "Oh, you're nuts." I said, "Harry, I'm going to go. I've had enough. If you don't like the idea, then I don't want to make it for you." He said, "Wait a minute, wait a minute, wait a minute. I know enough not to try and tell you how to make pictures." And we made it, and it made a lot of money.

Q: *You worked with Hecht on the script of* Underworld, *didn't you? There are several things in there that are similar to* Rio Bravo.
HAWKS: Yes, well, Ben and I worked on the story and a friend [Art Rossen] was to be the director. He went up to San Francisco, as I remember, to go up to the prison there, but unfortunately got tight, so they had to fire him. We had sketches made of every scene. We had sets built and we had a cast. Then we got Joe von Sternberg to direct the picture. He always remained a very good friend of mine.

Q: *Hecht said in his autobiography that he was upset about what Sternberg did to the script. He said Sternberg added "sentimental" things to it.*
HAWKS: I think it was a damn good film. Hecht kind of would resent somebody and find something to say about him. I got along with him, but I know that was a habit of his. And I think probably Joe's arrogance got to him.

Q: *I saw* The Criminal Code *for the first time recently, and a lot of the dialogue was pretty stilted, it didn't hold up well, but then there were some good scenes with really sharp dialogue that I figured you must have stuck in there, like the whole scene of Huston being shaved.*
HAWKS: Oh yeah, we wrote a whole bunch of stuff for that because the last act was absolutely no good. But I liked the beginning, I liked the story. So I got twenty convicts, got 'em a room, gave 'em a lunch, gave 'em a drink. I sat down and said, "I'm going to tell you guys a story and I want you to decide how it ends. I'll go off until you decide." I went off and they talked for about an hour, and I came in and said, "Are you ready to talk?" and they told me the whole ending; the whole last act.

Then I had convicts working for me. One time they got bored with what they were doing, so I put 'em on a dog trot and I said, "You're going to keep trotting until you decide to behave, and anybody who stops is automatically fired." So they made a couple of rounds of this place until they yelled out, "Hey, mister, we'll be good!" I said, "O.K., let's hear it from everybody whether they'll be good." And they would go by me saying, "We'll be good, we'll be good." So I stopped them and we became pretty good friends. I liked the picture because I liked

[Walter] Huston. I thought he was the greatest actor I ever worked with. And a wonderful person.

Q: *What kind of research did you do for* Scarface?
HAWKS: I made a contact with one of the best newspapermen in Chicago so that we could use the newspaper wire. I could ask him about people and things. If a man came into my office and said, "My name is James White, I was connected to the gang in Chicago, I wonder if I could talk to you," I'd say, "Mr. White, I know all about you." He'd say, "How do you know?" and I'd say, "Oh . . . I know. I know that you started as a bouncer and became a pimp, you ran a saloon, you carried a gun for so-and-so, did such-and-such a murder." I'd get through and he'd say, "I wasn't no pimp." And I'd say, "O.K., what do you want? Want work to pay for your passage out here?" He'd say, "Sure." I'd say, "How did you do such-and-such a thing?" And he told me quite a lot. Five or six of them came around and told me their stories. Of course we took liberties; we did what we wanted to do.

While we were making it, five or six of them came out and said, "The boss wants us to see the picture." And I said, "You go and tell him when it comes out he can buy a ticket. You don't scare me. Why the hell don't you come out and just ask to see it?" They reported to Capone that it was just great, and they invited me to Chicago to see him. They met me at the train, and they were late. One of the fellows said, "There was a killing last night and we had to go to the funeral." I said, "Do I have to ride with you if there was a killing last night?" They said I could ride in a different car. But when we went into a café, they would sit with their backs to the wall and I had my back to the door. We had some damn good-looking girls with us, a bit brassy but very pretty. When I saw Capone, we had tea and he was dressed in a morning coat, striped trousers. I was with him two, three hours. Then he came to see me when I was working out here and the cops came and arrested him right on the set.

Q: *Did he see* Scarface?
HAWKS: Five or six times. He had his own print of it. He thought it was great. He'd say, "Jesus Christ, you guys got a lot of stuff in that picture? How'd you know about that?" I said, "Look—you know how

somebody can't testify if he's a lawyer? Well, I'm a lawyer." And he laughed. He didn't give a damn.

Q: *I'm curious about the Vietnam film you were going to do. Could you tell us about it?*
HAWKS: I wanted to find out first what kind of assistance I could get from the Army. And it wasn't very much. They wanted to tell me how to make the picture, tell how to do the story. So I took a loss on that.

Q: *What was the plot?*
HAWKS: I'm going to use it, but not in Vietnam.

Q: *Did it make any statement about the war?*
HAWKS: I've *never* made a statement. I think our job is to make entertainment. I don't give a God damn about taking sides.

Q: *In a situation like that, though, wouldn't it be hard not to make some kind of statement? Because it was such an emotional subject, it's hard not to take sides in some way even if you're just making a story about two guys. There's bound to be implications.*
HAWKS: Oh, I don't know. You see, I don't look at it that way. For instance, in making a movie one time I had a bunch of colored musicians, and they [the studio] said, "Don't get the colored musicians mixed up with the white musicians." I said, "To hell with you. I'm making a movie and if you don't like it go get somebody else. As far as I'm concerned the colored people belong in music because they're part of this kind of music." I think they've gotten all mixed up. They've gotten so you can't have a Jewish comic because you're making fun of the Jews. You can't have an Irish comic because you're making fun of the Irish. There's more goddamn *minorities* . . . Nasser banned a picture called *Land of the Pharaohs* because he said it made it seem as though a Jew designed the Pyramids. It's hard enough to make movies without getting into all that stuff.

Q: *Was the trouble in dealing with the Army on the Vietnam film that they wanted you to make a pro-American statement?*

HAWKS: Look, when I've got an idea for a story I tell it the way I'm interested in it. I expect to make a picture in Russia. They asked me to come over there and make a picture. They've got a great cameraman over there, they've got good labs, and they've got good studios. I can go over there and make a movie. But I said, "I understand you're difficult to get along with." They said, "What do you mean?" I said, "Telling people how to make a picture." They said, "We wouldn't tell you." I said, "O.K.—two Americans are trying to get away from the Russian police and they go in the back door of the Ballet Rousse. The cops come in and they're dancing with the Ballet Rousse, in dancing costumes. Then they go from there and they get in with the National Symphony Orchestra." They said, "What do you want with them?" I said, "I want them to do the score for the picture." They said, "O.K. You can do anything you want to." I said, "Now, look, it costs a lot of money to get ready, to get started, and I have to make deals, become responsible for the picture. I'm going to send you a script and I want every page of the script initialed in front of the American consul." I still don't know if I'm going to have any trouble or not, but at the *thought* of any trouble . . .

I made a picture called *Air Force* during the war. Pretty good picture, taken from a true incident. I made it because I knew General Arnold. Christ, he even made me a general for a week. I was doing a bunch of things for him and the first general with a higher rank that I ran into, I called the general's office and said. "Hap, I'm sitting next to a guy who has three stars on his shoulder. He doesn't want to do what I want him to do. I'm not a general anymore; will you tell him to do what I want him to do?" The general turned around: "Boy, it didn't take you long to settle that." I told Hap, "I don't want to be a general—as a civilian I can ask for anything." Curt Le May wanted me to do the story that they made about the long-range bombers. What did they call it?

Q: Strategic Air Command.
HAWKS: Yes, and when a bunch of people started telling me what kinds of things I could do and what I can't do, I said, "I don't want to do it."

Q: *Is the Russian picture planned as a Russian-American coproduction?*
HAWKS: It's *my* production.

Q: *How did this come about?*

HAWKS: Well, I went to the San Sebastian Film Festival. I was the president of the jury and was very careful not to inflict my things on the jury. They chose a picture called *The Glass House* by Truman Capote. And I said, "I can't go along with you on that. I made it once better [*The Criminal Code*] and somebody made it better than I did, called *The Big House*. It's just old stuff. I'll go along with you if you'll give the Russian picture a special award." The Russian people were very happy to get it, and the head of their delegation came to me afterwards and said, "You've been invited to come over and make a picture."

Q: *One mystery which has never been explained is why William Wyler took over* Come and Get It *from you.*

HAWKS: The BBC sent me a telegram this morning, they're doing a picture on the life of Goldwyn and they wanted me to talk about him. [Note: this interview was conducted four days before Goldwyn's death.] I'm going to say that he really tried like hell to make good pictures, but we didn't get along too well. He didn't think a director should write. He was crazy about writers and he really tried to get the finest authors he could get ahold of. He got Edna Ferber's story because Edna Ferber was supposed to be a good writer, and there were a great many things that I didn't like about the story.

Goldwyn was going to the hospital and he asked me to make it. He said, "You're in charge." So I changed the little lame girl who sang so badly that the woodsmen hooted at her to a lusty wench, you know, and when he came back I had about a week more of work to do. He saw what I had shot, and it was a shock to him. He bought a story, and he didn't get it. He cast a girl in it and the girl wasn't used—I used Frances Farmer, who was getting seventy-five dollars a week, for most of it. So Willie Wyler was put on and Wyler photographed six hundred feet of the film, and Goldwyn gave him credit for being co-director.

Q: *What was Frances Farmer like at that time? Her autobiography is really a devastating book.*

HAWKS: She was probably one of the cleanest, simplest, hardest-working persons I ever knew. She came a couple of times to my boat wearing her sweatshirt and her dungarees and carrying a toothbrush in her pocket. She had no phoniness about her at all. She studied under a very fine teacher in Washington. When I told her the part I said, "I want to make a test." She played the mother and daughter roles in the picture, and she tried to do the mother by make-up, you know, things like that, and she failed. She was one of the first persons to see it. She said, "Does that mean I'm out?" And I said, "Hell no, you've got the part. I'll meet you tonight about eight o'clock. Where do you live?" And she told me. I said, "I can't find that; I'll meet you up on such-and-such a corner." We went to all kinds of beer joints, little places around town, looking for a woman of her type.

We finally found a marvelous one, and I said, "Now you do something. You come in here every night for two weeks. You get picked up; what'll probably happen is some guy will try to feel your leg. You're a strong girl, you can handle yourself. Whoever does it, talk to him, be that woman, with her mannerisms and everything. And then we'll make a test." She was just fabulous. She was a blonde, a natural, but she just used a dark wig; that's all she put on. No change in makeup, just her face changed. Her whole attitude changed, her whole method of talking. And she just really . . . the very first day I remember her working with Eddie Arnold, who was a real old trouper, and she said, "If you'd only speak that line a little quicker I could keep this thing going." And he looked at her, and he spoke it quicker, and the scene was better. He said, "Hey, look, she's pretty good." I said, "She's so good that you'd better get right to work or she's going to take it and walk off with it." And then she fell in love with a guy who ran away from her. She didn't take a drink before that, then she started to drink. She just went to pieces.

Q: *You shot part of* The Prizefighter and the Lady *without credit for MGM in 1933. Why was that?*
HAWKS: *The Prizefighter and the Lady* was a story that I worked on. It was written for Gable and Harlow. Gable was the dominant one and Harlow was the empty-headed blonde. They cast it with Max Baer and Myrna Loy—*complete* opposites. In other words. Max Baer was the stooge and Loy was the lady, the prizefighter and the lady. I said, "I don't want to make the picture." I wouldn't make it with them. And they said, "Will you help out, do a couple of weeks' work, give Baer a

start, teach him a little about acting?" Then Woody van Dyke will take over." I said sure.

Q: *Why did you do* A Song Is Born, *the remake of* Ball of Fire?
HAWKS: Because I got $25,000 a week, that's why. Goldwyn pestered me and pestered me. He said, "There's some way to do it." I came up with a way, then he wouldn't let me do anything. And it wasn't easy. Danny Kaye and his wife were separating and he was a basket case, stopping work to see a psychiatrist twice a day. It was an altogether horrible experience.

Q: *Did Goldwyn come on the set and try to interfere with you?*
HAWKS: Yeah, and I'd insult him as much as I could. I'd say, "You're spilling stuff on your tie again, Sam."

Q: Ball of Fire *looks like it was fun to make.*
HAWKS: We had a marvelous scene where Cooper had to come in to say something to the girl [Barbara Stanwyck]. She was in bed, you couldn't see her face, you could just see her eyes. I said to Toland, "How the hell can I do that? How can I light her eyes without lighting her face?" And he said, "Well, have her do it in blackface." So the next day I saw her and said, "Barbara, tomorrow don't bother making up. I want you to play in blackface." She said, "What the hell kind of scene is that?" [Laughs]. Oh God! It was a good scene.

Q: *That's a rare sentimental moment in your work, the professors singing "Genevieve" in the background of the scene.*
HAWKS: When you're doing a story about old people you can afford to be sentimental, you know. God, I was responsible for starting "Jeannie with the Light Brown Hair" up again, the theme music from *Barbary Coast.* I've regretted that ever since.

Q: *You said once that John Ford was better than you with composition and long shots. Is there anything you think you can do better than Ford?*
HAWKS: Oh, I think I couldn't do his brand of humor. His brand of humor was kind of a bucolic travesty of an Irishman, kind of overdrawn characters. I certainly know that I made better comedies than he did.

But I don't think I made better Westerns. I don't think *Red River* is better than his Westerns. He's a great storyteller. Many, many years ago we used to talk about what we would do, and he said if he had a scene that he didn't think was good enough, he'd do it in a long shot rather than try to punch it up. If I've got a scene like that I just try to do it as quick as I can.

Jack was quite a guy. I saw more of him than anybody, almost, in his last few months because I'd just drop over to the house. He spent most of his time looking at old, old Westerns on television—you know, those cheap westerns that were made in about a week. And he was still bright; he kept his senses.

The last time I went out to see him, he said goodbye to me. I walked out and stopped to speak to his daughter, and he yelled, "Is Howard gone yet?" She said no. "I want to see him!" He said, "I want to say goodbye to you." I said goodbye. He yelled again, "Is he still there?" And he said, "I want to say *goodbye* to you." So I called Duke Wayne and said, "Duke, you'd better get down here. I think he's going to die." Duke got a helicopter and came down here, and the next day he died. Peter Bogdanovich did a damn good story about that [in *New York* magazine]. He got it a little bit messed up, but it made a good ending for his story.

Q: *When young directors ask you for advice what do you tell them?*
HAWKS: Friedkin was going around with my daughter in New York. He asked me how I liked his last picture *The Boys in the Band*. I said, "If you're going to be making pictures you'll have to learn not to ask that. I thought it was lousy." He said, "I'm interested in why." I said, "It's too bad that somebody who has the talent you have should waste his time on junk like that." He took it all very, very well.

I said, "You made another lousy picture before that called *The Night They Raided Minsky's*. You're gonna run out of pictures. They're not going to let you make them unless you make something that people want to see. And then they're gonna tell you how to make them." And he said, "Well, what kind of thing do you mean?" And I said, "Well, people seem to like chase scenes . . ."

Hawks on Film, Politics, and Childrearing

CONSTANCE PENLEY, SAUNIE
SALYER, AND MICHAEL
SHEDLIN/1974

SINCE 1923, HOWARD HAWKS has directed over forty
motion pictures, including at least a half-dozen masterpieces—*Scarface,
The Big Sleep, Bringing Up Baby, His Girl Friday, Red River, To Have and
Have Not, Only Angels Have Wings,* and *El Dorado.* He has piloted some
of the most sophisticated scripts and high-energy performances in the
history of the American cinema.

Hawks rode the crest of Hollywood during its heyday and won nearly
every battle to maintain creative control over his pictures. In his non-
film life as well he is a man of High Adventure: he has been a stunt
flyer, an auto racer, a motorcyclist, a marksman, a horseman, a tennis
player, a baseball pitcher, a golfer, a skier. He went fishing with
Hemingway and hunting with Faulkner. He has built racing cars as well
as camera cars. He collects firearms and Western prints, he is a gun-
smith as well as a still photographer.

Since the Fifties, Hawks has been revered by French critics (Godard
listed *Scarface* as the Best American Sound Film), but until recently his
career has not been taken seriously by commentators in this country,
although his films have always been popular with the international public.

In the last five years, largely through the efforts of Peter Bogdanovich,
Robin Wood, and Andrew Sarris, Hawks's work has finally achieved a
respectable critical status. However, many of his films are still not recognized as parts of a single director's oeuvre—"the only oeuvre the

From *Jump Cut*, January/February 1975. Reprinted by permission.

American public can totally identify itself with" (Henri Langlois).
Twentieth Century, Sergeant York, Rio Bravo, Hatari!, Red Line 7000, Ceiling Zero, The Dawn Patrol, The Criminal Code, Air Force, I Was a Male War Bride, Monkey Business, Man's Favorite Sport, Gentlemen Prefer Blondes—
were all directed by the same man.

We had been asked by the Pacific Film Archive to escort the master during his two-day visit to the San Francisco Bay Area in connection with the Archive's definitive retrospective of Hawks's films.

"Glad to know ya," said the white-haired action director at the airport. He was accompanied by his secretary Nancy Reeves. As we drove to Berkeley Hawks regaled us with a dozen "irrepressible Hawksian anecdotes," including an account of his invitation to make a film in the Soviet Union and an appraisal of Marlene Dietrich's legs. He told us about Gloria Swanson completing the direction of Von Stroheim's *Queen Kelly* and dropped cryptic remarks about his hoard of unpublished Fitzgerald manuscripts.

Hawks speaks quietly and forcefully. He laughs often, interrupts often, listens intently and asks few questions. He is a curious mixture of taciturnity and loquaciousness. He seems to be a strong silent type and yet he talks almost continuously. During lunch we were perversely enchanted as we found ourselves hanging batedly on every scabrous John Wayne anecdote.

"If I want to have fun at a party," said the master over his chef's salad, "I'll tell the Duke, 'See that guy over there? He's a Red!' "

Later in the day we asked Hawks for a private interview. He agreed without hesitation. Nancy Reeves scheduled us for the following morning at ten.

We met an hour early to discuss strategy. In the last few years there has been an optimistic over-reaction to Hawks's conservatism. It has taken the form of a re-consideration of Hawks's women characters in the light of current feminist ideas, and a suggestion that he was in some ways actually a progressive social force. We *wanted* to see this aspect of him. On the strength of *His Girl Friday*, if nothing else, we were ready to suspend our aversion to his reactionary romanticism and hail him as a closet subversive, a repressed populist, perhaps even a right-wing anarchist.

In order to find these things out about Hawks we realized that we would have to circumvent the usual What-Was-It-Like-To-Work-With-Humphrey

Bogart approach. Most critics and audiences who have questioned Hawks have been respectful in the extreme. This is understandable. Hawks is an exceedingly dignified, steely-eyed big hombre. He wields a penetrating blue stare and a seventy-eight-year reputation for no-bull-shit. He is not the kind of man you niggle with.

We were, however, determined to probe into his personal philosophy and get beyond the anecdotal response. We decided to discuss our perspective straightaway and to ground all of our questions in our passions and our politics rather than attempting to set up a "comfortable atmosphere" in which he could be "drawn out."

Hawks considers himself an apolitical artist. He pooh-poohs Analysis and insists on the primacy of the untrammeled creative instinct. He told us that he thought Frank Capra got "no good" when he started to *analyze* his own pictures, to put "messages" in them.

He believes in the total omnipotence of the individual and consequently in the transcendence of art over mere social conditioning. And yet Hawks's movies reflect, transmit and are *created by* American history and American society. His work represents the apotheosis of macho fatalist individualist cynicism. His heroic characters (not the adolescents of his comedies) are stoic, tough, competitive and authoritarian.

Hawks expresses the dominant ideas of the American culture. His cinema is above all a male cinema—male values, male heroes, male activities, and male resolutions. Hawks believes in and glorifies such traditionally masculine pursuits as world war, trailblazing, killing Native Americans, cattle driving, gunfighting, airplane piloting, hunting and auto racing. With a few notable exceptions (*His Girl Friday, Gentlemen Prefer Blondes, Ball of Fire*, etc.), women in Hawks's films are entirely marginal to the operative reality except as attractions or diversion's to the heroes.

Hawks's fabled obsession with Men in Groups indeed exists, but the groups are always hierarchical and are often engaged in authoritarian or super-aggressive activity. Their solidarity is falsely defined by their romantic isolation from the rest of society. They are the "doers" who have, at best, disdain for the "watchers."

We are not suggesting that Hawks should have or could have made other kinds of films, we are simply outlining some of the codes of the dominant ideology which are inscribed in his work.

This interview was conducted on April 23, 1974, pre-Nixon's resignation, pre-SLA liquidation.

PENLEY: *Our bias is probably toward not just formal analysis of films but a somewhat political analysis—trying to figure out how films work and how they affect people and how they work to change your consciousness. So we're always looking for those kinds of things too. Of course we've always been interested in the way you've been able to do things like portray emotion between men, and people in communal groups, and collectivity, and the strength of your women characters. . . . And especially after Leigh Brackett wrote those articles in* Take One, *did you see them?*
HAWKS: Leigh's? I don't think I did.

PENLEY: *Well, they were very illuminating. She said some really good things. . . .*
HAWKS: She's a smart girl. I thought I was hiring a man.

PENLEY: *That's what she said. You were slightly upset when she walked in, but you got over it. . . .*
HAWKS: Well, when you expect a man and you get a girl who's been out playing tennis, tanned up. . . . I said, "My God, you write like a man, I thought you were a man." And she's done very well. . . .

SALYER: *Well, since we're coming to you as "film critics," we were interested. . . . Your films have been analyzed and discussed perhaps more than any other filmmaker. The* Cahiers *group in France. . . . We were wondering what you thought of the enterprise of film criticism, whether you've ever found it effective in thinking about your own work or explaining your films to a larger group of people, maybe that you wouldn't have the chance to talk to apart from thru your films. Have you ever in fact been helped by a film critic?*
HAWKS: I think that after I made my first picture, a fellow said it was lousy, and he said, "For God's sake make entertainment, make stuff that people would like." And he said, "You're never going to make it too good for them, so don't worry." And I've told a number of people the same advice. Bill Friedkin asked me if I'd seen his last picture, and I said I did. He said, "Well, what'd you think of it?" I said, "After you've made

a few more, you'll know enough not to ask that question." I thought
it was lousy.

SHEDLIN: The Exorcist?
HAWKS: No, *The Boys in the Band*. I said that the thing that made me
most angry about it was the fact that you showed that you had talent
and then you waste your time on junk like that. So he said, "What shall
I do?" And I said, "Make something that people will be entertained
and amused by, that's the sole function of motion pictures." "Any
suggestions?" And I said, "Yeah, make a good chase, they seem to be
beginning to like chases, and if you make something better than the
ones that have been made, you'll have a. . . ." So he won an Academy
Award. And he's still trying; I don't know if he's going to have continued success. . . . I don't think *The Exorcist* is something awfully good.
I've got a script written by William Faulkner that had just as much
blood, just as much horror and everything. And I decided I didn't want
to inflict it on people. I'm gonna sell it and let somebody else do it. But
I've listened to thirty French directors in a room, German directors,
Swedish directors, Italian directors . . . I think too many of them want
to *analyze* films. Too many of them want to find a motive for doing it. I
keep telling them, "you're just story tellers; if you've got a story, tell it,
tell it good." If you're any good at all, you won't think about where
you're going to put the camera or what you're gonna do—you'll know
that you want to get in close on this, you'll know. . . . And if you're not
any good, you'll use a lot of tricks and think that they're new. Just if I
like a story I don't say well it's about this and that's been popular
then. . . . It's more or less been the other way. When I came back from
Europe I wanted to make a western. Jack Warner said, "What do you
want to make one of those for?" I said, "It's time somebody started
making some good ones; there've been none made." He said, "All
right." Still making money. That was almost fifteen years ago.

   When they started making all these sick pictures, I didn't know
exactly what the audience was going to want, so I said to Wayne, "Do
you want to make a couple of westerns with me?" He said, "Yeah, like
to." So we made some westerns. With no analysis at all of what effect
they would have on people, just trying to make something that is
entertaining. I'm thoroughly on the side of tired people who want to go

down for relaxation, and don't want to think. I think that's why *The Sting* got the Academy Award. Sheer entertainment, and damn good entertainment, well done.

SALYER: *In light of what you said yesterday about the AFI filmmaker calling you up, and you said, "How could you invest in a film not having seen it," and also said you believed in making a film with a social purpose.*
HAWKS: *I* said that?

SHEDLIN: *"A film with something to say," you said. That there should be a purpose behind the film, it should mean something. Then you would invest in it.*
HAWKS: Oh, you mean in talking not about my work, but in somebody else's. Sure!

PENLEY: *Do you think that some films can serve that function?*
HAWKS: Well, I would say that the quickest way to show that you can direct is to learn how to tell a story and tell it in film. I know a few good filmmakers who can't tell a story. And most of those filmmakers are not writers or creators, they are stage directors—they take a script and interpret it beautifully, but they practically don't put anything of themselves into it. They don't mark it. . . .

PENLEY: *Do you think that films affect people, that films could change their attitudes? Do you think films should do that, or can do that?*
HAWKS: I think it's pretty goddamned dangerous, because who the hell are *you* to decide what is good for somebody, you know what I mean? And any more than I would want my boy listening to some people I know who are quite bright people. I feel like booting them and saying, "Get out of there and don't talk about things like that." I don't know. It's a public thing. For instance, I am certain that the media has turned people against Nixon, and they haven't any proof yet. They merely have proof that he had bad judgment in hiring certain people. And that's rather doubtful proof because I think that by the time the elections come around the Democrats are going to have a lot of things thrown at them by the Republicans who are holding off that will show you that the whole damn thing is lousy and rotten, you know? And I

just was saying that I don't approve of some of the textbooks that they pass around now; I don't approve of some of the stuff that the newspapers and television do. They exaggerate things out of all context; all they want to do is get a good headline. There are very few papers that report well. You know, I mean they're all biased. And if you start that going in motion pictures, in a field that's pure entertainment, how are you going to tell the people who want to go in for entertainment, "you're gonna be lectured tonight, you're gonna be told that this is a policy and that is a policy" and stuff like that. So you're out of luck.

PENLEY: *Don't you think though that all films portray some kinds of values, moral values, whether they're intended to or not?*
HAWKS: To who? To you or to another person or. . . .

PENLEY: *To everyone. . . .*
SHEDLIN: *To the audience . . .*
HAWKS: No, I don't think so. You're going to get an entirely different audience in the country than you get in the city, so who are you going to aim your pictures to?

SHEDLIN: *But don't you aim your films to be an expression of your deepest convictions? Wouldn't you say that if you invest your films with anything it's your deepest feelings?*
HAWKS: No, I think that they're full of the things that I *like*. If I finish a picture where I've gotten, by accident, too many losers in it, I don't like the picture at all. I didn't like *Red Line 7000;* I thought it was awful. I don't like pictures that. . . . It's so easy to go in and pull some bum out of the gutter and wash him off and an hour later find him dirty and down there again. But who wants to look at that? Who do you help by picturizing that?

SHEDLIN: *Are you saying that you portray positive values in your films? I feel that a lot. And I feel that one of the strongest ones is a tremendous sense of individualism. I mean, yesterday many of your responses to things were, "Well, I'm offered something—can I do it my way?" That's the same kind of control over one's own life that people are seeking today, and that these liberation movements that have grown up in the 60s and 70s are about.*

I sense a tremendous feeling of strength and need to have control over your life, and characters in your films to be able to choose the way they want to, free of outside coercion.

HAWKS: If people want to get that out of my films, they're very glad to get it out. I feel myself that I'm not going to cram it down their throats, I'll tell you that.

SHEDLIN: *But people have written about those values in your films, and people* have *drawn them out. Would you say that you do feel that way yourself?*

HAWKS: Well, that's a hell of a question to answer. I mean, I've read so much stuff written about me, and a lot of them make me laugh, 'cause I didn't intend that at all. It's just very simple. I believe in telling a story and I like to tell it about something that I know about. And in many, many cases I know the person that I put in there. I know a drunk or a bum or a liar or a cheat or something like that, and I put him in a picture. But it's so easy to have a villain that makes faces, or the music comes up like one of the old melodramas that they used to play on showboats. I get more fun out of a villain that is a little different. I had a lot of fun with Chris George in *El Dorado*. He was a good sport, he had a sense of humor, and he didn't do one bad thing in the whole picture. He died, and he said "You never gave me a chance." And Wayne said, "You're too good to give a chance to," and he died happily, because a man better than he had said "You're good."

I like the character in *To Have and Have Not*, the fellow who played the big fat fairy. He'd never done anything before; he was awful good. No motive at all other than to find a different kind of a heavy, just to try to do something that's amusing. I don't do it for any purpose whatsoever beside that.

SALYER: *Well, when you talk to someone or read something that someone has written and they say that they like a film that you like, and you read that they got a sense of enjoyment out of it in the same way that you enjoyed making it, and thought it was a good story the way you thought it was a good story—is that in any way inspiring to you to know that you have communicated to someone?*

HAWKS: I like it. I don't know if it inspires me more. It depends on who's saying it. It depends on whether I have any desire to inspire that person. If I like him, I have. If I don't like him, then I don't give a damn about inspiring him. Actually it's hard to say. I don't believe in analyzing my own work. I just don't do it. I know people who have gotten completely off base by trying to analyze their own work. I played a lot of tennis, with the world's champion; a brother of mine—I was sixteen and he was fourteen—we played ten sets a day with the two world's champions. We went on tour with them, and we were two of the best hustlers you've ever seen, 'cause he'd warm up left-handed, and he had knee pants on, and I bet $50 he could beat the state champion. Then he'd turn around right-handed and beat him 6-love, 6-love, and we'd be $50 richer. He'd *analyze* his service. After that, any girl could serve better than he could. He could still hit any other shot, but as soon as he analyzed it he couldn't do it. And I know a lot of people who. . . . Frank Capra, until he went into the army, was one of the greatest directors we ever had; made great entertainment. After that he couldn't make anything. He started to analyze his pictures, and put messages in them. He put messages into his other pictures, but he didn't think about it. He did it *naturally*. When he got to thinking about his messages, oh brother, he turned into really . . . ah, no-good. . . .

If writers get to believing all the stuff that's analyzed and written about their books, then they get no-good. So it's a dangerous thing. Because they're given a talent, they better use it and not try to use the thoughts that some other person has about their work.

PENLEY: *I'd like to ask you just one more question along these lines. Several times, yesterday and today, your disenchantment with politics in this country [HAWKS: affirmative grunt and "Sure . . ."], especially now. You said that you feel that politicians are the slimiest people around. Don't you feel that it is the place of film, of movies, to try to counter that in any way, or to try to have some effect on the corruption of political life in this country . . . even though it* does *bother you?*
HAWKS: No, I don't think it's movies. I think probably television has the right to do that. For the simple reason that you can turn it off, and you don't have to go out of your own room to get it. . . . If you go out and pay your money to get into a theater, you're entitled to *get what you*

want. If they have special theaters set aside to run foreign pictures, you know you're gonna get to see a foreign picture. But when you go to see the average picture, the average person is knowing they're not to be taught, not to be instructed, but just to be amused and entertained. And that's why I say that television has a better chance. I think some of the television things are good. They're on very unpopular channels usually, you have to turn them on special because only a few people want 'em. But they do a damn good job of what they do.

PENLEY: *And you wouldn't feel that that was too manipulative? You said earlier that you thought television had shaped people's attitudes about Nixon.*
HAWKS: *Oh yes, I think so . . . without a doubt. Television* and *the papers.*

PENLEY: *Then you think that there are possibilities for television to get across news about politics and social conditions in an unmanipulative way?*
HAWKS: I think they've got a chance. I doubt if they do it. I supported one politician about ten years ago. For state's attorney—Evelle Younger. . . . He was a lawyer. We rode out to a football game. Somehow, having a drink after the football game, some people I knew were talking about who would make a good district attorney. I said "What about that young fellow I rode out with, Evelle Younger?" "Well, my lord, he'd be a good one," they said. "Will you help?" I said, "I'll help, but after I talk to him." I talked to him, and I said, "I'll back you, and these people will back you, *if* you won't get up there and make election speeches and tell everybody what stinkers politicians are, and rank yourself with the same bunch of stinkers, you know. If you will just stop calling names or doing any of that kind of stuff, I will back you." I get a letter from him every year saying, "I'm still doing what you told me to do." I wouldn't want my boy to be a politician, because if he ran against anybody, there'd be eighteen dirty skunks who'd start saying what a louse he was. And the only reason they'd say it is 'cause they're one themselves. So I don't know *what* you're gonna do about that. I really don't know. But I think that if you can get a set that you can turn off, then that's the best thing about television.

SHEDLIN: *Um, it's hard to explain this, but we see your films as being very political. For instance Rosalind Russell in* His Girl Friday *is such a strong female character in a century women have not been portrayed like that at all—that's an intensely political thing to us.*

HAWKS: Yeah, but it's accidental. It just happens to voice some of the stuff that I happen to, you know, enjoy. Or else *portraying*—and it's not done with the intention of curing the ills of the thing or doing anything like that. If they do like it. . . . I wish a lot more women would act like the women that I portrayed because they're the attractive ones to me, and I like them when they're honest and when they're direct, and it seems as though other people do too. They like to watch the girls in the pictures. And as far as men go, I don't care about the size of them or anything, but I like the strength of them. I mean Bogart was a giant, but he was a little man physically. . . . Cagney is another one. What I don't like are the kind of—not effeminate—but sort of effete, kind of lackadaisical people, you know what I mean; it's no fun makin' pictures with that type in 'em. I don't know whether you'd say that you could teach people a lesson or not. I think if you're gonna get something out of a picture, it's because they like the movie, don't you think so? You wouldn't bother to analyze the stuff I make if you didn't like it.

SHEDLIN: *Well, that's true, but I also sense, for example in a film like* Scarface, *that you had a so-called* message *behind it, and that it wasn't the kind of thing that would make people feel light.*

HAWKS: Well, that is in the best novels or theater . . . I don't know . . . *something* that has existed thru ages of *evil*—the Borgian family, isn't that true? Hasn't that gone thru many, many generations? Well, all I was trying to do was say that the Borgian family today is Al Capone and his family. And we had a portrayal that showed just what gangsters are really—a crumb bunch. They're evil, double-crossing poisoners, that's what they are. So the picture turned out pretty good. I wish it had come out in a day when *The Godfather* did, because it's a better picture. I'd have made an awful lot of money too. I didn't find anything new in *The Godfather*, that wasn't in *Scarface*. It's a depiction of a phase in the country. . . . And you know one of the strangest things—there was a gangster in Chicago, a rather nice man, a very attractive man. Well-educated daughters. . . . He came out and he sent his name in and he wanted to look thru the studio. And I was interested in talking to him. The girls were well-schooled, good manners, and he was well-dressed.

He said, "Howard, where'd you get some of that stuff that you got?" I said, "What do you want to know for, you mad?" He said, "Hell no, I'm not mad. That's way past and gone. I was just interested in how you found it out." So I told him. He said, "Well, I'll be damned. People talk, don't they?" And I said "Yup." He said, "Why hasn't the picture played in Chicago?" I said, "No one will let it." He said, "You want it to play there?" I said "Yes." He said, "Can I use your telephone?" Came back and said, "You can run it in Chicago anytime you want to." Well, that's part of an evil system, isn't it? If a gangster can walk in and change the whole thing. . . .

But politics has gotten to where they want to control and tell you what kind of movies, what kind of books, what kind of everything. Who the hell is qualified to do it? I don't know how thru movies you're ever gonna get to tell people how this corruption works in the country. Because the whole media is just quoting all these people. It's a *story* for them. You know, I write a story and then somebody comes along and they say, "You're *changing* that." Well, I *wrote* the goddamned thing. "I know, but what are you changing it for? It's printed on there. Why not keep it. . . ." You know, they read stuff in the newspapers, they see stuff on television. I don't know what you're gonna do, but you're not gonna be able to do it thru movies, I don't think.

SALYER: *In once sense, though, I think you're* doing it. *I mean, it's . . .*
HAWKS: Well, maybe, but without knowing or trying to, you know, because I am making pictures that *please me*. The reason that I think that Bogdanovich and Friedkin are gonna make good pictures is because they're making pictures that please them. And they're not doing it for any other motive than to make entertainment. I told Friedkin that if he made two or three pictures like *The Boys in the Band* that he'd find he's not making another picture. Or if it was it'd be something that he didn't have anything to say about. I said, "If you want to make pictures and *enjoy* making them, you better go out and make something that a lot of people want to see. And then they'll turn you loose and let you make what you want. And *then* maybe you can do some of the things that you want to do. But as a beginner, you haven't got a chance. The best thing to do is to learn how to tell a story. Be careful that it isn't just something that *you* want to do, and then,

when people've got confidence, they will give you money and backing
to do it. . . . No sense in trying to make a picture that will be any form
of propaganda unless you've got somebody good in it, so that you can
get an audience in to look at it. . . . Because if you've only got fifty people in the movie theater, you're not getting anywhere. You have to get a
full house. Then you have a chance of convincing them. . . . Better than
that, if you've got a full house, and the other theaters are looking to
run it and you've upped your viewing audience to the biggest thing
going. . . ." I was very lucky. The average picture is quite satisfied if they
get almost 50% outside of the United States. I get 65, 67% of the money
outside of the United States. And it makes me very glad that the people
in Japan laugh at the comedies that I make, the people in France think
that they're great—they like the *best* the one that I think is the least
good. They like 'em in Spain, in Italy. And that means an awful lot of
people are getting some message that you say you got, isn't that right?

SHEDLIN: *Given your feeling of the corruption and general deception and
horribleness of the government, of the authorities, I would think that a rebel-
lion against them would be a more fully developed theme in your work. I
would think that you would turn some of your scorn for these authorities who
try to tell you that you can't make certain books and movies . . . that you
would put more of that into your characters.*
HAWKS: You mean set myself up as God, and I'm the judge of the
whole thing? Well, I haven't got any right to just say that my ideas
about something are gonna help the world out, 'cause maybe they're
gonna do a lot of harm to the world. So the best way to do it is to just
go away and do what I think is best and not try to get down to that
other kind of thing. Maybe you can call it fear, I don't think it's fear. . . .
Not to be egotistical, I mean I've started an awful lot of things, been
first in a lot of things, and other people have followed. . . . Just in an
endeavor to give people a *different side of things*. For instance, until
1930 all dialogue was the old-fashioned, melodrama emoting kind, in
everything. And when I did *Dawn Patrol*, it was the first picture of
understatement, you know—you didn't let people go. . . . And Irving
Thalberg, who was one of the few geniuses that the picture business
produced, said, "You son of a bitch. Everybody's gonna try to do it and
they don't know how. You're gonna *mess us up*." Well, in two or three

years, *they* began to do it, everybody began doing understatement;
people began writing it. Then Kazan came along and made one picture
where a guy went sky high—I think it was Dean—and everybody
thought, "Well, that was marvelous . . . here was a fellow blowing his
top." You know what I mean, *really* going back to the old fashioned
acting. But he didn't know when to quit. He made a picture that had
everybody doing it, and they turned it down, they thought it was lousy.
So now he's evened off again. I try in a picture to have somebody blow
off—if I can find somebody who can get hysterical. I've tried all kinds
of different kinds of comedy, all kinds of different kinds of pictures,
tried not to get stuck with one kind. Right now people seem to think
I'm a western director. I've only made four of 'em. And I've made quite
a few pictures. But—it's pretty dangerous when you set yourself up. . . .
Frank Capra *unconsciously* taught people a lot of great things when he
made *Mr. Smith Goes to Washington.* That was the greatest *Hurrah* opinion of politics that was ever made. Well, when he got out and started to
do it consciously, he didn't get enough people in to look at the picture
to pay for making the prints. So I couldn't advise anybody to try to do it.

SALYER: *When you referred earlier to "sick pictures," what exactly did you
mean by that?*
HAWKS: Well, I mean that it's rather hard to make good drama, but
awfully easy to make bad drama out of sick people. Sick pictures: pictures of psychopaths, pictures of strange people, pictures that are nause-
ating, people that you don't like to look at or follow—those are sick
pictures. Some dope comes out with the idea that he's gonna make
something. . . . They got a whole bunch of those pictures lying down in
Hollywood, that they can't cut or make a picture out of or release. I've
seen some of these boys come out from New York, who've made stage
plays and little off-Broadway plays, and try to make a gunman a psy-
chopath, a western gunman. Nobody's paid any attention to the pictures. They've stayed away in big herds. And I've heard people say that
the westerns that we make aren't true-to-life. Well, they're not dressed
exactly the same . . . but all it is is a dramatization of the things that
happened. All of the fellows who were good directors and made good
pictures, like George Stevens making *Shane*, were particularly impressed
with the settler who came out and ran into trouble, then violence

started picking on him. He did that story and he did it awfully well. In *Red River*, I did the story of people who wanted to get together a big herd of cattle and how they did it. They rode right over everybody. I almost made the story of the King Ranch; they asked me to make it. Then I told 'em something about the history of the King Ranch and they couldn't hardly believe it. And they said, "You're not gonna do that, are you?" And I said, "No, I'm not," and I threw it away and I made *Red River* instead.

I don't know. You people can have your ideas and everything, but I don't know how you're gonna be practical, how you're gonna get 'em across. . . .

PENLEY: *Well, there is quite a bit more independent filmmaking now. A lot of Third World countries, small European countries like Hungary and Czechoslovakia, have been finding ways to make films in such a way that you don't have to be dependent on having to make a million dollars. . . . I think there's some hope in that. . . .*

HAWKS: Well, I don't know what you mean by that. They've got an awfully small audience. They haven't gone very far, or else they'd be *making* some money. The growth of pictures in places like Hungary or Sweden has been great, but it's been a normal growth, it's grown up with the interest of the people there. I don't think there's any more independent pictures being made in America than there used to be. My lord, there were hundreds of little studios working full blast. . . . John Wayne made *fifty* westerns before he made *Red River*. As a matter of fact, I thought that small production had *gone down* a great deal.

PENLEY: *We're not so much talking about independent companies that make films for the mass audience, but making films that could communicate to one sector.*

HAWKS: Where do those pictures run?

PENLEY: *On college campuses, museums, special theaters. . . .*

HAWKS: Well, yeah, I know, but then you've got an extremely small comparative audience. Because for every student that goes in to see those, they go to fifteen films in big theaters outside. It all depends on what you want to make. If you want to make pictures for that, well go to it.

Did any of you see *The Donovan Platoon*, directed by Pierre Scheon-dorffer? Well, you missed something. It's the best short subject I've seen in years. I saw it in Paris. I said, "What are you doing with this?" He said, "I can't do anything with it." I said, "Let me have it," and I showed it. CBS has run it four times on prime time. Now he's got money enough to try other stuff. He's also learned an awful lot. He's also gonna shoot second unit for me, and if that's good I'm gonna let him make a picture. And he had a purpose when he made that thing. He got out there, he got shot at. Got beautiful stuff, but. . . . It has a fabulous beginning: Vietnam countryside, everything is just peaceful and very idyllic. Then you get closer. You hear someone singing an old folk song. It's a soldier, a Negro soldier. And all of a sudden all hell breaks loose. You're in a *war*. And he told stuff and told it beautifully. Now there was a short subject that turned into perhaps a half a dozen more things, and then it'll turn into pictures. And if he can tell 'em as good as he told that one, and I know he can, he'll be *good*. I'm trying to teach him not to just make local stuff. I wouldn't count too much today on your local stuff. And campuses change. They think different at another campus than they do here. We got two in Los Angeles—USC and UCLA—where they think entirely differently. I'm kinda betting on USC right now . . .

SHEDLIN: *Why?*

HAWKS: I think they're gonna teach people how to make films and I think they're gonna teach them better, not only films but commercials, all kinds of things. I think they're going to be pretty damn well instructed. But they're lucky. A woman put up an awful lot of money, it got them equipment, opportunities to work. Whereas the group up at . . . *AFI*, I think they came to kind of a standstill. They got too special about their own stuff . . .

PENLEY: *About two years ago, in a San Francisco interview, you were asked about your women characters. You were asked if you thought that women could ever develop as strong friendships as men. You said No, you didn't believe they could because women never had to get out there in the world and get involved in conflicts and struggles that would make them bond together the way that men do. Then, in the past few years of peoples' struggling with their sex roles, with role reversal, and people thinking about that. . . . Do you still feel that way?*

HAWKS: Some of the great friendships, or at least the friendships that I've used, have been true. One of my greatest friends—I ran him through a fence in an auto race. I won the race, and I thought, "Oh oh, here he-comes, I'm gonna have a fight." Instead of that he grinned and said, "That's pretty good, but don't do it again." I knew exactly what he meant. He'd run right into me if I tried it again. So we had a few drinks, and he had a girl he was trying to get rid of, and she was over in Europe. I heard she was coming back, and he was on location. So I said, "Why don't you step up to my house?" He stayed there five years. We fought and argued about everything. We were really good friends. I had another good friend who saved my life. I don't think there are quite as many *opportunities* for women to form that kind of an attachment. In *men* it brings you closer. . . . That's the only reason I said that I haven't even heard of more than a few reasons given by women as to why someone is their great friend. Mostly it's "I like 'em." But there's nothing that formed or cemented a bond, no incident.

SALYER: *Could that bond be cemented just by a common work project, like working on a film together?*

HAWKS: I don't know, I don't know . . .

SALYER: *Or is it only where you're risking your life, which is something that . . .*

HAWKS: I don't know. I would say that the risk thing and the other has a little more strength, but that'd probably be the man's viewpoint . . . I don't know. It'd be hard to answer that. What do you think?

SALYER: *I think that the actual risking of one's life, say in auto racing or wildlife hunting, can be sort of just a metaphor and, for me, risking my life is more involved in a sense of risking my integrity, or for me to compromise or to be dishonest or not be responsible is risking my life, where it's not losing my life or dying.*

HAWKS: Well, then you'd have to say you disagree with the remark that I made in San Francisco.

PENLEY: *No, uh. . . .*

HAWKS: OK, then *write* me a good relationship. I'll put it in a movie. I can't just make one up, I'll tell you that, but I don't have to make them up between men, I know why people become friends and why people become enemies. And I've used friendship so many times in plots.

REEVES: *Do you know why that bond forms? Is it to some extent because you are working on a common project?*

HAWKS: Well, write it down. Write a thing that kind of comes to a head that's strained by a certain thing, and why it's picked up again . . .

SALYER: *But it's even true that, say, during, WWII, when most of the men in this country were off to fight the war, a lot of the women filled the jobs that were vacated by the men, and did a lot of the kinds of work that women don't usually do. And even today, like women are working. . . . excelling in sports, and the Vietnamese women are fighting absolutely on an equal basis with men against the United States . . . I mean that is even on your own terms, where a women is risking her life, and yet you still say you don't. . . .*

HAWKS: And yet she's not willing to risk her alimony, is she?

REEVES: *I think that's a new field that you're talking about, and it's a changing field, and I think what Howard was saying before was that that opportunity has not been available to women because we have always stayed home and washed clothes and took care of husbands and had babies, and they weren't out engaging in that . . . kind of relationship.*

HAWKS: I know a girl who was modeling, and then she got sick and tired of modeling and became a photographer. My God, the stuff that she does as a photographer is just as good as any man's. She gets herself in worse trouble cause she can talk her way out.

REEVES: *If you're gonna look at the differences between men and women, there are many things that women can do, and relationships that they can form that men can't because of their attributes . . . as a man. And I think it should be utilized. I mean you utilize your femininity just as a man utilizes his masculinity. Why deny that? In the past, not only have women not used their positive attributes as women, they haven't even recognized that they were there.*

HAWKS: I think the women I put into pictures, or at least the characters, are a whole lot more along what you're talking about than the average.

PENLEY: . . . . *In* To Have and Have Not *last night, you know immediately Lauren Bacall is going to distrust other women . . .*
HAWKS: Well, I know, but I'll make you a bet right now that I can find ten jealous women for two who can overlook a thing . . .

REEVES: *Women were kept in a place where they had to distrust, they had to be jealous because they had not developed their own character to the point where they could navigate on those terms.*
SALYER: *Well, we really can't begin to realize what are the positive attributes of being a man or a woman until we've gone beyond the conditioning, and we haven't yet. . . .*
HAWKS: There were three women, three of the most beautiful women you could ever imagine, who were so chased and run after by men that they got just sick and tired of it and they turned to each other. That lasted for a certain time, and then all three of them got married and lived very happily. It just was an adjustment of the thing. I don't want to quite try that in a movie though . . .

PENLEY: *That might be really interesting. . . .*
HAWKS: If I could get Lillian Hellman to write it, it would be. . . .

PENLEY: *Just think how much more rich and complex films would be when we have whole, full friendships and relationships between men and women, among women, among men . . .*
HAWKS: Fine, but unless women start, in writing and various ways, letting the world know about some of this thing, how are you gonna guess what it is? They don't talk about those things, do they?

SALYER: *One of the problems. . . . Howard, you said you could help somebody get a film distributed, but there aren't that many people like you, and one of the problems is. . . . there've been several very interesting films made like this by women in France. . . .*
PENLEY: *Feature-length color films with professional actors, professional everything. . . .*

SALYER: *. . . . And the big distributors in this country, like United Artists, won't distribute them, because they don't like the kind of bonds women are forming. They said that to a woman who made one of these films.*

HAWKS: Well, I don't think that there's *any* motion picture company that've got enough sense to say that.

SHEDLIN: *Apparently the male distributors were offended by the rebellious women in the film. . . .*

HAWKS: OK, well they handed it to the wrong people. They didn't handle it right. If the Japs can bring karate pictures in here that all the distributors can laugh at—a whole organization can laugh at it, but one fellow says, "Well I don't give a hoot whether you don't like it or not." They just grossed $12 million with a picture.

PENLEY: *But the very strange thing about this is that one of the films we're talking about had been very successful in France, and had been distributed there, and was a very funny film, but there was something . . . these images of women were so threatening . . .*

HAWKS: Aw, I don't believe that at all. How many pictures made in France have been successful in the world? In the last ten years?

ALL: *A lot. . . .*

HAWKS: Oh no. Three or four pictures in ten years, that's all.

SALYER: *Yeah, but the reason why U.S. films get greater distribution is because the United States controls a lot of the distribution in foreign countries . . .*

HAWKS: I have never seen a picture so good that it couldn't get distribution. They get awful sick and tired of running a picture that only a few people are in there to take a look at.

SHEDLIN: *Wasn't* Scarface *suppressed?*

HAWKS: Suppressed into making an awful lot of money. They take a picture out, generally, and try it. If they can't get an audience, they say "What's the use in bringing this out, it just costs us money." There's a picture called *Walking Tall.* In the advertising there were typical scenes of violence, all that kinda stuff. They put it out, it didn't do enough business to pay the operator. But the fellow who made it said; "This is a good picture," so he took it in and he made entirely new advertising. Very clever, smart advertising. . . . How long has it been since you've seen an audience stand up and cheer for a picture?

SALYER: *Z was the last time I saw an audience stand up and cheer for a picture. . . .*
HAWKS: Well, that was just advertising, and they're gonna gross $30 or $40 million, and everybody's gonna go to see that movie. Just on a difference in advertising. Sometimes they'll try and sell a picture to women, and find out they're mistaken, they'll turn around and write ads directed at men. And sometimes the opposite way. And it's hard to tell what to do or anything. . . .

I gave a boy some money to make a picture of a horse and a mare and two young lovers, and the life parallel. And he made a movie. I wish all of *my* movies would do as well as that one did. Never played in a big town, but just played and played and played in the country, where they *understood* it. So all I'm saying is that you have to get something that will allow you to keep the theater open. I don't know if you know the new kind of theaters. They come in modules. They can set 'em up on parking lots. They can have four theaters running from the same place, all connected. . . . Plenty of popcorn, pop . . . and they're doing a whole lot better than the big theaters. So maybe there's a chance for a theater in there to take a chance on running this kind of stuff. You can't do it in the big theaters; costs too much money.

But, you see, what you're advocating really is a *minority* advocation, you know. In all of the United States, there are about twelve, fourteen maybe twenty theaters that run foreign films. Because they've found out that unless they had an audience, they lost money faster than they could put it in. . . .

SALYER: *Howard, to change the subject a little bit, but not to touch on something that we haven't touched on before, I'd be interested in what you think of the process whereby we go from the bonded friendship, right, which has an integrity, an honesty, and is a reason for living. . . . How we get from that kind of good, and how we spread that through society. At the opposite end of the spectrum is government, in a sense. The sleazy, corrupt, sniveling*

politician. I mean, in circles of government, you can't even talk about friend-
ship in the same way. It's who owes who a deal, who owes who a favor. Your
friend is someone who can manipulate a situation for you, in order to give
you more power. And it involves oppressing and hurting other people. How do
we take a couple of individuals and move out from there?
HAWKS: Go out and shoot 'em all and put some new people in. Take
'em five or six years to get the same bad habits.
(Laughter)

PENLEY: *So you think that people, innately, cannot have any sort of com-*
munity on a larger level?
HAWKS: No, I think that when a great many of the younger people start
in politics today, they start with good ideas. They find out that if they
don't do certain things, they're not going to be elected again. And pretty
soon, a gradual erosion takes place until they begin to think like the people that you see, for instance, in the Watergate. I haven't *any idea* how
you stop that. You have to be a master planner to do it. Because you've
got a generation that voted for somebody because they expect favors.
Everybody up there is trying to do something for his constituency; he
trades favors—he votes for somebody else if they'll vote for him. How're
you gonna stop that? The only way I know is shoot 'em all and start a
new bunch and then it'll take 'em five or six years to learn how to do it.

SALYER: *Who shoots 'em. . . ?*
HAWKS: Oh, *you* go out and do it. . . .
(Laughter)
HAWKS: No, I don't have any idea how you do it.

SALYER: *What about the Symbionese Liberation Army? Here's a group of*
people—men and women—who, in a very specific sense, are very strong,
and are fighting for what they perceive that they want. What do you think
about that?
HAWKS: You think it's good to break all the laws that exist?

SALYER: *In a certain sense you seem to advocate that.*
HAWKS: No, I don't at all. I don't advocate that at all. I think they're
breaking the law, and I think they'll catch up with them, and then

I think as soon as one talks they'll know who the rest of them are. And they'll make sure that somebody talks.

SALYER: *But if I went out and shot everybody I'd definitely be breaking the law. . . .*
HAWKS: Oh no, I was kidding when I said that. I didn't mean that. You know you can't do that.

SHEDLIN: *We were speculating that the Symbionese Revolutionary Army may be a conspiracy of the police or the Central Intelligence Agency. What interests me about the whole thing is that there* is *a true story, and yet there's all this information out in the culture from the papers, from the media, from everybody's own ideas of what it is . . . There's no way of telling what it really is at this point. . . .*
HAWKS: Do you believe, for instance, that a girl like that can keep hidden a relationship so that she could have been part of that all the time?

PENLEY: *I don't think she was.*
HAWKS: Do you think that outside of brainwashing that they could have turned her over? Don't you think that she made that statement . . . They've got her worn down to where she'd just about do anything. . . .

PENLEY: *You know what I think about it? I think it has more to do with something that you've been interested in in all your films. My idea about how Patty Hearst has become involved in the SLA, as a serious member of it—given what her lifestyle was previously—is that maybe when she was with them it might have been the first time in her life that she felt that she was part of a* group. *I mean no matter how crazy that might be, I think that she's always been pretty much isolated. . . .*
HAWKS: It's a pretty quick transition. I could much easier think that they are giving out these things, that they've got a plan to get a revelation (sic) by saying that she is part of it. . . .

PENLEY: *But it's pretty clear that the Hearsts did choose their money over their daughter, and if I was her, I think I would. . . .*
HAWKS: I think you're nuts. I think you're nuts.

PENLEY: *Because I think they could have done a lot more. . . .*
HAWKS: Your method of thinking would allow anybody to grab somebody and all of a sudden somebody would be broke. I don't think
they're broke but they spent $2 million. I don't think that they're terri-
bly wealthy. . . .

SALYER: *They also got a lot of contributions. It wasn't all their money. . . .*
HAWKS: Not out of the $2 million. No they didn't. They turned it
back. The other $4 million was going to be done by the Hearst
Corporation. They don't own the Hearst Corporation. They could probably benefit from it, but I don't think that Old Man Hearst was gonna
give that bunch of nitwits a lot of money. He just fixed it so that. . . .
I doubt that they have any more than they gave. . . .

SHEDLIN: *So you have no respect for the* adventurous spirit *of these nitwits?*
HAWKS: I have absolutely no respect for kidnappers or anybody else who
tries to get something that way, 'cause I don't think they've got a chance
in the world of getting it. I've yet to see that these protesters who come
into a place and tie themselves up are gaining anything by doing it.

SHEDLIN: *How would you suggest that people express their hatred for the*
authorities?
HAWKS: I don't know. Don't ask me. You think of a way. But not that
way, not by breaking the law. . . . Otherwise, pretty soon we wouldn't
have a country. Look, I have a youngster eighteen years old. I asked
him to trim his hair. He says, "I don't want to." I said, "OK, fine." I took
his car and his motorcycle away from him. He said, "Why'd you do
that?" I said, "I wanted to; I don't want you to have 'em." I said, "I have
a perfect right to think just as you do. You can do what you want to,
but I don't have to go along with it."

SHEDLIN: *But what was he withholding from you by not cutting his hair?*
HAWKS: Any desire to do anything I asked him to do. I didn't like the
way he looked. I just said, "You don't want to do it, that's quite all
right, I don't want to help you. You sail along." Didn't take him very
long before he said, "I'd rather cut my hair and have some of the things
that I get from you." I said, "Good. I think you're smart. If you know

the way to get 'em, I think you're doing the right thing. I think really the fellow that turned-him on was a very nice guy, a friend of his, who showed up with a very trim, neat haircut—it wasn't short, but it wasn't. . . .

They say that Patricia Hearst is old enough to take care of herself. What if it had been some five or six year-old? Would you admire them then? What the hell do they want, they have never made that clear.

SHEDLIN: *Well, in some ways I feel that they've been more clear than any other leftist group about their demands, and that they've been forceful in making the papers print their stuff. However, I'm not in favor of them kidnapping a non-combatant. I don't think that's a good plan. . . .*
HAWKS: I think they've turned the whole wrath of the people against a group like that, that attempts to dictate . . . you know, I don't think you can get away with that. . . .

SALYER: *Well, then, it's a very delicate line, or limit, that you have to perceive about breaking the law. Like, in a sense, Bogart in* To Have and Have Not *was breaking the law because the law was the fat fairy—he was the law of the land. . . .*
HAWKS: Well, you differentiate between laws. This group that did the kidnapping caused mental anguish. I don't think there was any mental anguish. . . . that was part of a big movement of the Free French—which laws were they breaking?

SALYER: *In other words, Bogart had popular support, the people were. . . .*
HAWKS: Well, he didn't like that fat man who came in and pestered him, so he went against him. . . .

SALYER: *Well, Cinque, by the same hand, apparently didn't like Marcus Foster. . . .*
HAWKS: No, but it's just one of those things. I don't take part in it. This is the first discussion of politics that I've had, and I might say it's going to be my last.
(Laughter)

I'm gettin' too old to try and figure out what to do about that. But if you people want to do it, I think it's fine, it's great, I like to see interest taken. But you have to figure out some way of doing it.

PENLEY: *To get a popular movement, to get popular support so that you're not just out there on your own trying to. . . .*

HAWKS: You're certainly not going to get it by those campus disorders. That really turned the trick against them, didn't it?

SHEDLIN: *Well, in some ways these "disorders" helped to end the Vietnamese war. . . .*

HAWKS: I don't think so at all. I think that when Nixon came in he knew that there was going to be no finish to that war. They didn't know what the hell to do with it. How long did the French fight over there? Years and years. Well, we've been doing the same thing. It's a kind of fighting. . . . You have the choice—you drop a couple of atomic bombs and it could've been over, boom, just like this, but they weren't gonna do that. Now, meantime, America lost all over the world by fighting there. And they'd have lost more if they just turned the country over to Russia. So who makes the choice? I think that whoever started it in the first place was wrongly advised. They should have said, "Go over there and drop a couple of big bombs, and if you don't feel like doing that, stay out of it."

SHEDLIN: *But wasn't it in great part the public pressure, the campus disorders, that kept the government from using nuclear weapons?*

HAWKS: I don't think they did anything but anger the people against them. That's my feeling about it. You hear an entirely different thing than we would hear. I think they angered people. . . . They found out that they were doing no good, so they stopped it, didn't they? They were smart to stop. And it had different phases, different effects, all over the country. There's some people trying to rehash that shooting on that southern campus. . . . Seems like a ridiculous thing. What are they gonna rehash?

PENLEY: *Those National Guardsmen at Kent State—In a way they broke the laws, they took laws into their own hands. . . .*

HAWKS: Well, you say that, but you know, they were being pelted with rocks and they were breaking things and they were being shot at by snipers . . . all the history shows that. . . .

PENLEY: *No. . . .*

HAWKS: Well, you've been readin' the wrong stuff. Not only were the people breaking the law and attacking. . . . and I don't approve of the firing, but . . . I know if I had a gun and was out there, and people started throwing rocks and bottles and slingshots and every kinda thing at me, I'd shoot 'em. Would *you* stand. . . .

SHEDLIN: *But would you be a National Guardsman with a gun out there on a campus?*
HAWKS: I don't know. I doubt it.

PENLEY: *Well, that's a political choice. . . .*
HAWKS: But once you're *in it*, and sworn to *obey*, you better obey. Otherwise, you're just gonna get into trouble. I think the provocation that needs to call out the National Guard is wrong, is completely wrong.

SHEDLIN: *But you talked about your son's obedience, and the obedience of these people who have sworn to the Armed Forces, and yet I don't get the sense that you're interested in obeying anyone but yourself. . . .*
HAWKS: I'm not interested in my *son* obeying me. Holy smoke! But I have exactly the same right as he has. If he doesn't want to do something for me, why the hell should I want to do something for him? That's where I stand as an individual. And he knows that there isn't any rank or anything between us. I didn't do anything to discipline him or to make him do anything. I just said, "If you don't want to please me, if you don't want to do something, why should I try to please you? I get no fun out of your automobile or your motorcycle, except you riding it. And if you don't want to please me, then I get no fun out of looking at you ride a motorcycle that I had to pay for." It's very simple logic. I don't think I was wrong, I don't think he was wrong. But he decided that he would—rather than show his independence—agree that he was a little bit dependent for some things on me. He didn't have to be, he could've gone out and earned it. I doubt if he would've gotten the car very quickly, or the kind of motorcycle he had to race with, or anything like that. But certainly if I provided those things, I have the right to ask him to think about me. We get along a hell of a lot better now than we did before. I think those things are very, very simple. I haven't anything against anybody doing their own stuff, as long as they don't insist that other people do their stuff. I'll tell you the way I feel. They talk about the Establishment. And I said to Greg: "What does an Establishment mean?" He said, "Well, everybody thinking the same way." And I said,

"The greatest Establishment I've seen in all the time that I've been living is you people. You wear the same clothes. You do your hair the same way. You think the same way. When I went to college, all you had to do was you had to put on a jacket to go to dinner at the fraternity house. You had to be clean and neat or else the guys told you that you'd better. . . . really. But you run around and you're so deathly afraid that somebody else is gonna tell you that . . . you know . . . if you want to rebel against this thing. . . . So *you're* the Establishment. Don't ever call us the Establishment." He turned around and said, "I guess you're right."

SALYER: *But we're just a small minority, and government and big business and the military are by far the largest percentage of the population. . . . And they're the people who have the power, who have control of the media. . . .*
HAWKS: But you're not gonna do it by having riots on campus, I don't think. I could be wrong about it. . . .

SALYER: *I agree with you. . . .*
HAWKS: By using common sense. By going into politics and sticking with it and getting somebody to follow you. I told you what I think politicians are. . . .

SHEDLIN: *If politics is such a horrible scene, and I agree that it is, how can you recommend that we go into politics, and that we not look for some other way. . . .*
HAWKS: You oughtta change it. . . .

PENLEY: *But you said that fresh new people with great ideas could go in, and five years later they'd be just like everybody else. . . .*
HAWKS: Until you get enough goin' on so that you take their place, and keep boosting those fellows out. How're you gonna do it any different? You're certainly not gonna have lightning teach—like Gary Cooper got religion in the middle of the road in *Sergeant York*. If you could only get politicians to get hit by lightning in the middle of the road and all come out singing songs, why everything would be fine. It isn't very practical . . . I don't know . . . I don't know.

Voices from the Set:
The *Film Heritage* Interviews

TONY MACKLIN/1975

BORN IN GOSHEN, INDIANA, Howard Hawks directed forty-six films during his career, including *Scarface*, *The Big Sleep*, *Red River*, *Gentlemen Prefer Blondes*, and *Rio Bravo*; he also worked as a producer and writer. Hawks received an honorary Oscar in 1975.

The Hawks interview was in his home in Palm Springs, California, in February of 1975.

INTERVIEWER: *One thing that's always been bothering me—now in the '70s people are going and looking at your films and saying, "Yes, they do have a vision, yes, they do have technique, yes, they do have a beauty and a structure." How many people recognized what you and Hitchcock and Ford were doing at the time you were doing it? At the time that you were making these films?*

HAWKS: That's a hell of a hard question. The first film that I made, first at Paramount and then at Metro-Goldwyn as story editor, with about sixty writers to tell what to do, and both studios promised me that I could direct. But then they said they could get all the directors they wanted to. So I quit and I went over to play golf and ran into the head of Fox [Sol Wurtzel] and he said, "What are you doing?" I said, "Playing golf." He said, "Aren't you working?" I said, "I'm playing golf." "Aren't you over at Metro?" "No." He said, "Well, you start work for

From *Voices from the Set: The Film Heritage Interviews*, Scarecrow Press, 2000. Reprinted by permission.

Fox this morning." I said, "No, I want to direct." He said, "You start to direct." So I went over to see him the next day and we finished the golf game. And he said, "Any story you want to do, just go and do it." I'd been kind of sour and I did a kind of a tragic story [*The Road to Glory*] where a famous keystone comedian got killed by a brick falling off a building on him and the girl lost her eyesight. It took place up at the house where a girl, a very pretty girl, drank some bootleg liquor and all of a sudden she said, "I can't see." She was pretty bitter that nobody wanted to sleep with her just because she couldn't see. And I wrote a pretty good script and story, and the critics thought it was just great. The fella at Fox said, "Now you showed you can direct. No one's going to like that picture. For God's sake go out and make some entertainment." So I went home and that night I wrote a story called "Fig Leaves" and it got its cost back in one theater. I've gotten away from your original question. What was it?

INTERVIEWER: *The original question was how many people at the time real-ized that there was a vision in the films . . .*

HAWKS: Oh, they realized that—about the men that you spoke of. The first four or five pictures that I made were very successful and then I angered the head of Fox, not the man who gave me the job but the New York head [Winfield Sheehan] who used to be a police commissioner and I made fun of policemen in a picture. And then talking pictures came in and they asked us what did we know about—they called it the "stage." And I said, "I've never been backstage." "What do you know about dialogue?" And I said, "I know how people talk. That's all." And I didn't make a picture for a year and a half. So then I wrote a story called "Dawn Patrol" and Dick Barthelmess heard it and he wanted me to do it. I did anything that Dick said and I made that and it was the biggest picture of the year. Ford had the same trouble. They wanted him to make a two reeler to prove that he knew how people talked. If you try things as I did, a picture like *Twentieth Century* with Barrymore the great idol making a complete dope out of himself and beautiful Carole Lombard running around like a nut—critics didn't know what to think of that kind of stuff and they, for the time being, kind of passed it up, and then they become sort of landmarks. They become famous later on. That happened to me on a number of pictures.

The first talking picture I made, *Dawn Patrol*, I had forty letters from the front office I had saved just for fun saying how I had missed on scenes because I underplayed them. They were doing everything broadly, ham acting. And then when Irving Thalberg saw the picture he said, "You son of a bitch. Now everybody's going to try and do this, and they won't know how to do it. You know how to do it, but they won't know how to do it." And he said, "You cause us more trouble." Irving was a good friend of mine. As a matter of fact he got me my job. I didn't know who he was. He used to come up to the house and talk stories with me, and he told Jesse Lasky that I knew more about stories than any man he knew. And so Lasky gave me a marvelous job writing forty pictures at Paramount for good money. He took me for a walk around the stages and all the electricians were saying hello and he said, "How do you know all these people?" I said, "I was a prop man over here. You've given me quite a jump from fifty bucks to three thousand. Pretty good."

You see the fellas that we think are directors are the ones that have a style. You certainly never could say that Capra didn't have a style or that Leo McCarey didn't have a style. Ford had a style. They said I had one. The ones that we didn't give too much to were the people that didn't pick their stories; they were given a story by a studio and given a great writer and great people to work with and then made a picture. The ones that we thought were good were the ones that decided what story they were going to tell and went on and told it because we think that directing is a storyteller's job. Willy Wyler made a lot of fine pictures but he never had a style. And Mike Curtiz made a lot of good pictures, but he never had a style. And there were a number of fellas that when things started to go wrong, who'd been good directors, who couldn't work on their own, couldn't pick their own stories. I only made stories that I liked except when I tried to do a friend a favor, when a friend would beg me to make a picture, and I'd say, "Look, I don't know how to tell the story. I won't be any good at it." And I'd make a louse.

I made a comedy for Zanuck [*Gentlemen Prefer Blondes*] because Zanuck asked me to come over and he said, "We've got a girl, Marilyn Monroe, that you could put in a picture. We put her in two or three pictures, we lose money on them. Tell us what we're doing wrong."

And I said, "Well, she's as phony as a three dollar bill, and you're trying to make her real. She belongs in an outrageous comedy or in a musical or something." "She can't sing." I said, "Yes, she can sing." "How do you know?" I said, "I go to Palm Springs a lot and I run into Marilyn. She's at a cocktail party and nobody'll take her home. And she comes up and says, 'Mr. Hawks, can I get a ride with you?' and I say, 'OK.' So one day I said, 'Marilyn, if you can't talk, the radio is playing, sing.' And she sang." And I said, "She sings good." "Will you make the picture?" I said, "I'll make it if I can get somebody to hold Marilyn up." "Like who?" they said. And I said, "Like Janie Russell." They said, "You can't get Jane Russell." Originally I found Janie in a dentist's office getting ten bucks a week. Duke, Janie, and George Raft are the only ones who are still grateful. So I said, "Get her on the phone." I said, "Janie, got a picture for you." She said, "When do we start?" Zanuck was sitting there. I said, "How much do you want?" She said, "Do you think I can get fifty thousand dollars?" I said, "You'd better keep talking." "Seventy-five?" "Keep talking." "A hundred, a hundred and fifty? Two hundred?" I turned around and said, "She wants two hundred thousand dollars." He said, "Tell her that's OK." So I said, "Janie that's as high as we'll go—two hundred thousand." And she was pleased as hell. I said, "Now I'm going to make this if I don't use your musical department, if I don't use your method of making musicals. I want to make it my own way. If you want to make some musical numbers when I get through, you make the musical numbers, but I don't want anything to do with thirty or forty chorus girls." And I made a bunch of intimate little songs that worked very well. They let me do it. And actually every picture was successful that I could choose.

I made one for Sam Goldwyn [*A Song Is Born*] that I never should have made. But he was stuck for a story and he said, "Howard, what can I make with Danny Kaye? I'm stuck. Now, Howard, you've got to do this." I said, "I'm not going to do it, Sam," He followed me down to Palm Springs. Annoyed me and pestered me and everything. I said, "Sam, I won't do the picture." "Isn't there some way you'd do it?" "Yes, if you'd give me $25,000 a week, I'd do it." "OK, you've got a deal." I said, "You're a goddamn fool." I said, "There's one thing—I don't use Virginia Mayo." Well, I got Virginia Mayo, and he was so mad at having made such a silly deal that he didn't—oh, I don't know—he just didn't like me at all. He'd made a deal with a writer and the writer wasn't any good. He didn't like the writer, he didn't like me. I've never seen the picture. I didn't want to see the thing.

But it wasn't really until the French, English, and Italians, for instance as far as I'm concerned, started saying, "This guy Hawks is good," then America which was way behind began catching on. See, directors were not given things here until Harry Cohn of Columbia started it. The studio didn't want to have to pay a director. They wanted them to do what they wanted them to do. Of course, Metro-Goldwyn was very successful mainly because of Thalberg. But Cohn couldn't get stars. Vic Fleming came to me and he said, "I just made a deal with Cohn. I got 100,000 bucks for making a picture." I said, "What's the matter? Is he nuts?" "No, he can't get any stars, but he thinks I can get them." "Well," I said, "you can." He said, "I told Cohn that maybe he could get you. He was going to phone." So he did and I went over to see him and I said, "I want to hear you say why you want me." "I want you to make pictures for me. You make good ones, and you can get the stars. And I think the director's the important thing." I said, "OK. Fleming stuck you, but I'm just going to ask you for just what I got on the last picture because I like the way you think." Now he started that business of letting a director do what he wanted to. Capra and I, when we were working there, our pictures made more money than the studio did. They lost money on all their other pictures. They did one thing though—they kept the nucleus together and kept their work in the studio, so that was worth something. But, I don't know, I made five pictures with Cary Grant; every one of them's been successful and Cary never thought any of the stories were any good. John Wayne never in his life thought much of the stories, not one story that I made with him. I told him, "Duke, it doesn't bother me one bit that you don't like it. You can act. That's all you know about it. You don't know how to produce, you don't know anything about stories. Just do what I tell you to do and it'll be all right." He says, "I'm doing it." But he says, "I don't know how to do your stuff." I tried to help him on *The Alamo*, and I wrote a whole bunch of scenes for him. He read them and he said, "They're great scenes, but I couldn't do it. I couldn't do it." I was going to have the girl in *The Alamo* raped by twenty or thirty people and want revenge. It would have been a hell of a good story. "That's a good scene," Duke said, "but I don't know how to do those things." And he did a corny girl. That's the only way you can answer that question.

INTERVIEWER: *Yes, that's part of the answer. What I'm also asking is it seems to me if you do make a film with personal qualities and people don't recognize that it's personal, they haven't in years gone past, it would be a terribly frustrating experience.*
HAWKS: No, because I would always tell a producer, "Look, I don't know how to tell that story." Now, for instance, Jack Warner assigned *Sergeant York* to Mike Curtiz, and he wanted me to do *Casablanca*. Now that was before Bergman and Bogart were thought of. So Curtiz and I had lunch and he said, "I've got a story about people in the hills. I don't know anything about them." "What is it about?" He said, "Sergeant York." I knew a little about the story. I said, "Mike, I got one that's a goddamn musical comedy. They stand up and they sing something about the party. How about trading? You take *Casablanca*; I'll take *Sergeant York*." And we were up against each other for Academy Awards. They came out in two different years though. But Jack Warner said, "OK, if you guys want to do it." I said, "Jack, poor Mike doesn't know anything about Tennessee hillbillies." And it was just that I found stories that I liked and made very few stories that I was given.

INTERVIEWER: *Did you make pictures for the public or pictures for yourself?*
HAWKS: I don't think that's a fair question.

INTERVIEWER: *Oh, I never ask "fair" questions.*
HAWKS: I make them for the public. If you ask me do I like a drama or a comedy, when I go and hear them laugh about it I like the comedy. Two years later when the drama has taken hold and people come up and say, "I'll never forget *Red River*," I like *Red River*. Ford and I used to talk about the fact that everything that you did had been done before, and the only chance that you had was to do it differently. And one way was to make it fun. Now I got so sick and tired, I went over to Europe

for about two or three years. And I came back and I did *Rio Bravo*. It had some stuff in it that hadn't been done before—Dean Martin rolling around in manure and Walter Brennan saying, "There's a guy around here that smells pretty bad. I think he ought to take a bath." When he finally took a bath that was what made things start. Also they asked me what I thought of . . . what was the Western that Cooper made that they thought was so good? He was the sheriff.

INTERVIEWER: High Noon.
HAWKS: They asked me if I liked that. I thought it was lousy. "Why?" And I said, "He was a joke as a sheriff. He wasn't a sheriff; he wasn't a pro. He ran around like a chicken with his head off asking people to help him. Then his wife who was a Quaker saved his guts." Another one, *Five O'Clock to Yuma,* or something like that.

INTERVIEWER: Three O'Clock. *I think it was.* [3:10 to Yuma.]
HAWKS: Well, make it *Four.* That was a picture where the prisoner taunted the sheriff and said, "Wait till my friends catch up with you." And I said, "That's a lot of hogwash because a good sheriff, if somebody wanted to help him, would say, 'How good are you?' 'I can shoot.' 'Are you good enough to go against the best man they've got?' 'No.' 'Well, then you'd just be trouble. I'd just have to take care of you.'" In that *Yuma* thing, when the prisoner was taunting the sheriff saying, "When my friends catch up . . ." the sheriff would say, "You'd better hope they never catch up 'cause the first man shot is going to be you." So I was telling that to Leigh Brackett who wrote for me. I said, "Hey, let's do a picture the exact opposite of those things." And so we did. We got so many good ideas in doing it that I wrote them down and so when we came to *El Dorado*, we just did the opposite. Instead of a guy who was good with a gun we had a guy who couldn't shoot. Instead of a drunk and his friend the sheriff, we had the sheriff as the drunk. We just did exactly opposite.

INTERVIEWER: *And* Rio Lobo *was a third?*
HAWKS: *Rio Lobo* was a mistake because they didn't have the money. We needed two good people. Otherwise my story wasn't any good. I saved the story and just wrote that damn piece of junk and made it.

INTERVIEWER: *A lot of the lists of best ten Westerns of all time have either* Rio Bravo *and/or* Red River *and Peckinpah's* Wild Bunch. *I know that you didn't like* Wild Bunch. *Right?*

HAWKS: No, I don't like it.

INTERVIEWER: *What do you think about people that relate to both those films? Do you think it's possible to relate to both of those films, really?*

HAWKS: Somebody that likes Westerns, that's all. They've asked me what I think of Peckinpah and I said, "Hell, I can shoot three men, get them to the morgue, and bury them before he gets one down to the ground." There's no doubt about it that he makes a picture with a certain thing, but I think he overdoes it. It doesn't meet reality; it's just being tough. I try to do almost exactly the opposite to what he does. And I miss humor in his pictures.

INTERVIEWER: *His humor is often kind of "nasty." I think there's humor. Like "We Shall Gather at the River"—instead of a song of celebration he used it ironically to make a kind of fun of the people who are singing it. I think that's a quality of his humor.*

HAWKS: I like things like—I think it was in *Rio Bravo*—Wayne went over to a man and said, "So nobody ran in here." Some man said, "Nobody ran in here." And Wayne went like this and hit him right across here with a gun so blood was coming all over his face. And Dean Martin said, "Take it easy, Chance." And Wayne turned and said, "I'm not going to hurt him." The audience laughed so at that. Wayne said, "That's one of the best lines I've ever had." I said, "I know. You've used it about three times since."

INTERVIEWER: *One of the lines that I like most is in* Rio Lobo *when Wayne was in the dentist's chair and the dentist actually pulled his tooth out and said, "I have to do this because you aren't a good enough actor." Do you kid Wayne a lot in that way?*

HAWKS: Oh, sure. Any actor—for instance I believe it was in a Cary Grant picture, Cary was supposed to be telling a blonde that there was a man waiting in a car down there. "What does he look like?" Grant said to me, "How'll I say—what does he look like?" I said, "Tell her he looks like Ralph Bellamy, the actor." And everybody laughed about it. This was the only decent answer I could give him. I think too many people take themselves too damn seriously when they're making pictures. For instance, there's one director, a pretty good director, who said to me, "I never can get over, Howard, seeing in *Scarface* when there was a raid going on, bullets were flying, and Vince Barnett was answering the telephone saying, 'Speak louder. I can't hear you. This is Mr. Camonte's secretary. Speak louder, I can't hear you.'" And then we shot coffee, hot coffee came out and burned his behind. And they said to me, "Anybody that'd be a damn enough fool to use that kind of stuff in the middle of an exciting sequence . . ." That's when you can get your laughs, when something like that happens.

INTERVIEWER: *They don't do that much any more, do they? Get laughs in the middle of a dramatic scene? That's one of the qualities that's missing many times from modern pictures.*
HAWKS: They did in *The Sting.* I thought *The Sting* was one of two good comedies that have been made in the last four years—*What's Up Doc?* and *The Sting.* I think the people are getting so damn sick and tired of this junk that they're looking at, kind of sick stuff, that I thought they'd vote for *The Sting* to win the Academy Award, and they did.

INTERVIEWER: *What have you done in the last couple of years?*
HAWKS: I helped a boy I know [Max Baer Jr.] make a little picture called *Macon County Line.*

INTERVIEWER: *Yes. It just came out last year.*
HAWKS: About eight months ago. And they told me the other day it's going to gross fifteen million to eighteen million dollars. Cost one hundred seventy-five thousand. It's just got the qualities to interest people. *Easy Rider,* I didn't think much of. My boy who's nineteen said, "How about going to a picture tonight?" And I said, "OK." He looked it up and he said, "There's nothing playing here that's any good except *Easy Rider.*" I said, "You've seen that." He said, "I know. I'll see it again." We went down to see it. He lasted about fifteen to twenty minutes, and he went out to have some popcorn, etc., for a reel to a reel and a half.

He came back in and looked at the stuff and went out again. I said, "I thought you wanted to see this again." He said, "You can't look at it the second time." He said, "I like your pictures the second time, but I don't like this."

INTERVIEWER: *That's a real test, isn't it? That you can go back.*
HAWKS: Yes.

INTERVIEWER: *How did you advise the maker of* Macon County Line?
HAWKS: I didn't advise it. They had a true story that had a certain shock value and a certain honesty. There was something about the story that I would say was a good story.

INTERVIEWER: *But didn't you say you helped him?*
HAWKS: Yes.

INTERVIEWER: *In what way?*
HAWKS: Composition of scenes and afterwards in cutting. They had it all cut wrong. They didn't know how to do it. I helped and made suggestions, some of them that they probably didn't even realize were suggestions. But they did them. I worked with Max Baer's father when he was champion. Max Jr. just made another picture. He came to me at first, and I wrote down eight or ten pages of what I would do about treatment and that kind of thing. I don't know whether he followed them or not.

INTERVIEWER: *Have you seen* Macon County Line—*the finished picture?*
HAWKS: Yes.

INTERVIEWER: *And some of what you did suggest is in there?*
HAWKS: Oh, yes. And I helped them sell the picture. I wrote a letter saying it was a good picture. He published it and he got five calls the next day. I didn't say it was a great picture. I've got two stories now. One of them is a wild, crazy comedy with every blooming thing that they used to make. It has a toughness, and yet it has the quality of things like *Bringing Up Baby* or a couple of Cary Grant things that I've

done. It'll take a second unit about six months to do their work because it's in about five or six different countries in Europe.

INTERVIEWER: *What part does sentimentality play in motion pictures? It seems to me that it played a big part in Ford's films and it plays a part in your films, especially things like* Sergeant York *and* Red River.
HAWKS: You mean almost corny?

INTERVIEWER: *Almost corny.*
HAWKS: Corn to me is somebody whispering sweet nothings to a girl in the moonlight and all that sort of junk. I certainly have never had anything that even resembled that. The women were pretty self-sufficient, pretty sure of themselves, pretty honest, happened to be the kind of girl that I like. I wouldn't know how to do the other stuff. Ford has been admittedly corny. But he got away with it. Very corny. My comedy and Ford's are entirely different. Ford's is corny and mine is sarcastic. I could never do Ford's kind. Wayne gets corny but doesn't get away with it. You've got to do stories about something, and I've been very successful doing stories about the friendship of two men. When I was at Metro I wrote some lines for *Test Pilot* with Gable and Tracy, and Vic Fleming who made it came around and said, "How are those guys going to read those lines?" I said, "Have lunch with them and I'll come wandering in and get them to tell me about it." The lines were, "What are you doing this for? Because I love you." They said, "We can't read lines like that. How would you read them?" I said, "No wonder, if you're any good as actors you'd know how to read them." And I showed them. "Oh, that's different when you read them that way." And they did it, and they thought it was great. You can't tell about these things. One fella—I don't know what his name was—in writing about the picture said that usually I was so close to being truthful that when I made *Only Angels Have Wings* I certainly went too far, that that was just beyond the stretch of anything. I wrote him a letter. I said, "I agree with you perfectly except for one thing: I didn't make it up. Everything in there was absolutely true." And I started in telling him the things. Of course, he was amazed. I said, "This is one of the cases where truth is stranger than fiction. I didn't exaggerate, I just did it. And you thought that I was going too far."

INTERVIEWER: *Let me follow up on that. If you do have a personal style and you do have events that actually happened in history, doesn't the personal style distort or change them?*

HAWKS: I don't know whether I can answer that. I asked Sergeant York two thousand questions, and I got answers. "How did you get religion?" "I got hit (H-I-T) in the middle of the road." I said to Johnny Huston, "How do you get religion in the middle of the road." Well, after a couple of drinks we finally decided he was riding a mule and lightning hit him and the mule's shoes were all curved up and his rifle was bent, and he heard music coming. He walked in and Walter Brennan was leading the congregation in "Give Me That Old Time Religion," and he became religious.

INTERVIEWER: *That's not what the Beatles say one does in the middle of the road.*

HAWKS: All I'm saying . . . York made a pretty good answer. "Did you see the picture Hawks made?" He said, "Yes." "What'd you think of it?" He kind of grinned and he said, "Well, I supplied the tree and the branches and Hawks put the leaves on it." And I think that was a pretty damn good answer. It's just like the French. I go over there and about thirty directors want to have dinner and a few drinks and talk. And they're absolutely astounded at the fact that I say, "I never think about that." "What do you think about?" I said, "I think if I like it, I do it; if I think it's funny, I do it. If I like an actor, the audience likes him; if I like a girl, the audience likes her. I don't apprehend or go through all that stuff."

INTERVIEWER: *In other words, your act of filmmaking is almost intuitive.*

HAWKS: Completely. Unless it comes to things like . . . *High Noon* is lousy because that isn't the way a guy acts. I like to deal with pros unless I'm dealing with a bungler purposely. For instance, Zanuck wanted me to do a story called *A Man on a Ledge*, a guy that had the whole country . . . he stayed out for two to three days on a ledge. "Oh," I said, "I don't want to do that." "Why?" I said, "I don't like suicides." "Oh, Howard," he said, "that's a silly way . . ." I said, "I'll do it in one way. Cary Grant's in bed with a very good-looking girl and her husband comes home and he crawls out on the ledge and pretends he's going to commit suicide." "Oh," he said, "you can't do that." Afterwards he said to me, "I wish we'd done that."

INTERVIEWER: *I read in Joe McBride's book, and I absolutely can't believe it, that you had the rights to* The Sun Also Rises *and you couldn't understand how you could make it into a comedy. That can't be made into a comedy can it?*
HAWKS: I don't think I ever said that. [McBride now agrees. Ed.]

INTERVIEWER: *It didn't make any sense to me at the time.*
HAWKS: I bought *The Sun Also Rises* because I really figured that anything Hemingway wrote I could make a movie out of, and I got to working on it. I could make it today if I wanted to, but not at that time. I sold it to Zanuck who thought he could make it.

INTERVIEWER: *How could you make it today?*
HAWKS: I'd be pretty frank about it. There's no reason why you can't make a picture today about a man who was shot in the wars and was impotent and suffers with the thing. You could do that today if you wanted to. I wouldn't want to. I worked on that for a long time before I sold it. And then Zanuck went around talking about how he had gotten the best of me in buying it. I sold it to him for four or five times what I paid for it. And then six months later he came to me and he said, "How were you going to do that picture?" I said, "Darryl, you've been running around saying how you got the best of me. Give me fifty thousand dollars and I'll tell you how I was going to do it." And he said, "No, I'm not going to do that." And I said, "OK." After I saw the picture I told him he'd have been a lot better off if he had given me the fifty thousand dollars.

INTERVIEWER: *But you couldn't have done it, could you? Could you have told him how? How would you have approached it?*
HAWKS: Today?

INTERVIEWER: *No, when he wanted to make it.*
HAWKS: Oh, I had it. I've forgotten exactly how I was going to do it. But you could have explained—I don't know if it would have stood

up—but you could have explained the injury, and if you'd written good enough dialogue to go with it, you could get around it.

INTERVIEWER: *The last line of the book is, they're riding in the car together—the nymphomaniac, Lady Brett Ashley, and Jake Barnes who's the soldier—and she says, "We could have been so much together." And he says, "Isn't it pretty to think so." Just ironically. And they have that scene two-thirds of the way through the film. And at the end of the film they're going off into the sunset to do God-knows-what together.*

HAWKS: I know. Zanuck didn't know how to make that kind of a thing, and the people he gave it to didn't. You can get away with things. For instance, Howard Hughes wrote a story about two brothers, one was a cop and one was a gangster, called *Scarface*, and he wanted me to do it. I ran into Ben Hecht and said, "Ben, do you want to do a story with me?" He said, "Yes. What about?" I said, "It's a gangster picture." He said, "You don't want to do that." I said, "I've got an idea. This Caesar Borgia is in Chicago today with Al Capone." He said, "We'll start tomorrow morning." It took us eleven days to do the script and write the dialogue and make the whole thing. Now the censors said that the scenes between the brother and the sister were too beautiful and shouldn't be done by a gangster. They didn't realize that it was our version of incest. So you can get away with a lot. You can absolutely turn stories around like that and still get something out of it. What you do is you get a different scene. You don't get the usual scene. Every time I make a scene, before I make it I start trying to do it the opposite way because everybody's been trying, a lot of good people have been trying, for years to tell a very few stories. I thought *Rio Bravo* was a damned good picture because everything in it was completely different. Yet look what happened in *El Dorado* when we got Jimmy Caan, who couldn't shoot a gun, to shoot a fellow who was running away and the sign fell down and hit the fellow and knocked him down. It just turned it. Whenever I worked with Hecht and MacArthur we'd go dash right to a story, and then we would have what we called a name-calling contest. We'd sit around and try to think of different ways to say things so that the dialogue wouldn't sound the same. I remember one day somebody said, "Oh, you're just in love." And Ben Hecht said, "Oh, you're just broke out in monkey bites." You know. And out of it comes a certain quality. The audience doesn't know exactly what you're saying, but they suspect it or something and it becomes interesting. Any time you can do a thing the way you'd do it, you put your mark on it. So I work right with writers, and they don't seem to mind it. I say, "Yes, that's a good way of doing it, but there'd be another way too. You could do it this way." They say, "That isn't a whole lot different." I say, "Here, let me do it."

Now Hemingway, I wanted him to write for me because I said, "Ernest, I can make a picture out of any damn thing you write, even out of *To Have and Have Not*." "Oh, you can't make a picture out of that junk. You couldn't do it." And I said, "OK, what about the relationship between Harry and the girl? It's a great relationship, isn't it?" He said, "Yes." I said, "How did they meet?" So we sat around for a week or ten days to figure out how they met. And I made the movie and saw Ernest and I said, "Now the fellow paid you ten thousand dollars for doing it. I paid him eighty thousand to buy it from you and I sold it to Warner Bros. for half the profits of the picture, and I made about a million and a half." He wouldn't talk to me for a year and a half. But all you need is a little jumping off place to change a story around. We changed *His Girl Friday*; it was *The Front Page*. I was telling half a dozen people that the finest dialogue of the times came from Hecht and MacArthur. The hardest, quickest, funniest dialogue. And to prove it after dinner we got up. I had two copies to *The Front Page* and I gave one to a girl and I said, "You read the reporter; I'll read the other part." And in the middle of it I said, "My God, the lines are better coming from a girl." So after a few days I ran into Harry Cohn and I said, "You said anytime you want to make a picture . . . I want to make one." He said, "Good, you started today." And I said, "No, I started a long time ago. I'm going to do *Front Page*." "A remake?" he said. I said, "Yes." He said, "You don't want to do that." "OK, Harry, I'll go some other place. I've already bought the story." "Now wait a minute, wait a minute, if you want to do it, do it." And he said, "Walter Winchell could play the editor and Cary Grant could play the reporter." And I said, "You're batting pretty well. You're .500." "Why?" he said. And I said, "Cary Grant, I'll get him to play the editor and a girl to play the reporter." "Are you nuts?" he said. Well, we made it and it was a very successful picture.

INTERVIEWER: *It certainly was.*

HAWKS: And the only thing that helped was I called Ben Hecht up and told him what I was going to do, and he said, "I wish I'd thought of that." And he said, "You want some help?" I said, "Sure." He said, "I need some help. I'm working on a story I can't solve. I'll come up there, and you help me and I'll help you." Well, he helped. He suggested that they had previously been married. And it made a whole great big difference in the whole bloomin' picture. And I helped on his story, so we got along fine.

INTERVIEWER: *Everybody who has seen* His Girl Friday *and compares that to the recent* Front Page *has said it makes* Front Page *look paltry in comparison.*

HAWKS: I'm quite amazed that Billy [Wilder] tried that. I haven't seen it, but I would think that it's a little too old a story. There's nothing you can do to bring it up to date. I brought it up to date by putting a girl in there. That's as far as you could go. But he usually does do it.

INTERVIEWER: *But this time I think he hasn't. You weren't especially happy with* Hatari *and* Red Line 7000. *Is that right?*

HAWKS: *Red Line* 7000, Paramount needed the picture. Something happened to Wayne—oh, he had an operation. I had to wait for a long time. So they wanted me to do this and do it in a hurry. I cast the picture in an awful hurry. I didn't get the right people. And another thing that was wrong was the fact that I was trying something that we tried years and years ago—to put three stories together and make it jell. We called it *Bits of Life*, and it was a flop. It made me mad. I didn't direct it, but a damn good man directed it and the stories were good. I never could figure out why, and then when I made *Red Line* I found out why. Just when you get people interested in one story, you jump to another story. Just when they're interested in that, you jump to another. By that time they've forgotten the first one. They're all mixed up and they say, "The hell with this thing!" Now the English think it's a great picture. I don't. I think it's lousy. I think it was my fault and mine only. I think the stories are good. The people are good enough. The stories were all taken from life. I was trying to make up my mind which I would do as a racing story and I said, "Well, I'll put all three of them together." And it was my fault. Now *Hatari* was just simply—the story did not live up to the great stuff that was around it. Actually, it was partly my fault, for doing it, for getting the people that I did. I'd seen the young Frenchman—he did very, very well. I'd seen the German boy that played in it. But Wayne just blew them off the screen. There wasn't anything left to do. He just took charge; they were just barely there.

INTERVIEWER: *Is there anything that you could have done to keep him from taking charge? Or wouldn't there have been anything in the picture then?*
HAWKS: Then I would have hurt it. Wayne was the money ball. He and I worked together, and the scenes that we made were good. It was just that there wasn't anything left to do.

INTERVIEWER: *Tell me about Wayne and* Red River.
HAWKS: Wayne was trying a little too hard in *Red River*, and I said, "Look, don't, this is just a story. Wait until I tell you, and then you try. Because if you do two good scenes in the picture and don't annoy the audience the rest of the time, you'll be good. If I can do five good scenes in the picture and not annoy the audience, I'll have done my job as a director." After that he always used to say, "Is this the one where I try?" He took that to heart, and he tells people that. He told it to Ford, and Ford quit trying on the little scenes, just went over them easy. They have to be there to tell the story. You have to say that we're going to move from St. Louis to Kansas City. You have to have something moving.

INTERVIEWER: *Did you know that the Montgomery Clift and John Wayne relationship would work as well as it did? Did your intuition tell you that?*
HAWKS: I wouldn't have cast that if I didn't think they'd work. I thought they'd work good because I thought he was good— Montgomery Clift was good. Wayne came to me and said, "I don't think this kid'll work." Oh, Wayne was afraid of his size and everything about it. He was worried about the fight at the end. And I told him Monty would kick him in the head. "Kick me in the head?" I said, "That'll even it up, won't it?" But after we got to working, we had a lot of fun. Monty

was a sort of an Actors' Lab guy. Preconceived ideas of doing things—
things like that. We astonished him by saying, "Monty, you pick out a
scene. Just tell me a scene and Duke and I'll do it." And he told me a
scene, and we were lucky—we hit good dialogue. He turned and looked.
He couldn't believe that it could be done. He thought that you had to
study and learn. He had it all worked up to get mad in one scene, to get
very angry, to get really upset. He said, "What'd you think of it?" I said,
"Monty, I've seen that done so many times that I can't even remember
who did it. But I'm sure that they must have done it better than you're
doing it now because it was new when they did it." "What do you
mean?" I said, "Instead of getting angry, do a scene and fight against
your anger." So when it came somebody was going to kill Wayne and
Monty threw him a gun and said, "Go ahead, go ahead." The fellow
didn't want to. Monty came over and said, "You're a lucky man. That's
how close you came to dying." He played a hell of a good scene. There
was a man who was really angry, not just phony noise. And you knew it
was because he wanted to do it for Wayne. I had two, three people tell
me that the end of the picture wasn't any good. I said, "I agree with you.
But how in the hell would you end it?"

INTERVIEWER: *How about if one of them had died, which obviously must
have passed through your mind.*
HAWKS: Oh yes. I tell you—I made *Dawn Patrol*, and one of them died
when he was fighting for his country or he was living up to a thing.
They put the other guy in charge. I did that story really twice, one
called *Road to Glory*, where you start with one commander who's in
trouble, and then another, and then finish with the third. So I kill off
somebody that the audience has just gotten to like. They don't like it.
What do you gain by it? I didn't mind a bit killing Paul Muni in
Scarface. But just to kill somebody to finish a picture . . .

INTERVIEWER: *Don't you think Wayne was fated to die in a sense in that
picture? Obviously you don't.*
HAWKS: Oh no. I'll tell you one reason why: if he'd died he'd have
been a loser. I don't like losers. I don't make pictures about losers. Steve
McQueen asked me about a picture that he made, a rodeo picture or
something like that [*Junior Bonner*].

INTERVIEWER: *For Sam Peckinpah.*

HAWKS: Yes. "Did you like it?" I said, "I thought it was lousy." "Why?" I said, "Everybody in it was a loser. I hate losers." "My God," he said, "you're right. Everybody was a loser." And I said, "That was a lousy picture, wasn't it?" And he said, "Yes." I said, "What are you going to do with a picture about a bunch of losers?"

INTERVIEWER: *But that's film today because so many people in society feel that people are losers because they are vulnerable or they are victimized or they aren't strong enough to take on the onslaughts of whatever there is.*

HAWKS: Yes, but pictures are not successful for the reason that people who are tired and want to go and see a movie, they go and see it for entertainment. And if they are losers, then they're not entertained a bit. If they're not losers, they see an image of themselves and like it. Then they go on.

INTERVIEWER: *Let me ask you a question, though. Maybe there's an inconsistency here. Joanne Dru wades in and stops them fighting and says something like, "Oh boys, you should stop it." Now isn't that some-what like the Quaker woman interfering in saving Gary Cooper's life?*

HAWKS: No, it wasn't. But one of the things that was bad about it was Joanne Dru. She was meant to do comedy. And the girl that I had that was ready to play and under contract was a big, tall Irish girl that learned to play cards and could deal you any kind of a hand so that you knew she wasn't a whore. She had a lot of guts and everything. She came in the day before we were supposed to go to Arizona and said, "I'm pregnant." I had no one to put in the picture but Joanne Dru, and I thought she did a very good job for what she did but she didn't inspire you a bit trying to make scenes.

INTERVIEWER: *No. I'm not sure she made that last scene believable.*

HAWKS: I'm not sure anybody could. I was thinking of Walter Brennan doing it. I was really thinking of letting Walter do it.

INTERVIEWER: *You mean to stop the fight?*

HAWKS: Yes.

INTERVIEWER: *Then why didn't you?*
HAWKS: I thought the girl was OK doing it. It's a tough situation. Lot of people liked it. Lot of people didn't like it. All you wanted was to stop the fight.

INTERVIEWER: *She stopped it in a way that was almost hysterical where Walter Brennan might have kidded them out of it.*
HAWKS: No, I think if Walter had done it that you'd have played it with him mad.

INTERVIEWER: *But the way he gets mad is funny.*
HAWKS: Yes. Well, she was funny. She was crying and at the same time trying to do it. It's a tough scene to do. I did something of the same kind of thing in *Rio Bravo* with Angie Dickinson. She's drunk and crying. "You make fools out of yourselves. Go out and get shot and everything." That's the way women behave.

INTERVIEWER: *I believe Angie Dickinson and I don't believe Joanne Dru.*
HAWKS: Oh Angie's better, Angie's better. About the ending of *Red River*, you can't always come out right just on a single scene, a scene that's way past somebody's capabilities. Like one of the best actresses that I ever starred was Frances Farmer. And she was a girl that really had ideas of her own. She had to do a crying scene. I said, "Get the menthol." "What's that for?" I said, "To make you cry." "An actress does not need those things," she said. I said, "OK." We did it her way. You make close-ups, make medium shots, you make another shot. She had to cry all the way through. I said, "Now, Frances, we'll try my way. I'll show you both, show you what happened." She saw it, leaned over and said, "Kick me. You're right." The difference was that my way her nose was running, which it does when people cry. You know what I mean. It didn't dry up all the time. She didn't have to just do things. A much better scene. You can't tell what the devil's going to happen when you put new people in a scene. Carole Lombard was a second cousin of mine. When I came out here and got successful, Carole came out—she wanted to act. Her family had some money; she didn't have to worry about earning anything. I adored her. She'd come around. She was just as nutty as she was in pictures. She'd hang around the house; she might

stay overnight. I got stuck for a girl to play with Barrymore. I couldn't get one in all of town. You couldn't find anybody to play with Barrymore. So I said to Harry Cohn, "I want Lombard." "Oh for God's sake, you can do better than that. The most she's ever done is five lines in a picture. Played a clotheshorse." I said, "OK, Harry, then you find somebody better." He came in in three or four days and he said, "I got Lombard." So when we started I said to Barrymore, "Jack, I want a favor. Up until four o'clock this afternoon, it's on me. After that you say any goddamn thing you want." He said, "OK, Howard." They started to rehearse and he looked at her. Oh, God, she was awful! He had his arms around her, looked at me and held his nose. I went over and I said, "Now you made me a promise." "I'll live up to it." So I told the cameraman to get twenty minutes—I needed twenty minutes to think up some excuse. And he made the announcement there'd be a twenty minute break. I said, "Carole, let's take a walk." So we walked around the stage. I said, "You've been working on that story." She said, "I'm glad it shows. I've worked hard." I said, "You know your lines perfectly. What do you get paid for this picture?" She said, "Five thousand dollars." I said, "That's pretty good." She said, "I think it's great." I said, "What do you get paid for?" She said, "Why, acting, of course." And I said, "Supposing I tell you that you've earned the five thousand. You don't owe a goddamned cent and you're not going to do any more acting." And she just stared at me. I said, "What would you do if a man said such-and-such a thing to you?" She said, "I'd kick him right in the balls." I said, "Barrymore said that to you. Why don't you kick him?" She just stared. She couldn't think of anything to say. I said, "What would you do if a man said such-and-such thing?" She waved her arm in a typical Lombard gesture. "Well," I said, "he said that to you in the third line. You didn't wave your arm. If you go back in there and act, I'm going to fire you and get another girl. If you kick him, if you wave your arms, if you do any goddamn thing that you feel like doing, we'll go ahead and make the movie." She said, "Howard, you're serious, aren't you?" I said, "You bet I'm serious." She said, "OK." And we went back in there. I said, "We're going to try a take." And Barrymore said, "Oh, we're not ready, Howard." I said, "Will you tell me who's running this thing?" He said, "You are." And they got in there. I had three cameras on them. It was a little place. I didn't know what they were going to do. And he said this line, she made a kick at him. He started talking to her and staying away, and she ended up on the couch and kicking at him like this and yelling at him and doing everything like that. They played twelve pages of dialogue and he finally made his exit speech and walked out. I said, "cut and print it." He came back in and said, "That was magnificent. Have you been kidding me all this time?" She broke into tears and ran off the stage. And he said, "Howard, what the Christ goes on around this place?" I told him about it. He said, "I can't believe it." I said, "Jack, she is one of the most attractive women going. She hangs around the house. She says any goddamn thing that comes into her mind. She's utterly uninhibited. She's a complete extrovert." He said, "She's fabulous." I said, "I know it." And he said, "She's going to be a star." I said, "I know that too. I'm going to need some help from you." "Oh, hell," he said, "I'll do that. Is it OK if I make a pass at her?" I said, "Make all you want." I talked to Carole; I said, "For God's sake, don't say yes until the picture's over."

INTERVIEWER: *I really don't know what to think acting is any more. Whether it's training or skill or a natural quality or a genuineness. Now what is it? What is acting?*
HAWKS: If the camera likes you, it's easy. If the camera doesn't like you, there's not a goddamn thing you can do. You can get away with murder if the camera likes you.

INTERVIEWER: *But some people's cameras do like you and some people's don't. I'm thinking of Elliott Gould. For Altman he gives performances that are totally different than the ones he gives for somebody else. So it's not exactly the camera. I think maybe it's the person behind the camera as much as it is the camera.*
HAWKS: Yes, but if the camera doesn't like you, you're not going to do any good in pictures. It may like you in different degrees, but I've tried tests of girls that I thought were just fabulous. Nothing came out of them. In making a picture with Gary Cooper, I'd make a scene and I'd just turn around and say, "Oh, God." I'd look at it the next day and everything was right there that I wanted. I couldn't see it because the camera did it for him. Now Marilyn Monroe couldn't get a date. She'd sit around half-dressed, and nobody would look at her. And a pretty

extra girl would walk by and everybody'd whistle. But when you said, "All right, camera," something happened, and she became attractive to millions of people. Not to anybody who worked with her, not to anybody around her. But the camera liked her. That's how an actor like Bogart . . . he's a homely man, you know. But the camera liked him.

INTERVIEWER: *Now I would imagine that Bacall is beautiful and distinctive in person as well as in front of the camera. Or am I wrong?*

HAWKS: Bacall came out here because my secretary made a mistake and sent her a ticket. I'd just seen her picture. I wanted to find out what schooling she'd had, what training. In came the little girl. "I'm very glad to meet you, Mr. Hawks." Nasal, high voice. But she was enthusiastic so I said to the secretary, "Look, get a car and send her over to some studios. Let her see some people working and then send her home." But she didn't want to go back; she wanted to start working. I told her, "It doesn't make any difference how old you are or anything. But you have to be able to read the lines that we write for girls. And you can't do it through your nose that way." Didn't bother her a bit. She just said, "How do I change my voice?" I told her how Walter Huston told me he got his voice because he had one of the finest voices that I've ever known. Any man, the first time he sings a song gets a gold record, you know has to be pretty good. And she disappeared, and I said, "Where in the hell is that girl?" The secretary said, "She called in today and said she's not ready to come in." And when she walked in she said, "Good morning" [low, deep voice]. Well, I couldn't throw her right out, you know. Anybody who'd . . . she'd been working every single minute for three weeks, and she had her voice changed. I asked her to come out to the house. We had parties Saturday night, and she couldn't get a ride back home. She said, "I don't do too well with men." I said, "I like to have a few drinks at my own party, and I don't like to drive somebody home. If you can't get a ride, don't come any more." I said, "What do you do to men? Are you nice to them or are you nasty or what?" She said, "I'm as nice as I can be." So I said, "Try being the other thing." The next party she came up to me and said, "I've got a date to drive me home." "What'd you do?" She said, "I insulted the man." "What'd you say?" She said, "I asked him where he got his tie." And he said, 'What do you want to know for?' " And she said, "So I can tell other people not to go there." So on Monday I went over to the studio to a friend, a writer. I said, "Jules, we might be able to do a new character of a girl who's really insolent and people like it." He said, "That'd be fun to try." We just changed the whole character of the girl and I tried the scenes out on Bacall. And she did them so well I said, "I'm going to put that kid in the picture." "Oh," he said, "you're nuts." I said, "No, she's going in." And she became a star in her first picture. Those are things that if you get lucky, you can do. I told her—she admitted she was falling in love with Bogart—and I said, "Now look, he isn't love with you. He's in love with the part that you're playing. For Christ's sake, act that part, always, every time." And she did that and still does it today.

INTERVIEWER: *Sounds like you've had tremendous success. What are some of the times that you thought things had a quality when they didn't?*
HAWKS: Only a couple times. One was Jennifer O'Neill and the other was that girl in *Red Line 7000* [Gail Hire].

INTERVIEWER: *What happened with Jennifer O'Neill?*
HAWKS: The less I say about her the better. Jennifer was a great mistake. I had a great girl chosen for *Rio Lobo* and the Guild said that she couldn't come in and work because there were other people that should be first. So I was stuck and I talked to Jennifer O'Neill. Everything the girl did was wrong. She worked for about two days and then she thought she was so good she didn't have to work. She was fighting with her husband, getting a divorce. She had her children, three dogs, and her allowance didn't cover all that. She acted like a star, and she wasn't any good because she didn't work. She could have been. She was a lovely girl. But she just couldn't take direction of any kind and didn't want to. But she thought she was good, she wanted to do things her way. And she wouldn't come out and fight and argue with you. She would just quietly do it. Oh, there were a whole bunch of gags that we wanted to do. They were sleeping at night out in an old abandoned Mexican hut, and I think they told her that it had been used as a funeral pyre.

INTERVIEWER: *Oh yes. That the Indians were buried underneath.*
HAWKS: And she got up to go and get into bed with Wayne, and I wanted her blanket to catch on a bush and show her bare-assed, you

know, that kind of thing and get some fun out of it, and she didn't want to do it at all. Actually, during the whole picture she just depended on her sense of humor.

INTERVIEWER: *Does she have any?*

HAWKS: No. She just messed up things. She told me that she was a great horsewoman and when we fixed up the scenes of her riding she looked like she was making a comedy, the way she bounced around on that horse. I know the cowboy that had charge of her horse asked me, "Can she ride?" And I said, "She says she can." He came over and said, "Oh Lord, I close my eyes every time she's going to turn that horse because I think she's going to fall off." I had an option on her. When we finished the picture I said, "About that option—forget it. I don't want you or anything about you." which I very seldom say or do.

INTERVIEWER: *How do you cover up for that? Do you do it with the camera?*

HAWKS: There's very little you can do. You're stuck with it. You've got scenes, you've got to make them. And every once in a while things go wrong. I had a girl that I thought was just going to be one of the best that ever was [Gail Hire]. She was a rebel in the way she dressed; she was a rebel in the way she thought. She was just exactly what I wanted. We made a test of her; it was one of the best tests I've ever made. When she got the job she said, "I'm going to be a star and everybody should like me." She wanted to be loved by everybody. The last thing that I want is to have a woman in my picture loved by everybody. And I just couldn't get anything out of her. So I just told her, "I'm just going to stop making close-ups of you and show you how lousy you are after the thing's finished, and then see if you can't do any better." She tried, but she'd been infected by those things.

INTERVIEWER: *Were you too much of a gentleman with these two women? Do you think if you'd been harder . . .*

HAWKS: Oh no. Some people you can get tough with and help out. I remember one girl she'd been three weeks in a Goldwyn picture, and he threw her out [Constance Cummings]. I had seen the stuff and I thought that I could do something with her. She came to see me and she was still sensitive and hurt about this thing. I just said. "Now stop this goddamn nonsense just because somebody threw you out. I'll tell you one thing that makes you lousy: you toss your head when you speak. You speak like this. Now I want you to go out and study and get a dictionary and put it on top of your head and come in for the scene." She did and did it well. She started out and she was just really good. The only trouble was she was working with Walter Huston who was the best actor I ever worked with. All of a sudden she realized how little she knew. And all of a sudden in the rehearsal of a scene she just ran around and she started to cry and wedged herself between two sets and didn't want to come out. Huston went over to talk to her and get her out. I called her a yellow little son of a bitch who didn't deserve anything, and it made her so mad that she went to work and she did something. Now that time, it worked. But there are other people . . . Jennifer O'Neill is too stupid to do that with.

INTERVIEWER: *Let me ask you—do you think the story has gone out of film?*
HAWKS: No, I think they always have to have a story, but they have to have different ways of treating it.

INTERVIEWER: *I'm saying is the narrative gone? What we used to go to the movies for, which you have spoken very eloquently about—the story, the appeal and excitement of the story.*
HAWKS: You have to remember that they've been making pictures for a lot of years, and there are only a certain number of plots. The only reason that some directors and some writers are different from others is because they change. They don't change the story, but they do change the method of writing the plots—who plays them, what kind of people play in them.

INTERVIEWER: *"Losers" play in them now.*
HAWKS: Yes, that's one thing and I hate losers. I was at one studio and they said, "Now the scene on page twenty-five: moonlight on the water. We've just done that in four pictures, so there's no trouble at all doing that." I said, "Wait a minute. That's not in there. I'm going to think of something that's going to make you really work to do." But the writer actually had put, "Moonlight on the water sifted through her hair," or something like that.

INTERVIEWER: *Isn't that one of the reasons that the Western genre is exhausted? That since there are no new ways of telling the tale except to debunk it and show the West as not being heroic . . .*

HAWKS: Oh no. There's a lot of great stories about the West that haven't been told. There are three kinds of stories. The story of the founding of the West—the historical thing of which *Red River* was a fairly good example. Then when law and order came to the West—your bad sheriff, your good sheriff. I've done that; I've about exhausted that one. But there are others that can be done. Good stories. And they will be done because when I made *Rio Bravo* Jack Warner said, "You don't want to do a Western, Howard." I said, "Yes, it's about time for a good one. There's been nothing decent made for about two or three years and I like to make the kind of money that that made." In the future you're going to have to use different characters; you're going to have to change. That's all.

INTERVIEWER: *What about Walter Brennan?*

HAWKS: Walter Brennan first came into my office because a very smart man said, "I know a guy that was just like what you were describing, but oh, what the hell, he's just an extra man." And I said, "I'll tell you, bring him in. Give him some lines. Get him dressed up so I don't have to talk to him two or three times, and have him in here." And in came Walter Brennan. And I laughed. I looked at him; I said, "Mr. Brennan, they give you some lines?" He said, "Yes." I said, "You want to read them with me?" He said, "I'd like to." I said, "OK. Begin." He said, "With or without?" I said, "With or without what?" And he said, "Teeth." Well, I started to laugh at him. He was supposed to work for three days. I kept him three weeks. When it came to *Red River* I called him up and said, "Walter, I've got a picture." He said, "I'll be right over." He came over. He said, "Where's the contract?" I said, "I was going to tell you the story." He said, "Where's the contract? Sign that first." So I said, "Come tomorrow and sign the contract." He came and signed it and he said, "Now let's hear about the story." I said, "Now you son of a bitch I don't have to tell you the story. You signed up. You read it and your parts is Groot." There was one line in the script. The cook's name was Groot. That was all the part he had. He came in and he had a grin and he said, "Gee, Howard, that's a good story, what are we going to do?" And I said, "We're going to go right back to where you and I started from." "What do you mean?" And I said, "Do you remember saying, 'With or without teeth?' " "Oh, yes," he said. And I said, "This is going to be with or without teeth. You're going to lose your teeth to an Indian in a poker game, and every time you want to eat you have to get the teeth back." "Oh, we can't do that!" he said. "Yes, we can." Every time I'd think up a scene I put him in with Wayne. I put Walter in pictures where he didn't have any part. He won two Academy Awards and got nominated for three others that I made with him.

INTERVIEWER: *Hollywood has given you an honorary Oscar. How do you feel about?*
HAWKS: It means very little to me because of the choices that have been made. I just can't bring myself to think that the Oscar means anything. I have not been in accord with the Academy and their voting. I believe that anybody is allowed to vote as they choose, but I just don't like to be a part of thing that I think is wrong. There have been too many cases where I thought that the best picture was not chosen. Because of that I have stopped voting and stopped being an active member of the Academy.

INTERVIEWER: *Would you have felt honored ten, twenty, thirty years ago—or do you feel they have always been bad choices?*
HAWKS: No, I think they used to make good choices. Then politics began to enter into it. And heads of studios realized that it meant another couple million dollars for the gross, and they got everybody together and put pressure on you to try and vote for their choice. Zanuck would put a great deal of pressure on people to try and get one of his pictures in. I remember Jack Warner once asked me to vote for a lousy picture that he had made. I said, "I'm not going to vote for that bunch of junk." "Who are you going to vote for?" I said, "I'm going to vote for *Casablanca*, another picture you made." *Casablanca* won and Warner was trying to drum up trade for another. Of course, nobody knows really what picture is going to go and which is not going to go. No way of telling. You can say, "I like this," and I'd say, "Well, like it— that's OK. But I don't." Or you'd say, "I don't like that," and I'd say, "That's funny. I thought that was good." We'd both be right.

INTERVIEWER: *Do you still vote? Did you vote* The Sting *versus* The Exorcist?
HAWKS: No. I stopped eight or ten years ago.

INTERVIEWER: *You don't even vote for director?*
HAWKS: No.

INTERVIEWER: *Do you see enough movies that . . .*
HAWKS: Oh yes. I see enough movies. A number of us started the Directors Guild; we fought for it, everything. And then I don't think they showed very much courage, and I think they suffered greatly because of it. I just didn't want any part of it. I think that they've been very cowardly in their dealings with the producers. Everybody else has gotten a great deal more than them.

INTERVIEWER: *You mean the directors?*
HAWKS: Yes.

INTERVIEWER: *Everybody that I've talked to—directors, cameramen, people who do music—they all look at the studio heads as the enemy, don't they? That's the way it strikes me.*
HAWKS: It depends on when you're talking about. If you were talking about the old-time producer who was a good showman like Jack Warner, Harry Cohn, Irving Thalberg, like Zanuck—they weren't enemies, they were good. I think they talk about the present day bunch because I don't think they know what they're doing.

INTERVIEWER: *They're all corporate people.*
HAWKS: Your old-time producer was a showman. He wasn't worried about how a picture was made. I remember one time, oh, I had found Lauren Bacall and put her in a picture with Bogart. Warner had never seen any of it. We went to the preview together. And at a certain point after they started the picture, I got up and left to get a drink. I came back and Warner said, "Where have you been? Aren't you interested in what happens?" I said, "I know what's going to happen. They like her. And if they like that, they've going to like her better in the rest of the film. It's they like that, they're going to like her better in the rest of the

film. It's going good, isn't it?" "Oh, it's going fabulous," he said. I said, "Well, why do I have to stay? I've seen it a lot of times." On the way home he was very quiet and all of a sudden he said, "Howard, I want you to make another picture with those two. Do you know a story?" I said, "Yes." "What's it like?" I said, "A little like *Maltese Falcon*." "Buy it and make it," he said. I said, "OK." I never saw him again until I showed him the finished picture [*The Big Sleep*].

INTERVIEWER: *How did you get this control? By being devious or . . .*
HAWKS: Oh no, I've had control most of the time for a long, long time.

INTERVIEWER: *How did you get it when so many others haven't been able to get it?*
HAWKS: Oh, I don't know. Those that are any good got it. Capra got it; Stevens got it; McCarey got it; Fleming got it. Any of the boys that were good, they got it. Billy Wilder got it; Ford got it.

INTERVIEWER: *But Ford lost it.*
HAWKS: I don't know how to answer that. I went to dinner one night; there were a bunch of agents and producers there. They started to talk about Ford and they said, "He's finished, he's through." And they ran *The Quiet Man*. I got up and I said, "I sat and listened to you nitwits. Do you want to stand up and talk now?" I think that toward the end Ford was . . . I don't think he was working as hard.

INTERVIEWER: *Did you see* Seven Women?
HAWKS: No.

INTERVIEWER: *Why not? Now why did good friends of Ford not see that film?*
HAWKS: Well, I'm a good friend of Peter Bogdanovich. He sat on my set for three years. He made a picture with a little girl. I never went to see it. He said, "Why didn't you go see it?" I said, "I hate children in pictures. I love them in real life, but I hate them in pictures. I don't want to see your goddamn picture." That's why. We know and we don't want to see somebody we like make a bust. I haven't gone to see the

picture he made in Italy. Peter has a great deal of talent. He just had it too easy the first couple pictures.

INTERVIEWER: *Some people have said that* Daisy Miller *is a beautiful film. But it is hollow. It doesn't have anything except the visual. I don't know whether that's enough.*
HAWKS: It depends on how the visual is used. Ford, one of the things that I stole from him was he said when you have a scene that plays better as a tableau—for instance with dark skies—stay away from changing it.

INTERVIEWER: *Why does it take Hollywood so long in so many cases to recognize excellence?*
HAWKS: I think Hollywood has been too close, and I think they still are. I think if somebody makes a picture and that picture is successful, then they follow it. They asked me in an interview the other day what I thought of Howard Hughes, and I said I had a very high regard for Hughes. He was an individual. He made what he wanted to and did what he wanted to. The average producers and associate producers all sit around and have lunch together. They develop a jargon, and they talk about pictures being downbeat, and this being that, I don't know what the hell they're talking about. Now a picture like the *Poseidon* picture is successful, so they make one about a burning building, they make one about an earthquake, they do all these things just because they think that that's the thing. I don't believe in that.

INTERVIEWER: *Blockbusters smother personal style.*
HAWKS: It's too many cooks. People are butting in. It would be pretty hard for a man to do what he wants to do.

INTERVIEWER: *And this wasn't the way in the '30s and '40s and '50s.*
HAWKS: No. I just think that . . . I know one studio that's got four pictures they can't release. They let men make them and they don't make sense.

INTERVIEWER: *Is your Hollywood gone forever?*
HAWKS: I'm afraid it is.

Howard Hawks: A Private Interview

PETER LEHMAN AND STAFF/1976

IT WAS A COLD, rainy saturday, so Howard Hawks decided not to go on his planned fishing trip. I thought that perhaps it was just as well, since I was supposed to interview him during a lunch break, and I wondered if a devoted fisherman and sports enthusiast would want to talk about films at a time like that. As it turned out, the interview took place at the apartment where he stayed during his visit to Athens. His son, Gregg, had gone fishing, so Mr. Hawks was alone on a rainy afternoon (a situation that may have contributed to his talkative and congenial mood).

At age eighty, Mr. Hawks is an extremely alert, lively man. He speaks eagerly, not only about his wealth of past experiences, but about contemporary situations and his own future plans as well. Those future plans include several projects for new films.

During the course of the interview, several members of the *Wide Angle* staff dropped by and joined in the conversation. Marilyn Campbell, Lynne Goddard and Giulio Scalinger all contributed to the more than two hours of discussion. We present the interview here essentially as it took place. We have retained not only the order of the questions, but also the conversational language.

Marilyn Campbell helped in the editing process, since space requirements necessitated a few deletions. Richard Harbert, Lynne Goddard

From "Howard Hawks: A Private Interview" by Peter Lehman. *Wide Angle* 1:2 (1976), 29–57. © Ohio University School of Film. Reprinted with permission of The Johns Hopkins University Press.

and Barbara Fisher all worked at the often difficult task of transcribing, typing, and preparing the manuscript.

PL: *What do you think of the ninety minute standard length that most Hollywood films were at the time that you started working? Do you think that there was something appropriate about ninety minutes to tell a story?*
HH: No. We sort of grew up with that. I don't know if I ever got it done in ninety minutes. I don't think I did. I think I was around 100–112 minutes or something like that. I think it's ridiculous to say that you can . . . a writer doesn't write a book to try to write something ninety minutes. Some of them are long, some are short. And the next or any picture I make in the future will have a clause in it so television can't cut it. They can run it on two different nights and maybe only three spaces during each night for the commercials. And we'll designate where the spaces should be, because just as you get things going good they cut in one of those things.

PL: *I frequently don't watch movies I like on television just for that reason. It is very disturbing to have the rhythm broken up by the commercials.*
HH: I imagine people are getting used to it, but I don't think they can have the same thing any more than that silly thing where they put a laugh track in so that actors and actresses think they're funny.

PL: *Do you think that is part of the problem of why they aren't? You've made the point in the last couple of days that the comic talent is much less now than what it used to be. Do you think that the laugh track on television is partly responsible for that?*
HH: Well, they think they're funny.

PL: *Without really having to prove it?*
HH: Oh, they don't see it without that track in, so they get big ideas about how funny they are and then they begin to make damn fools out of themselves. And worse than that the girls get cute and that's the worst thing that can happen. I mean, if you saw Lauren Bacall do it, would you say that any place she was cute?

PL: *I screened* To Have and Have Not *last night and she was just tremen-dous in it.*

HH: But she isn't cute.

PL: *No. No. What do you think it is about television that makes them start acting cute?*

HH: The laugh track.

PL: *Do you think the laugh track is responsible?*

HH: Sure. And it is horrible. I saw a girl in a series. She was the girl from U.N.C.L.E. I thought she was really good and then she got cuter and cuter all the time. I had her in to see her and told her very frankly, "You're making an awful mess of things by getting cute. Do you think you can read this part without the cuteness?" She said, "I'd like to try." She came in and read it and I said, "That's too bad."

PL: *Do you think vaudeville and burlesque were much better training grounds?*

HH: Oh sure. They had to get laughs or else they didn't get paid. Nobody was there to do the laughing.

PL: *Do you know about Cary Grant's background? He is so funny in your films.*

HH: Archie Leach?

PL: *Archie Leach?*

MC: That is his real name.

PL: *Right. I hadn't heard that for a while.*

HH: One day he was sitting in an airplane all by himself waiting for something to be done and I had a hook up with him. He had things in his ears and I changed my voice and said, "Mister Archie Leach, we will now sing "I've Named My Pillow After You." And he leapt to his feet and said, "Who said that? Okay, I'll sing it." And he sang this awful song. Oh gee, it was terrible. Oh, he told me some very funny things. When he joined the pantomime thing in England it was a very big thing. You know that Christmas pantomime thing?

LG: *Yes, very well.*

HH: And he belonged to one of those troupes. And he was supposed to disappear. He was supposed to jump through a trap door but the trap door closed too quickly, left his head stuck above and he didn't get out of it. He just had to face the audience. We were going to do a pantomime.

LG: *They are tremendous fun.*

HH: I did a script and I was going to do Cinderella with men playing women parts and women playing men parts. Prince Charming was going to be the girl with the best looking legs I could find, and Cary Grant was going to be the mother of the two ugly daughters and Jimmy Durante was going to be in it. So were Hope and Crosby.

PL: *You've had a lot of fun over the years by turning around sex roles. How did you first get into seeing this as a possibility for having fun?*

HH: I don't have any idea. I just started doing it. I probably saw somebody else do it. Oh, I remember that I saw a fellow called Julian Eltinge who was the greatest female impersonator. I don't ordinarily like men playing female parts, unless they play it as Grant did in . . .

LG: *I Was a Male War Bride?*

HH: Yeah.

MC: *And* Bringing Up Baby?

HH: I think I was funnier than he was. I have funnier looking legs.

LG: *I think that is really what makes the man and his walk; unless a man naturally has a slightly mincing feminine style of walking. It's the walk and the legs that absolutely finish me, and Grant is very masculine and has strong cheek bones and heavy eyebrows, if I remember correctly.*

HH: I know what it was. It was the red wig; something that looks good.

PL: *Traditionally, the impersonators try to act like women, don't they, their movements and everything?*

HH: Yes. But not all the comics do it. They can arrive at a good spot where they must impersonate a woman. Then they do it like a man.

They asked me to do a picture over in Russia. And I said, "No." They asked, "Why?" "Well, you tell people how to do it." "We wouldn't tell you." I said, "Two Americans try to get away from the Russian Police and they run into the back door of the Ballet Russe and then the cops come in and they're dancing in there." They started laughing and said, "Okay, you can have the ballet." I said, "I think you're serious. I'd like the National Orchestra too." And they said, "You can have anything you want."

LG: *And strangely enough, I think men are more successful at imitating women in an amusing way than women are at imitating men.*
HH: Yes. They are. They definitely are.

PL: *I'm trying to remember, Mr. Hawks, if you used in your films any places where women tried to imitate men. Were there any that you can think of?*
HH: None that I can think of.
PL: *That's interesting because it is usually a very funny thing.*

LG: *Usually a woman is good at imitating Chaplin because of that sort of pigeon-step walk which is easy. But there are only a few stars that women can imitate with any success.*
HH: It must be done very broadly and they have to try to do it so that . . .

PL: *Some actresses like Marlene Dietrich sometimes used to dress in masculine clothes, but you didn't do it, did you?*
HH: Yes, I did.

PL: *Which one?*
MC: Hatari!

PL: *Oh yes, but that isn't really masculine clothes.*
HH: Josef von Sternberg came to me and told me that he was terribly interested emotionally with Marlene Dietrich, and he wanted to know how he should introduce her. I asked him what he had in mind. He said, "Well, she's coming down for *Morocco* where she's to

be on the stage, and then she sings, and I thought I'd make it lovely: flowers, trees, background and put her in a lovely gown." And I said, "That's something new; a great way to introduce her." He said, "Okay, God damn you. What would you do?" I said, "Put her on a bare stage with no props, a chair and a man's evening clothes. Let her lean on the back of the chair, sitting backwards, and sing a song and then get up and walk through the audience and have a pretty girl applaud her and have her look at the pretty girl with interest, grin, and go on. The audience won't know what the hell they found the first time they see her." And he did it.

PL: *Why did he come to you to ask about that? Did you have a close relationship with von Sternberg?*
HH: Ben Hecht and I wrote the script, handled the set design, casted it. A director friend of mine got drunk and they had to throw him out and get somebody new. And I said, "Well, let's try von Sternberg." And he did it. A little cheap picture, you know, very much like Bogdanovich did. And it was a damn good picture and he never forgot it. We were always friends. Oh, some of his antics I didn't approve of, but he was good.

PL: *You didn't "steal" from him like you did, once in a while, from John Ford? Did you ever take anything from von Sternberg?*
HH: Well, what do think about calling the girl Feathers?

PL: *Feathers? Right, but I thought that was yours originally.*
HH: Yes, but it went around . . . like the money in the spittoon. If anything is good I hang on to it.

PL: *What are some of the antics of von Sternberg? There are so many people that always refer to his carrying on. In his book he makes it sound like everyone else carried on.*
HH: You see, he was good. He stamped his pictures and you knew damn well it was a von Sternberg picture. He got interesting people and he picked out interesting stories. So I for one will have to say that he was good. Dietrich is a . . . Oh, we were sitting one night having a couple of drinks and she said, "Every picture I make is no good." And I said, "The

trouble is that you don't like the story unless it has a big party and nice dresses and somebody says, 'The most beautiful girl is coming tonight. Wait till you see her.' And then another says, 'Here she is now. You're right, she is beautiful.' You make people say that and you make an appearance." And I told her of the way she used to do things, and she went off and did a very good Western right after that. Changed her whole act. But, for instance, in *Morocco* she came in and found Gary Cooper sitting with a couple of tarts, one on each knee, and she went up and said, "You're doing very well." And, gee, it wasn't that other kind of stuff. I wrote a scene for von Sternberg one time for Cooper. Cooper was in the room and saw a picture and Dietrich had a fur coat on and he said, "That's a good looking coat. Do you still have it?" She said, "No. I wouldn't be here if I had that coat." And then she kissed him and said, "You'd better go now. I'm beginning to like you too much." That was a good line, you know. Von Sternberg had a scene and I said, "This is just silly. Dietrich's just going to rape Cooper and it won't be anything but rape."

So I solved it by having her send Cooper out and having him attacked by a couple of thugs outside and then she ran out to watch it. And he walked back and picked her up and carried her into the house in a long shot.

PL: *Yes, I remember that.*
HH: It was a rape on his side. No, von Sternberg was good. Well, he was particularly good with Dietrich.

PL: *The films she worked on with other directors just didn't have the magic she had with von Sternberg.*
HH: They didn't know how to play her. They were impressed by her beauty and they commented on it instead of letting her play the bad girl her own way.

PL: *Lee Garmes seemed to think that the way he lit her face was very important in terms of what happened with von Sternberg. He said he started to light it like Garbo, like Garbo's face was being lit, more from the side and he went to the North light and he thinks that was really important.*
HH: He made her look awful good. She is an amazing looking woman today with a good figure and everything about her.

PL: *When you were talking to students yesterday I was really interested in
the observation you made about the unions and what it is like making movies
in Hollywood now with the extreme unionization. You worked in Hollywood
for so many years, do you think that things have reached the point, with so
many different kinds of pressure from studios and unions and from the
re-editing of your films, the length and everything, that it is more difficult
now to make the kind of pictures you made?*

HH: The big studios no longer exist and neither do the showmen who
can recognize a story. I think I told the story about Jack Warner. I told
him I knew another story something like the *Maltese Falcon*. He said,
"Good-bye, go make it." And I never saw him again until after I did it.
And I used to go to Harry Cohn, head of Columbia. I met him on a
train going to a football game and he said, "Why don't you come and
work for me?" I said, "I don't know who the hell you are." "Well," he
said, "anytime you walk into my studio you tell me and you can start
to work that morning." "What about a story?" "Any story you want
to do." And finally Vic Fleming said, "I was talking to Harry Cohn
today and he needs to do a picture. He says that a director is more
important than a star." Then he admitted he couldn't get the stars
unless he had the directors. So he called me up and I went over to
see him.

And I said, "Do you really think the director is more important than
the star?" And he said, "Yes, you can make anything you want to, hire
anybody you want to, get it, get people." And he always said that to
me. One time I went in and told him I wanted to make a remake of *The
Front Page*. And he said, "Oh, you don't want to make a remake." I said,
"Okay, I'll go some other place and make it." He said, "Oh no, now wait
a minute. You stay here." He said, "We could use actors. In fact, we can
use Walter Winchell as the editor and we can use Cary Grant as the
reporter." And I said, "You got a good average today, you're half way
right. I'm going to use Cary Grant as the editor and get a girl as the
reporter." "Are you nuts?" he said. I said, "Okay, I'll go some other
place. Stop calling me names!" Cohn said, "No, go ahead and make it.
[Laughter] They were like that, you know. I mean . . . they didn't bother
about telling you how to make it or how to cast it. Oh, once in awhile
someone would make a suggestion. I made *Only Angels Have Wings* for

Harry Cohn. I went in to see Frank Capra about something. We were two officials of the Directors Guild.

PL: *Capra was always very pleased with his relationship with Cohn, wasn't he?*
HH: Oh well, he had to be. I had the same relationship with him. Cohn always had a thing that if anybody came into the studio he got word they were in there. He asked me to stop by and said, "I need a story for Cary Grant and Jean Harlow . . . not Jean Harlow . . ."

MC: *Jean Arthur?*
HH: Jean Arthur, and I said, "I was writing one this morning." And I had about six sheets of yellow paper in my pocket and I said, "Read this." And then Capra came back and he [Cohn] said, "When can you start this?" "Oh," I said, "I don't know. In a little while." He said, "No, you have to start it pretty soon," I said, "Okay, but it'll cost you more because I'll be slower doing it." And we made *Only Angels Have Wings*, which was a pretty good movie.

PL: *You were referring yesterday to the fact that you would go to Mexico now if you could to get away from the cost of pictures that have been driven up so high with the number of people sitting around the set that don't seem to do much of anything or that you would rather rope them off and get them out of the way. At what point do you think that began to develop where you were hampered with the cost going up?*
HH: It began to happen when the showmen and the men who owned the studios died and the organization tried to carry on with people who were incompetent. They didn't make as much money on the good pictures. The star system was out because the stars wouldn't sign with the new people, you know. Metro was the biggest studio in town principally because they had all the great stars. That was due to Irving Thalberg.

PL: *I'm not quite sure what the union had to do with that though.*
HH: Well, a weakness of the people who were running the studios. The old studio was owned by Jack Warner. Warner wasn't going to give in to the union.

PL: *Oh, they wouldn't give in to the union?*

HH: NO! They weren't going to give in. They were tough old boys who had grown up with it. When the new fellows came in they didn't know anything about it. They gave in to the unions and they never got one single thing, but they gave away everything.

MC: *You're talking though about the time that television came in and various other things were coming in too, aren't you?*

HH: It started before television came in, but also they were silly in not realizing that television was going to work.

MC: *Everyone but Walt Disney.*

HH: Oh, I know it, but, for instance, I was slow about it. I made *Red River* and I sold *Red River* for a half a million dollars and it's run forty times. I didn't realize it was going to get that big but also I discounted the fact that prices in the motion picture theater were going to go up and television was for free. And so altogether it changed Hollywood, but you can't even get a good man to go to work for the studio.

PL: *It seems that Aubrey of MGM and Robert Evans of Paramount were the strongest studio heads, and many of the directors that worked for them got into terrible fights with them and left, and both of them were constantly re-editing films and things like that. They seemed to not to have had that showman touch you were talking about that some of the original studio heads had.*

HH: I don't know, Evans has some qualities.

PL: *Yes, Evans seemed to be much better. Do you think that like Paramount which is now part of Gulf and Western, the big conglomerate corporations are getting into that industry?*

HH: I don't know. I play golf with the Vice President of Gulf and Western and he tries to make deals with me all the time. I said, "Well, do you want me to work with your people over there?" "Well, won't you do it?" I said, "No! you're going to have to hire me and make a deal with me to make the picture." And he always says, but he's got to go back to New York and talk it over. And then he comes out and I say, "What about it? You know, what did you find out in New York?" Well, he wanted to know about it before they agreed to it. And I said, "That's the trouble, you know, with these fellows. What the hell do they know about a story? I know the President of Gulf and Western. He made contracts left and right and decided that in the end not one of them was a good contract. As far as I'm concerned he doesn't know anything about it. You got a deal as long as he doesn't end it, interfere and all. I'll make a good picture here." I suppose that I get too interested in that. But I can't make a picture just because somebody wants me to. They have to let you tell the story your own way. The only person I ever had any darn trouble with was Sam Goldwyn. I made two pictures for him without any interference, and then all of a sudden he came in and just messed up the thing. Ooooh! It was horrible. I used to get very amused by him. He introduced me to a good looking girl one day who was going to be a scriptwriter and he said, "I want you to co-habit very closely with him." And I looked at the girl and said, "That wouldn't be hard to do." And she just laughed and said, "Does he. . . . is it the kind of English he uses or do I have to satisfy that kind of interest?" [Laughter]

PL: *He's become famous for that, hasn't he?*
HH: I know it and his publicity men probably helped that out.

PL: *Why did he change his mind all at once and interfere with what he previously had left alone?*
HH: He wanted me to do a picture and I didn't want to and he said, "There's one way that you'll do it." And I named a completely exorbitant sum and he said, "Okay." And then he was so mad at himself for doing that. He knew he'd made a fool of himself.

PL: *Do you think that people like Cohn, Mayer and so forth had a flare for showmanship that came from their background, from knowing what people wanted?*
HH: Cohn, yes. Warner, yes. Mayer was just sharp and slick. He picked Thalberg. Thalberg had more brains than anybody in the picture business. Thalberg owned half of the thing by the time he finished and he dictated the whole thing. He was the one that knew about what kind of story the director was going to make, he knew about what kind of cast was going to be in it, and he paid no attention to it until it was finished. They had about twenty stages and they could leave the sets up.

People were under contract, so it didn't cost them anything to add to the picture. And he would tell them in a way that the directors never seemed to mind to remake two or three weeks' worth. And that's what made his pictures good. And he didn't allow the stars to have one word to say about what they played in or to use their judgment. Nowadays, stars have messed themselves all over.

PL: *Do you think they've taken too much interest in their . . . think they know more about their career than. . . .*

HH: Oh, they think just because they can act they can pick a story or they can do everything. John Wayne said, "When I make a picture with you or Ford, it turns out to be good but when I make one by myself . . ." He said, "What's the matter?" I said, "They're always as corny as the devil." But, that's what's changed Hollywood and it will, of course, remain changed now.

PL: *I think a few days ago we were talking about Wayne's sixties films and we agreed that they weren't any good in comparison to the ones he made with you and Ford. And didn't you tell me that you thought he was asking so much for his own salary that there wasn't enough left to hire good, strong . . .*

HH: Well, no. I told him, I said, "You are asking so much that you get people with you that aren't good enough. You get directors that aren't good enough and you make bad pictures. And I don't want to make a picture with you and across the street have them play one of those things you made." So I said, "You cut me out of it."

PL: *Do you think it would be bad for the box office or don't you just think he could act as well now in a film of yours as a result of these films in the mid sixties?*

HH: Any actor makes three or four good pictures he becomes a great big star, right now. If he makes three bad ones he becomes nothing. He or she.

MC: *I think I've heard that's why talent agents have so much to say in putting together stories and directors and everything, because supposedly the stars have so much box office pull. Though there aren't very many stars that will guarantee box office anymore.*

HH: Practically none.

MC: *I was reading in* Variety *that you can't really have guaranteed box office even with stars.*

HH: Oh, no. They can fall right on their faces. No, actually the choice of story, director and everything went right over to the agents who had put together a package. They wanted to sell a star, story, director or some supporting people. They put it all together.

PL: *Didn't the studios, back in the early days when the star system was going well, didn't the studios put together the vehicles just for the stars?*

HH: No, they were smarter than the agents. That's why I told you Metro made the best pictures.

PL: *There used to be a line at Paramount: if the earnings weren't doing well to go and do another Alan Ladd movie. They made vehicles especially for those people, didn't they?*

HH: Oh, they catered to, not catered, but they really put on hunts to find the ideal vehicles for the people. Especially the women stars. I couldn't use a woman star for the very simple reason that they would tell you first that they looked best on the left side of their faces. [Laughter] And then they wouldn't want to do something because they'd say the public wouldn't like them to do that kind of thing. They wanted to be liked. They wanted everybody to say, "Isn't she lovely?" You know. This girl I used in *El Dorado* could have been a really big star. She was such a beautiful girl but I finally found that she used to go to a movie and look at a woman star and say, "Boy, isn't she just lovely? She is just so nice." And I couldn't get her to do anything unless she thought it was nice. One girl I had in a picture was a complete rebel; the way she wore her clothes, the way she spoke, they way she read her lines and everything. And I hired her. The moment I hired her she said, "I'm going to be a picture star," and she wanted everybody to like her. Oh God, she was awful. She really was so bad that she threw the whole story out of plumb. There was nothing you could do with it.

PL: *Someone like Robert Redford these days will really build his picture around him, much the same way John Wayne did in the sixties, where he'll decide the story and he'll even decide the actors.*

HH: He does now.

PL: *And do you think that is really bad for someone like Robert Redford and wrong in the long run?*
HH: Well, do you think that a man, just because he has the ability to act, he can, you know . . .

PL: *Judge these other things?*
HH: You just can't . . .

PL: *I wouldn't think so. No, that's why I'm asking because . . . no, I agree with you. I don't think acting ability is at all comparable to these other things you have to decide on when you make a picture.*
HH: I told Wayne, I said, "If a writer. . . . I'll have to change the language a little bit. And Big Joe was six foot three or four, physically endowed with many things, you know, women . . . every woman liked him, wanted to sleep with him and everything like that." He just said, "Oh, that's a part for me. You don't need to read the rest of this stuff." [Laughter]

PL: *Would you think the women stars cared more about those things than the men? You haven't had those problems with the male stars you've worked with? They don't care where you've got the camera or how good looking they are?*
HH: They don't care a bit about that.

PL: *They don't care about that?*
HH: And if I put a new girl . . . that's why I've used so many new people from the beginning with Carole Lombard, Rita Hayworth, Joanne Dru. Oh, I can't remember all of them. I've used a new girl in every picture.

MC: *Weren't you the first person to use James Caan?*
HH: Yes. Not only that but I ran into him in New York and he said, "I came back here to do a test for *The Godfather* and they can't make up their minds. I'm going home." And I said, "Now wait a minute. *The Godfather* ought to be a pretty good picture and you'd better stick around a week or so. If you got a part in that you've really got it going." So he always comes to me. He says, "When are we going to do another picture together?" I said, "Well, you get too much money," He says, "Well, I won't ask for very much money." But it's quite different, you

know, for Germans. They've got some laws over in Germany that have to do with taxes that make foreign investment very good for them. I don't know what it is. I've never understood it. "Would you make a picture for us?" And I said, "How much money you got?" "Five or six million," they said. "Yes, if you'd stay out of it." "Oh, we don't know how to make a picture. You're supposed to make it. Would you use Wayne?" And I said, "Why?" They said, "Well, every picture you make with him makes a lot of money." "Well," I said, "I don't know. I don't think so. Wayne's getting kind of old and he gets a lot of money and so forth for playing an old man." "Well, we'd just as soon pay him."

MC: *In those three movies you made with him, I'm not counting* Red River, *he has these two shirts, a red shirt and a blue shirt, and he changes them only about three times in the whole movie. But they seemed very important.*
HH: No, you're wrong. In *Rio Bravo* he started one place in a blue shirt and ended up there in a red shirt. I happen to think he looks good in those things the faded blue, the faded red.

MC: *He seems to be centered in the frame the way everyone . . . he seems to be reacting to everybody else in those pictures and he's just the center . . .*

HH: Well, he's very fortunate. For instance, in *Rio Bravo* he said, "Howard, what am I going to do in that picture? Dean Martin's got all the good scenes. What do I do?" And I said, "He's your best friend and you are watching him to see how it comes out. You're supposed to be very concerned." He thought a minute and said, "Okay, that's a good enough part." And he did it. And you felt that there was a friendship between them.

PL: *He can give the feeling of strong, emotional warmth.*
HH: Yes, some of the looks . . . I hadn't seen the picture for a long time, some of the looks that he gave . . . the look on his face while watching Dean break up and everything. As a matter of fact, you have to have a pretty good person playing with Wayne or he blows them right off the screen and you don't have any story left.

PL: *Do you think that's part of the trouble with his films in the sixties? He never really had anyone good working with him, actors either.*

HH: Well, I made one with him called *Hatari!* and Gable was supposed to be in it. And I couldn't get anyone strong enough and I got a French star, a good actor, German star, good actor, but he blew them right out. Didn't mean anything. It changed the storyline and everything.

PL: *Didn't that incredible strength in the characters he plays begin with* Red River? *In* Stagecoach *or in his Republic Westerns of the thirties and* Fort Apache *he made with John Ford about the same time you made* Red River, *he's never a very forceful person, I've never seen that before* Red River.
HH: No, well, actually Ford said, "I never knew that big son-of-a-bitch could act." [Laughter]

PL: *What gave you the feeling that maybe he could or that you could bring that out?*
HH: I can't explain those things.

PL: *Did that come out on the set or did you have the feeling ahead of time that if you hired him for the part you'd. . . .*
HH: Well, if I hire somebody for a part I have a pretty good idea that I can get out of them something. Once in a while I go wrong.

MC: *I saw him on TV just this last weekend, and he said that you were the first person who ever told him he could act in* Red River.
HH: Oh, he's one of the few loyal people, you know. I call him up and say, "Duke, I've got a story." He says, "When do we start?" and I say, "Don't you want to hear the story?" "No, hell no!" [Laughter]

PL: *He doesn't study the script much ahead of time, does he?*
HH: No, he wants me to tell him the attitude that he's to take, what I hope to accomplish by the scene. You know, like I tell him, "Well, you meet somebody and I want to start the two of you in a kind of fight. I don't want you to agree. I don't want you to be nice to her." "Okay, that's easy." And he studies his lines with that in mind and we go out and do it with practically no rehearsal at all.

PL: *Does he have his lines memorized or does he have people hold up cards?*
HH: Oh no, he can memorize a long scene in ten minutes.

PL: *Really?*

HH: Yes. No, twelve minutes at the beginning of the picture and eight minutes at the end. (Laughter)

PL: *That must make him very nice to work with then, considering . . .*

HH: Oh, he's nice to work with. If he blows a line I say, "Okay, tomorrow put in about two more minutes will you? And we'll leave out the line." But, I don't care if somebody blows a line as long as the thought's there, because it's more natural. The only reason for the search for naturalness is to make a better scene. As I told Wayne, I said, "If you can't be natural you're going to irritate, antagonize or bore the audience. So for God's sake be completely natural. And don't try to get too much out of the scene." And so he always says to me, "Is this one of my good scenes or do I get it over?" I said, "You get it over." And he can really go through a scene. I think he's a good actor.

PL: *He's one of my favorites. He seems so spontaneous the way he interacts . . .*

You made an interesting point earlier. You said you didn't think actors should be involved in politics, for better or worse, they did it. But first of all, how did you manage to stay out of it, seeing that you were in Hollywood so long and you worked with people who got notorious reputations for their political views publically well known? How did you manage to stay out of it?

HH: I told them to shut up and not to talk to me about it. [Laughter] I told them, "I'm just not interested."

MC: *Did Hughes ever offer you that notorious script* I Married a Communist *that he supposedly offered to several directors?*

HH: I never heard that Hughes was interested politically in anything.

MC: *Oh! Well, he shut down RKO for a whole year while he investigated the backgrounds of all the people working for him.*

HH: That could have been natural curiosity, but you can't tell about anything that Hughes did. He just wanted to find out about them.

But Duke was rabid about Communists and Reds. He'd start in and I'd say, "Hey, go over there and talk about it." I only got interested one time and it was on a bus going to a football game. I was talking to a young lawyer. I liked the way he talked. That night at dinner Ed Lasco, my attorney, said, "Howard, do you have any idea who would make a good district attorney?" And I said, "What about that fellow I was talking to today?" He said, "By God, he would make a good one. Will you help?" And I said, "What do you mean help?" And he said, "Oh, give a few luncheons and get people, you know, and that would be good backing, just generally help. That's the way somebody gets started." I said, "I want to talk with him first." So he came out to see me and I said, "I'll get behind you if you'll do something for me. Never in your campaign start talking about a liar, thief, or all of those names they call each other when they're running against each other." And he says, "Why do you say that?" And I said, "Because you would automatically fall into the same class."

PL: *Did it bother you that many talented people in Hollywood were having their careers disrupted and in some cases almost ruined by those political events? Even if you didn't agree with what those people were doing?*
HH: Well, it didn't bother me, but if someone wanted me to use Jane Fonda I'd say it's too God damn much trouble.

PL: *No, I meant during the McCarthy hearings and the House on American Activities Committee in the fifties.*
HH: I'll tell you. To be perfectly honest with you, I think politicians are the slimiest, dirtiest form of humanity that we have on earth. Now that answers it.

PL: *You just don't like them one way or the other?*
HH: I just don't like them anyway. Roosevelt, Johnson, only Eisenhower I thought . . . Maybe he did some things that he shouldn't have done, but he didn't do. . . . Kennedy I had no use for at all. . . . and Nixon. And you can see when you watch them it's an act all the time. I talked to a bunch of students at Berkeley. They asked me but I didn't want to answer. I said, "I'd rather not talk about this." They said, "We'd like to have an answer." "Well," I said, "you fellows are making damn

fools out of yourselves running around campus causing a lot of trouble. You're never going to get anywhere doing that. Why don't you get together and put the same amount of work into getting some decent, nice person, and electing him. You can do it easily."

PL: *That's what they're doing now.*
HH: Sure, I know it. I know they are. I said, "It would only take you about twenty years and you'd get rid of the slimy ones and get some pretty good guys, because you'll get some guys that are pretty good and they'll turn slimy on you. But if you keep at it for twenty years it will work out okay."

MC: *One of the most anti-political movies I've seen was* His Girl Friday
HH: I always make fun of them.

PL: To Have and Have Not too. *Humphrey Bogart doesn't care about the political events. He just doesn't know what is going on.*
HH: I've seen too much of them to want to praise them or anything like that. But actors have been spoilt by newspapers. The minute somebody becomes successful they come and ask them for an opinion. And their press agent is sitting around there in front of them and says, "Hey look, you'd better have an opinion." And then they're quoted and so then they begin to think they're smart.

PL: *I'm in total agreement with that. I think that's one of the most admirable things about your career. It's silly to think that even if you're a good storyteller, a good actor, a good anything that you should be an expert in solving the world's problems or that your opinions should count for more than anyone else's.*
HH: Hell, I'd be entirely wrong. But, you know, I made a picture with Rita Hayworth, her first picture, I think she was one of the most beautiful women in the world. She was a dancer so she moved well. She couldn't act for anything. Harry Cohn asked me, "Who are you using in this part?" I said, "I think I'll use Rita Hayworth." "Oh good, make a test of her." I said, "If I make a test of her I'll never use her but if I get her out there I'll have to make her good, you know." And we went through a lot of tricks to make her good. One scene she was supposed

to cry and we worked till about 11:30 on it. When we quit for lunch I told her to rig her rain set outside the porch of her room so that when she walked up the rain would hit her and water would run down her face and then you wouldn't know if she was crying or not. She looked pretty good. In one scene she was supposed to be drunk. I said to Cary Grant, "What the hell's the matter with that girl?" He said, "Oh, I don't know, she didn't know what I was talking about. She didn't listen." Well I said, "Make the scene again and you watch, and whenever it's a good time just look at her and say, 'You don't know what I'm talking about do you?' Because it's not in the script, I think you'll get a reaction from her that's true. Pick up a pitcher and fill it full of water and ice cubes and throw it right on her head. And I'll dissolve and you'll be drying her hair, and you'll be saying, 'What you want is to say this.' And then you take her lines and your lines." And we did it and it was a good scene. He finally sent her out and said, "Here, blow your nose." He threw a towel at her. Harry Cohn said, "I don't know what I can do for you. You got a star for me, a new star." I said, "YOU can do something for me." He said, "What?" And I said, "Don't put her in a picture for six months." He said, "Why do you say that?" I said, "Get people to ask her what she thinks of the President. Out comes a question and she'll start giving the answers. She'll get a lot of confidence and she'll be a different girl." And he waited six months and she sailed right on through it. You know, because she began to think she was something and what she said meant something.

PL: *Do you think that's inevitably going to happen with the star system?*
HH: Sure.

PL: *They're going to think they're important in ways that they really aren't. . . .*
HH: Sure.

PL: *. . . and make decisions they really aren't qualified to make?*
HH: Sure.

MC: *How did you get that performance out of that child actor in* Gentlemen Prefer Blondes? *Did he have some prior training?*

HH: By using a great amount of restraint and not choking him. [Laughter] He'd usually get a comic book and go in and sit on the toilet and read the comic book and come out when he felt like it. What could you do with him? You couldn't beat him up. [Laughter]

LG: *Aren't all child actors like that? I mean, one has this picture of them as being very precocious and you feel like really throttling them and yet you can't because . . .*

HH: Oh, I know it. I started making a movie written by Bill Faulkner, made in England, so I wanted some children playing as a beginning for the picture. I had some idea for it, I don't know why, I can't remember why I wanted it. So they tutored them, taught them English accents, and they were horrible. I said, "Those little things, they're the most horrible things I've ever known in my life. I'll never make a picture with a child again." But in that thing, that boy with the voice that talked down like this [deep voice], you know, he was very funny.

PL: *That really was the way he talked?*

HH: Yes. That's why I hired him.

PL: *That's a little bit like the kind of fun you have with the sex roles we were talking about earlier, isn't it? Dressing the little boy like a man and having him talk like that.*

HH: The most fun you can have is making fun of people, you know. You can get a doctor and get laughs out of him, a psychiatrist, where you drive a psychiatrist crazy like in *Bring Up Baby*. A scientist like Cary Grant, I made him a bone specialist and then he starts monkeying with the bones he lost. I said, "We'd better see this. Now can you build a dinosaur by the time we get done with this?" He said, "Sure I can." And we had the dinosaur set up.

PL: *I see, so you shot the opening scene of the movie after the whole thing was done. You mean, you didn't originally have that big dinosaur in the picture?*

HH: No, no, no. We just thought of it. I used it in another picture, the second picture I made, I used a dinosaur. People laughed at it . . . animals in the Garden of Eden took exercises in front of the window and [some-body] looked out of the window and yelled, "Shame on you for tearing down fruit from the trees." The dinosaur hung its head and tears came out of his eyes. [Laughter]

PL: *Is it true that you don't like* Ball of Fire? *You don't care for that picture?*
HH: No, I like it.

PL: *Oh, because I like it very much.*
MC: You had seven professors instead of one.

PL: *That's the kind of fun you're talking about.*
HH: Well, no. That picture was very funny. Brackett and Wilder are marvelous writers and they told me a story about seven professors. And I went fishing down in Florida and came back and they hadn't done anything with the story. And I said, "What the devil is the matter with you?" "We don't know what we're telling." I said, "It was your story from the beginning." "I know but we don't know what we're telling." I said, "Snow White and the Seven Dwarfs." And they looked at me and said, "Oh, for Christ's sake." And they didn't ask me another question and they went out and wrote it. The gangster was the big, bad wolf and Snow White was the girl singing with a band. They wrote it for a strip-tease dancer and a burlesque show worker. I went back stage in a bur-lesque show and I said, "I've never smelt smells or seen people as dirty as this bunch, you know. They wanted to do that so I got a good bunch of musicians like Gene Krupa to work with.

PL: *I was wondering what he was doing in there.*
HH: Well, I sort of knew him and I asked him if he'd come over. "Got any new ideas?" And I said, "I don't know. A couple ways for you to drum." And he did a real good job on a matchbox, drumming with matches, doing "Drum Boogie."

PL: *You had Hoagy Carmichael in* To Have and Have Not, *and you've used musicians several times. We were talking about Ricky Nelson and Dean Martin in* Rio Bravo. *It's interesting that you've managed to bring that music right into the movie. Frequently when you're watching a movie with singing stars you get the feeling, "Oh, here comes the boring song. Dean Martin's got to sing, Ricky Nelson has to sing." I never get that feeling in your films; the song really fits the story well. Do you try to work the song into the story?*

HH: Oh, way back in *Dawn Patrol* I had a boy sing a song I'd heard and he took a drink while he sang. But when we signed a release for it he said, "I didn't write it." It was an old Yale tune. I didn't know Rudyard Kipling wrote the lyrics. He wrote it. And we sang that and I had a boy sing it. And I'd forgotten who wrote the song we sang in *Rio Bravo*. Was it Hoagy Carmichael. . . Tiomkin?

PL: *Yes, it was Tiomkin. Was it in the contract of the stars because they were singers that there had to be a song whether you wanted to put it in or not?*

HH: I wanted to. Ricky Nelson could sing and wanted something to do and I said, "If you write a good enough song we'll put it in here." A lot of people who would come up there and help some, Hoagy Carmichael playing the piano, and Melt Powell playing it, the greatest pianist. He was pianist for Benny Goodman, Benny Goodman playing with Kreisler and Piatigorsky . . . saying strange remarks "Hey fishface, play" to the violinist. Hell, they even made me play one night.

PL: *Are you interested in music in general by the way? Do you like classical music or do you listen to music yourself?*

HH: No, I don't listen to some of the new music. I leave the room when Gregg (Hawks) plays some of that stuff. I like banjo players. I like Dixieland. Hoagy Carmichael was visiting a little while ago and he brought a man with him and he said, "This fellow's one of the biggest music publishers in the country." Hoagy played five or six new tunes and they were just fabulous. I said to his fellow, "When are you going to put them out?" "You can't get enough for them to pay for the covers." But Hoagy called me the other day and said that the trend is changing, and his songs would be out pretty soon.

PL: *Do you have that feeling frequently in watching a movie, that the music is just there because the star happens to also be a singer?*

HH: Yes, but you try to . . . Martin's lying on the bed making no effort to do anything and then people joined in. They liked the old man singing better than anybody. But it's more likable of you listen to people just fooling around.

PL: *What's nice in that scene is that John Wayne doesn't join in.*
HH: You've never heard him sing, he's really bad. [Laughter]

PL: *He used to be a singing cowboy but they had somebody else sing the part.*
HH: I don't think I've heard that.

PL: *Oh, it's terrible, I've seen it. He walks down the street singing a song during a gunfight.*
HH: He sang in a picture that I made, I can't remember what it was. He was out of key and he sang.

PL: *I vaguely remember that, but I can't place it now. Which one was it?*
HH: It seems to me that maybe it was *El Dorado*. I don't know.

PL: *But it's a little bit like . . .*
HH: Seeing *El Dorado* last night made me wonder what the deuce I was doing trying to read that poem in there. But I think it made a character out of the boy, out of James Caan.

MC: *I've heard a very elaborate explanation of that poem. He was trying to explain it.*

PL: *Yes, some critic once remarked that you were paying your respects to the French critics . . .*
HH: Who?

PL: *. . . who recognized you just like they had recognized Edgar Allen Poe before he was recognized in his own country. Is that a favorite poem of yours, "El Dorado"?*
HH: I like it.

PL: *Yes, It's a beautiful poem.*
HH: Yes, it is a great poem.

PL: *It worked very well. It's very unusual in a Western to see two cowboys riding along, one of them reciting a poem.*

HH: Yes, I know. Well, he made a good character. Their relationship was pretty good, you know. But that ending, holy smokes. I don't know where we fouled that up. And the funny thing is that very often in a big audience they cheer when the cripples win. So they must be on your side.

PL: *You try many more things than many directors would . . . all these things we're talking about. Many directors would be afraid to think of having a cowboy recite a poem to another cowboy, but it works when you do it, like some of these comic things we're talking about.*

HH: Well, you search and search for an idea that will make a character a little different from all those others or you'll fall into the same thing. People said, "You're nuts for putting Ricky Nelson in *Rio Bravo*." He added about two million to the gross. Over in Japan they had Ricky Nelson in the middle of the posters, great big ones, over at the side were Wayne and Dean Martin.

MC: *Were you ever asked to do a movie with Elvis Presley?*

HH: The Colonel [Tom Parker, Presley's manager] asked me to, but I said, "I don't think I'd be any good. You'd better get somebody else."

LG: *Why did you think you wouldn't be any good? Because you didn't relate to his kind of music at all?*

HH: No, to the type of picture.

LG: *They were always very zany, weren't they?*

HH: Corny.

PL: They were corny, right. They were mostly very . . .

LG: *They were very romantic and he would burst into song and then . . .*

HH: John Ford was the only person who could do corn good.

PL: *Did you know the Colonel by the way?*

HH: Oh, he was working at the same studio I was.

PL: *They worked mostly with MGM, didn't they?*

HH: No, they worked all around. This was over at Paramount. Or else he would just happen to be over there and we'd just start talking, you know. He did a fabulous job with Presley, you know. Hell, Presley is still going. He's a little lame, he can't do quite as many twists as he did but . . .

PL: *I saw him a couple of years ago. He sounded very good still. You probably never cared for him in the first place but he's still going very strongly.*

HH: Oh, you never know why you put something in a movie. Except I always figure if I don't like it I can always cut it out. We had a funny thing in *Rio Bravo*. So many of the bad guys got shot and so few of the good guys got shot. I cut out a scene and Jack Warner said, "Holy smoke, why did you cut out that scene? It's a great scene." I said, "Jack, there's too many bad guys shot and it's going to get funny. Anyway, I'm going to use it again in another picture." He said, "For us?" I said, "I don't know." And it wasn't. It was in a Paramount picture. And we did it in exactly the same place and we knew exactly where to put the cameras and how and what to do.

PL: *At what point do you begin to start thinking about things like where you're going to put the camera and how you're going to light the scene? Because it sounds like most of your advance thinking is on the story and the characters, right?*

HH: All of the advance thinking.

PL: *The other stuff you do right on the set?*

HH: We usually go out . . . if we're working on the set I don't change it, but if we're going to a new set the next morning I go over with the cameraman and . . . "How about if we start this way?" Okay, then I get there in the morning they've done it and sometimes I change it.

PL: *You mentioned yesterday that the opening shot of* Scarface *was not as difficult as it might seem because the set was constructed right. I was just wondering how much you participate in the way those sets are constructed so that you can do the kinds of shots you like.*

HH: Oh, I've had seven years of architecture and . . .

PL: *Then you'd say you used your architecture experience when you . . .*
HH: Yes. You know what to do about building a set and usually the easiest way to do it is to build a model of the set and that gives ideas as to what you're going to do. Or a drawing.

PL: *Do you do that yourself frequently, for a film?*
HH: No.

PL: *You have somebody you work with do it?*
HH: But I understand blueprints and things like that. For instance, there was a studio manager at Warner Brothers, quite a nice guy, we were good friends and we made *To Have and Have Not*. So when we decided to make *The Big Sleep* I said, "You got any suggestions?" And he said, "Yes. What if I get about four good set designers." Let them read the story and tell them, "Maybe we can use something that's standing here but change it." And they then came to me and said, "Can you use an office building instead of this." And I said, "Sure." It cost about $800,000 less to make that picture with the same cast. And it had started because he said, "Do you want to go down to the ocean to make this fishing stuff?" And I said, "No, I get seasick on a boat. Do you think you can do it in a tank here?" And he said, "You mind sending a camera down and getting a long shot of the boat out in the ocean? And you'll have to get your fish shot. We can't do that." And I said, "Can't you send out a good fisherman?" And we worked right on the stage. A big tank, brought in the boat, turned it around in there. Nobody could tell the difference.

PL: *That's one location you didn't want to work in?*
HH: We hadn't anything we were going to gain by it here, you know, we wanted to get it over with. We had an idea for a scene. In Hemingway's story Harry was a fisherman so we kept him a fisherman.

LG: *One interesting thing that I've noticed in the last week while we've been screening these really quite old movies, is that I've heard much more audience applause in the cinema than I have watching more up-to-date movies. And I have heard audience applause in the cinema, but certainly I've heard a lot more in recent days than normally.*

HH: No, I told you I thought they liked to laugh and almost every-thing you ran down here had quite a few laughs in it. Was there any serious one that you liked?

LG: *Not really, no, I mean even ones with perhaps a thread of seriousness through it let me laugh.*
HH: But, many of these kids want to get laughs. You know, for instance in *Red River*, Walter Brennan is disagreeing with Wayne and says, "This is going to hurt," and pours whisky on the wound and then Wayne winces. And then he pours some more on it and audiences always laugh at that. We started in *Rio Bravo*, and the second time we made the movie we put funnier things in it. For instance, *El Dorado* had more laughs than *Rio Bravo*.

PL: *Your earlier comedies seemed more traditional in the sense that they did start funny and you knew you were watching a comedy. The screwball come-dies you did in the forties, those were comedies from the word go. It wasn't until the fifties that you began a combination and played with the audience.*
HH: You couldn't do much with *Bringing Up Baby*. That was just nuts. And Lombard, the one on the train . . . What was the name of that one with Lombard?

PL: Twentieth Century.
HH: Yes, of course. I tell you those were a little ahead of their time. People didn't know quite what to make of them.

MC: *Something like* His Girl Friday *has, for instance, a very simple scene where Earl Williams comes in through the window and it suddenly becomes very dramatic, I think, maybe, because it is one of the few long shots . . . and then the lighting changes.*
HH: I would say the value of the play was the fact that it was about a murderer, an escaped murderer, and against that background it was very easy to get the cynicism of the reporter to make you laugh. And I carried it a little further.

PL: *Do you think the fact that you made so many Westerns in the same period during the fifties was part of the same thing? Don't people think they*

know what to expect when they go to a Western? You can play with those
expectations like you play with the expectations of comedy.
HH: Well, I don't know if they really know what to expect. They do
in most of the Westerns. When I made *Rio Bravo* I purposely stayed
away from working for a couple of years and when I came back Jack
Warner said, "What are you going to do?" and I said, "A Western." And
he said, "Oh no, my God, Howard." I said, "Okay, I'll go someplace
else." "No," he said, "make it here." And it started a whole new trend of
Westerns. And then I didn't make another Western for a couple of years.
I don't hang out around Hollywood and I don't hear the talk and I don't
hear what to make and what everybody's doing. And so I don't hear the
talk that there are too many Westerns and pictures should be downbeat
today, you know, all that stuff that these guys sit around at lunch and
talk, They're talking for the boss, really, you know, to impress the boss.

PL: *That's what we were talking about earlier. Most people's bosses are too*
far removed from the showmanship to know what the people want.
HH: I got married and took my wife to the studio and Jack Warner let
us go walking around. He made a joke and everybody laughed and she
looked at him and said, "Do they always laugh at you when you're not
really funny?"

PL: *Obviously she wasn't looking for a job.*
HH: He liked her.

PL: *I think that is one of the reasons why those films are so popular today,*
why they seem so modern and so fresh. They really did start a whole new cycle.
HH: Well, actually, I like to think that they were told a little differently. You know what I mean, I had a little different idea about making
it. And also I had Wayne, because it's really hard except for Wayne and
Cooper to talk about a good Western. They were about the only two
who made good ones.

PL: *You've remarked several times that you really hated* High Noon, *which*
I do also, and just listening to you talk now it occurred to me that High
Noon *really doesn't have that sense of humor either.*
HH: Oh no, it doesn't make sense.

PL: *It's no fun. There's never any comedy or any humor in it.*

HH: If they had built up a character for Cooper, a man that had been elected sheriff by accident or anything, but when you start making him run around like a chicken with his head cut off trying to get people to help him, I just said, "What the deuce? That's silly!" Actually the studio thought they had a lousy picture and they did. Dmitri Tiomkin wrote a beautiful, beautiful score for it and that made a movie out of it.

MC: *What did you think of the Anthony Mann Westerns with Jimmy Stewart?*

HH: That ease and everything of Jimmy's doesn't apply to the Western. You know, it was a violent, wild place and the brawling and the stories with no guts in them, I didn't like them.

PL: *Borden Chase wrote those. We were talking about him the other day, and he wrote some of those screenplays for the Anthony Mann Westerns with Jimmy Stewart.*

HH: He had a lot of jobs after doing. . . .

PL: Red River?

HH: *Red River.*

PL: *After not doing it, right?**

GS: *What about the Sergio Leone Westerns? What do you think of those?*

HH: I only saw half of one and walked out. All the good guys wear white hats and all the villains wear black hats. All the equipment wrong, and they didn't know what cowboys did or anything like that.

PL: *Do you think Clint Eastwood might become a successor to John Wayne, if he handles his career right?*

HH: I thought he was going to be, but I don't think he's John Wayne, no. In the first place he's making his own pictures.

---

* Chase was angry with Hawks's changes in the script.

PL: *He's going in that same direction, then. He's directing them, too.*

HH: He was nice enough to ask me to direct a picture, and I said, "What kind of a story?" and he said, "I'd rather have you choose a story." And I said, "What's your idea?" And he said, "I want to see how you work. I'm directing myself." He was very nice about it.

PL: *That's interesting, because he struck me as someone who was probably fairly intelligent.*

HH: He would like to do the story I'm working on now. And what's his name, Steve McQueen, wanted to play the other part, and everybody said, "Why don't you use them?" And I said, "For a very simple reason: neither one of them has a sense of humor. I'm supposed to be making a comedy and I can't make a comedy with those who don't have a sense of humor." Duke Wayne hasn't much of a one, but I usually manage to blunder him through a scene, and it works out okay, you know, by having somebody with him to play against.

PL: *It does work out, because it seems like he has a sense of humor.*

HH: Yes. He has. I'm not saying he hasn't. But he is not a comedian.

PL: *Right. He's not a comic actor.*

HH: You have to attack him, and the fact that he's strong, you know, completes everything. There's a good scene with Dean Martin talking about the girl, "Aw, you know, you don't want to do what I did." "Why would I do what you did? You made a damn fool. . . . " "I know, but you're about to make a fool out of yourself." You know. That kind of stuff. What they've gone through is a reversal.

PL: *You love to do reversals in your films. You mentioned to me a couple days ago you didn't like* True Grit. *Was it because it made fun of John Wayne, or doesn't he have the comic character he was trying to play?*

HH: I read the story, and I couldn't make sense out of it. One moment it seemed real, and the next moment it seemed to be a complete satire, and the next moment it would be something else. And I think when they made it the director didn't know.

PL: *Many critics said they thought it was the first time in John Wayne's career that he acted. I thought that was probably very insulting.*

HH: No, I think they were right. I think John Wayne's been playing John Wayne, but playing it awfully well. But this wasn't John Wayne. This was a burlesque show with John Wayne, you know. And I told him, "Be careful about it; you're going to play old men now." He said, "You got a story?" And I said, "Yes, but I don't know whether we're going to do it if you keep on making lousy pictures." He said, "What's it about?" And I said, "Two guys grow up together and they're in competition. One of them—the one that you play—is power and money crazy. The other fellow is not. You meet a girl in a bar-room, fall in love with her and she falls in love with you, but you walk off and leave her and marry a rich girl, and she marries the friend, who knows that the girl is in love with you and still loves her. And you make a damn fool out of yourself with the girl's daughter because she's so much like the girl." "I could play that," he said, "I don't know if the audience would like it." It's just an idea I had.

PL: *Who would you have gotten in a film like that to play the other part? To play the friend?*

HH: Somebody who had a good sense of humor, and was funny. I never went through and worked it out much. I envisioned a good beginning, competition, growing ranches, and one fellow marrying a rich girl and everything. I knew a real character like that. His friends stuck with western horses and he went on and bought show horses and all that kind of stuff, and lived in a great big house. He enjoyed himself much better going to the little ranches. But something tells me that a couple old men aren't terribly interesting in stories unless you've got real good characters.

PL: *Do you think that Jimmy Stewart was inappropriate for John Ford's westerns like* The Man Who Shot Liberty Valance? *Did you think he was miscast there, too?*

HH: I thought Jimmy was good. I was going to sign him. I had him back in New York. He was just out of college. I'd have liked it very much to sign him. I agreed with everything you said. I made a test, though, at Metro Goldwyn, and they had another week to decide whether to take me. They took me. So I never worked with him. I wouldn't have let him get as stylized as he was. I would have gotten much more of a Cooper out of him.

PL: *There really became two sides to that stylized personality of his, because first it was authentic, then it became almost psychopathic, and he'd do that transformation into a raging maniac almost.*
HH: It's really hard to find somebody like him.

MC: *Have you ever worked with Henry Fonda?*
HH: No. He was not my type. A good actor, he's fine, I've enjoyed him, but he just doesn't fit into the pictures I do.

PL: *It's interesting, because John Wayne is the only one you and Ford both liked to use, isn't he? You didn't share the other actors that Ford . . .*
HH: Oh, I wouldn't use Ford's . . . you know, they were corny.

PL: *Ones like Victor McLaglen, maybe, or . . .*
HH: Oh, I used Victor McLaglen, but what I meant is . . . I used Ward Bond in a picture. But I wouldn't use a lot of . . . Although I've used some fellows who worked for him. But I wouldn't use any of Duke's stuff when he made pictures, and he never asks me either.

PL: *I guess it was true of the lead actors, too. Wayne was the only one that you really both shared in common time after time. And Ford would never use the type of women you used either. He would never use women like that in his films.*
HH: No, no, no. I wrote a good scene for Duke for *The Alamo*. Found a girl. It was a girl who when the Mexicans came forward had been caught and raped by about 30 Mexicans—army, you know. Damn good reaction. She was ready to do anything, and she dies for trying to help them, and was glad to die for it. And Duke read it and said, "That's a great scene, but I can't do it, and I'm not going to do it, so don't try to talk me into doing it." I said, "Are you going to do something corny?" and he said, "Yes." And he had a really corny thing there.

PL: *Did you do anything in* The Alamo? *Did you visit him at all while he was making the film?*

HH: Well, both Ford and I saw it and said cut fifty minutes out of it. And he took it off someplace and he came back and said, "Howard, the audience says you're wrong." I said, "Where'd you take it?" I think he took it to St. Louis. I said, "They have a lot of previews there, don't they?" "No," he said, "this is the only one they've ever had." And I said, "And you're basing the fact on an audience that's seeing its first preview and liked your picture." And he put it out, and we were going to go and make *Hatari!* He said, "Howard, I'm going to lose every nickel I've got." And I said, "Well, there's one man who can help you. I got this fellow." He said, "I can sell a picture if you don't try to sell it at advanced prices and reserved seats." This was a Columbia picture. And then I didn't talk about it, just said cut about fifty minutes out of it. So Wayne talked to these fellows and he said, "Will you cut that fifty minutes out for me that you told me about." And I said, "Yes. But it's going to cost you a whole lot just for a new orchestration." It cost him six or seven hundred thousand dollars. He recut it and made new prints and everything. But he got his money back. Didn't make any.

PL: *He had a lot of his own money in that production. Isn't that right, that he sank a lot of his own. . . .*

HH: A couple million from friends in Texas, and three or four million from the bank. The bank got the money first, then friends, and then Duke, and there wasn't going to be anything left for Duke.

PL: *So you did help him out, recut what he took out. . . .*

HH: Oh, yes.

GS: *Do you think he was a good Davy Crockett?*

HH: Oh, well, I don't think Duke can direct.

"You're Goddam Right I Remember"

KATHLEEN MURPHY AND
RICHARD T. JAMESON/1976

HOWARD WINCHESTER HAWKS was home the afternoon of July 12, 1976. For some time there, it looked as if it wouldn't happen. Kathleen Murphy had finally taken the leap and declared *Howard Hawks: An American Auteur in the Hemingway Tradition* as her dissertation subject. Then she decided she'd better talk with the man himself. Phone calls were made, and friendly sounds, but Hawks could never plan "that far ahead" because he was "working on a story." When "that far ahead" got cut to a little over a day and a half, it was on, and there was a frantic scramble for a borrowed tape recorder (courtesy of Ron Green), plane reservations, and an L.A. home base (provided by Rick and Leslie Thompson). That was Saturday; Sunday, we flew; Monday morning, we were driving in a rental car to get to Palm Springs by noon.

When we walked in out of the 98° air about five minutes late, three dogs checked us over while our host continued strongly to advise the person on the other end of his phone line that the air conditioning equipment he'd installed wasn't working, and that he, Hawks, had come to the conclusion "you're a goddam crook." Serious doubts about the enterprise set in when I took an indicated seat on the edge of a Relaxacisor chair and inadvertently tripped the activator switch, precipitating a non-Hemingwayesque movement of the earth beneath me; and when I failed to locate the switch by conscious means, I became the object of an icy blue stare that made me feel distinctly like the "Fancy Vest" who'd been dumb enough to sidle toward his rifle under

From *Movietone News*, June 1977. Reprinted by permission.

the assumption that Cole Thornton wouldn't notice. An attempt to start recording with side two of the first cassette almost came as an anticlimax after that.

Still, we were there—and we stayed there. We had brought along about three and a half hours' worth of tape; we could have filled nearly twice that, despite several gestures of willingness to depart if we were being too much of a bother. Mr. Hawks, who had turned eighty just over a month before, had driven 350 miles the previous day, taking his son to and from a motorcycle meet in the desert; and he frequently kneaded a stiffening hand he'd once broken on Ernest Hemingway's jaw. He talked. We talked. Whenever he left the room to find a sketch or article that had come up in the conversation, we prowled around looking at the original Red River D belt buckle on the wall, the title painting from *El Dorado*, the mugs painted HOWARD, FROM DUKE. The dogs clicked in and out of the immediate vicinity on the cool flagstone floor, occasionally crowding up to Hawks for special attention; he put on his sternest manner to dismiss them, but when, about the third time it happened, we managed to remark out loud that he wasn't being very convincing, he broke into a richly pleased smile, and from then on there was a lot of laughing.

We didn't go to Palm Springs to interview Howard Hawks for *Movietone News*, but in listening and relistening to the tapes and seeing the more-than-pleasure they brought to other people, we finally decided what the hell. The following represents but a portion of what we recorded. The Hemingway material, while valuable and provocative, has been left out here. We heard some of the anecdotes that previous Hawks interviews have included, and some of them are reproduced here yet again—partly because they will be new to some readers, partly because they're wrapped around other material, partly because even many months later they still seem *different* to us because we heard them from Howard Hawks himself and watched him while he told them. There are scads of questions we wish we'd asked. Some we did ask didn't go anywhere (like what happened to Malcolm Atterbury and Harry Carey Jr., listed in the credits of *Rio Bravo* but not on view in the film itself). Sometimes the ways Hawks misconstrued, or chose to misconstrue, the questions were almost as interesting and suggestive as more direct answers might have been; but mostly these have been edited out.

As days go, it will be hard to top. Just about the time the cassette went into the machine right, Mr. Hawks was looking at a copy of *MTN 26*, containing the John Ford memorial, and remarking that he'd "seen it before—about 150 times." He meant the Monument Valley butte on the cover. We'll let July 12 take it from there.

John Ford, John Wayne, Acting Like an Old Man, etc.

A: Well, Ford and I guess I were the only people that worked with Wayne that he didn't want to know what the story was or he didn't want to see the script—he just said, "When do we start?" . . . And of course he adored Ford. As a matter of fact, Ford came down here to die. And I used to stop in at his house and have a drink on the way to playing golf. One day I went in and he was laughing like hell, and I said "What are ya laughing about?" and he said "I was just remembering all of the things I've stolen from you." I said, "I'll make ya any kind of a bet that I've stolen more. Hell, you'd be dead before you'd even find out." And one day—he was really laughing—he said, "I just thought of the best thing I ever stole from you. I had just a fair-to-middling picture up for an Academy Award [*How Green Was My Valley*] and you had a real good one [*Sergeant York*] and I beat ya out of it!" And when I went over to see him and he said goodbye to me about six times, I knew that something was happening and I phoned Wayne and I said, "You better get down here and see Pappy. If I were you I'd *fly* down." He came down and he saw him just two or three hours before he died.

My opinion was that he was the best director in the picture business. It was very strange because we were both very pleased that the other one would steal from him. We didn't have any feeling of jealousy or anything like that. When I made *Red River* with Wayne, Ford saw it and said, "I didn't think the big son-of-a-bitch could act!" And he put him in two really good pictures immediately after, and within a year and a half Wayne was one of the biggest stars in the picture business.

Every time I made a picture with Wayne, Ford used to come down and stay with us on location, watching. And I'd say, "Can't you wait to *see* it to steal something from it?"

Q: *It's amazing how Wayne manages to age in* Red River—*and I don't just mean in terms of makeup, but in terms of his behavior and the way he walks and moves and speaks.*

A: Well I'll tell ya a funny story. He wasn't sure about how to play it. He said, "I don't know about playing an old man, I don't know whether I can do it—I'm not that kind of an actor." I said, "When we get to the old man part I'll tell ya how to play it. But in the meantime we're gonna start the picture while you're young." So we made all those scenes and we were talking and out on location getting ready to make a shot; and we were squatting on our heels the way, you know, the way cowboys and western people do. And he said, "Ya gotta tell me, how the hell am I gonna play an old man?" I said, "Watch me get up." He watched me and he said, "OK, I know what I'm doing."

Q: *It's a shame he doesn't seem to be working with anybody who challenges him now—I mean, a director. His recent films . . . they're always ready to hand him anything and know that he'll carry the picture, which of course he can do—*

A: No, he can't. He needs opposition; and without opposition, it's very difficult to make a picture with him. He blows the rest of 'em right off the screen.

I was going to make *Hatari!* with another star [opposite Wayne], and the studio couldn't afford it. So we had to hire—I hired a German boy and a French boy to play the parts, and Wayne just went [*makes a quick shrugging gesture*] and they were gone. I had to change the story. But when I put him with Bob Mitchum and Dean Martin and Montgomery Clift, we got a story.

Q: *I was curious how he—and you—got along with James Caan in* El Dorado *because James Caan seems to be of such a different acting style than John Wayne. I mean, if I may say so, he's got a kind of smartalecky, very modern style of acting—*

A: I didn't think he came out as smartalecky and modern in the picture *El Dorado*, did you?

Q: *Well, there's a real difference between his style of acting and Wayne's, it seems to me. That business of dressing up like the Chinaman out in the alley behind the bar is the kind of improvisation that I associate with a more modern school of acting, you know what I mean?*

A: [*Long pause*] Well, it wasn't in the script and . . . Matter of fact, Jimmy didn't realize it but he was playing a comedy part. [*Chuckles*] I don't believe in people trying to be funny. And as long as he didn't know, I didn't tell him. And he was quite amazed at the way the audience laughed at him. And he said, "I learned more on this picture than I ever knew before. I thought you had to try to be funny, but when I played it serious, they laughed!"

But people are not funny if they try to be funny. *I* don't think.

Q: *Paul Newman can be very witty, very amusing, but when he "plays it for laughs" it can be dreadful.*

A: Well, Wayne, ya really have to jump on him—although he's getting smarter about everything. Except directing.

Working with Writers

Q: *[Between cassettes Hawks started talking about an author who had objected to Hawks's revision of his story—until the film was released and proved successful, giving the director the opportunity to say, "I guess you don't think we messed up so badly that you want your name taken off it."]*

A: . . . But that's the only trouble I ever had. I never had any trouble with Hecht and MacArthur, or Dudley Nichols, or Leigh Brackett . . . I don't *change* the story, I don't change the scene: I just make it the way that I think it should be made, and that means that you just do little things with the dialogue, and that ya run into a place where ya can make something funny, and you add that to it because it's awfully hard to get anybody today who can write funny. They try to write dialogue that's funny, and no, I don't trust dialogue at all. But I can write *action* that's funny. I made one-reelers . . .

Q: *These "little changes" you made—it seems to me that a lot of what's funny in your films has to do with the fact that people are having trouble with dialogue, they're having trouble talking; it's as though your movies were about—*

A: I haven't any idea. I don't analyze them—I just go ahead and do it. I see too many people that I thought were so good get into trouble by starting to analyze their own stuff. . . . I read one of Frank Capra's things where he told you how to make pictures. *I* wouldn't know how to make pictures from the way he talked about it—and I don't think that *he* did. . . .

I liked Capra; I still do. . . . He came to me one time and said, "This kind of dialogue that you do, Howard, what's the principle of it?" I said, "Going round Robin Hood's barn in order to tell something. And then the next thing, being absolutely direct." And we discussed it and I said, "Funny that you come around, 'cause Noel Coward came and introduced himself on the set—nobody brought him in or anything—and he said, 'I wondered if I could talk to you about some of this dialogue that you do. Whaddayou call it?' I said, 'Hemingway calls it oblique. I call it three-cushion.' " Capra went out and did a marvelous scene between Jean Arthur and Tommy Mitchell [in *Mr. Smith Goes to Washington*] where she gets tight and tries to get Tommy to marry her because she's in love with Jimmy Stewart and . . . It went clear around like that. He did it better than I did it—that one time, and he never did it again.

But Coward, whom I admire so much, was very interested in talk, and talked about it. And then I said, "If you like my dialogue you'll like Hecht and MacArthur. They've got a story—called *The Coward*, no, *The Scoundrel* . . ." And when Hecht and MacArthur got ready to do it, they called me up and said, "Howard, ya have to come help. We hadn't realized what directing means. Could ya come back a couple weeks and help us?" and I said Sure. So the first thing I had to do with Noel was this scene where he turned around and walked back through this . . . thing, and I said [*sighing*] "Hey, Noel, you can't wiggle your behind like that—it shows up too much." "Oh my God!" he says, "Tell me if I do that!" I said, "You're goddam right I'll tell ya about it!" [*Laughter*]

Q: *I wanted to ask you who Seton I. Miller was or is. He worked a lot with you early on.*
A: He was a boy at Yale with my brother who sent me some stuff that he wrote. I worked a lot with junior writers that I thought were

good, because they're so easy to work with, because I'm gonna change it anyway. He was a good plodder, ya know what I mean, he worked, he studied. He really worked on—not very many talking pictures, I don't think . . . John Lee Mahin was one of those boys. He worked for a newspaper—so did Hecht and MacArthur—but he was good, so I hired him. Introduced him to Victor Fleming and he did great work for Fleming and for me. But he was a peculiar type of a writer. He had to be told what to write. Then he did it well.

Q: *What do you mean when you say "he had to be told what to write"? Do you say, "I want a scene in which this gets established between these characters"—?*
A: Tell 'im what the scene's for, tell him a little of the attitudes of the people and everything, and then he wrote beautiful dialogue. He worked with me on *Red Dust* [dir. Victor Fleming] and *China Seas* [dir. Tay Garnett]—I was producing over at Metro for a while . . .

Q: *He worked with Jules Furthman on* China Seas, *didn't he? Another writer you've worked with—*
A: I can't remember. I can remember them if I directed them. I was producing for about fifteen directors and eighty writers over there.

I had fun when we wrote *Rio Bravo*. My daughter was getting interested, and she had one good idea about throwing dynamite. I said, "Look, I'll write the story and give you a credit and it'll save me money on income tax and you'll get enough to buy a new house." So she's listed as the writer.

Q: *That's B. H. McCampbell?!*
A: Yes! [*Laughter*] Barbara [Hawks] McCampbell!
But I used to work with a kid who was beginning writing, and pay him five or ten thousand dollars for the writing, and I'd rewrite it myself. And if it was something I didn't want to do, I'd sell it. I could charge off the guy, I didn't get credit for being a writer and you could charge those things off.

On *The Sun Also Rises*

A: I bought *The Sun Also Rises* and kept it for twenty five years. And
then I just decided that I couldn't do it. With the condition of pictures
at that time it was pretty damn tough to show that a man had had his
balls shot off, ya know. We tried all kinds of ways of figuring how to tell
it, and it didn't turn out very nice with the characters . . . So I sold it to
[Darryl F.] Zanuck. And he went all over town saying he'd got the best
of me, 'cause of the way he'd bought it. About eight months later he
came to me and he said, "How were you gonna do that?" Well, I said,
"I'd be very glad to tell you—for $50,000." "Oh I'm not gonna pay you
that." I said, "Go and make it then!" He made it and I sent him a wire
saying, "You'd have been a whole lot better off if you'd paid me the
50,000 bucks because it was a pretty bad picture."

Source Material for *Only Angels Have Wings*

A: One critic said that usually I was pretty much to be relied on, but
when I made a picture called *Only Angels Have Wings,* now that was just
too much for anybody to believe. I wrote him a letter and said that—I
kept a copy of this letter and I'm thinking of publishing this letter—
every single thing in that picture was absolutely true, there wasn't anything I invented. I invented how to *use* it. I got back a very nice letter.
   The whole story was about . . . I was down in Mexico hunting with a
bush pilot. You know, there weren't any landing fields; they land anywhere. He had some homemade things that he dropped, and smoke
would come out, and he could see which way the wind was blowing.
And we'd go down and land and run our wheels on the ground to see
whether it was mushy and marshy or what. And I went to dinner, and
there was a guy there whose face had been burned in flying. All scarred.
No expression on his face. Just talked to ya—nothing happened on his
face. There was the cutest girl. The dinner was for a pilot and this girl.
They were married, and they met in exactly the same way that the two
people in *Only Angels Have Wings* met. And the only thing I couldn't
use was the fact that the fellow with the burnt face got up and said, "A
year ago tonight you were married. You went to bed about ten minutes
to two. You got up at two o'clock. There was a pause of about fifteen
minutes, then you repeated this thing," and the girl said, "Damn you,

you were peeking!" And they brought out a German machine used to keep the hours on flying; and it recorded when the motor started on a scroll, it recorded the takeoff run and recorded in the air, change of altitude, and landing bumps, so that they had a complete record of the time. And he'd hung it under their bed. Instead of being angry, the girl was so pleased and so proud of it, she put it up over the fireplace. . . .

The *Dawn Patrol,* Richard Barthelmess, and a Toast to the Dead Already

Q: *When you were talking about the guy with the burnt face and* Only Angels Have Wings, *I naturally was reminded of Richard Barthelmess, who was great in* The Dawn Patrol *and gives a magnificent performance in* Only Angels. *I wondered if there was any story behind your using Barthelmess. He was past his peak as a star, wasn't he, and yet he was so fine . . .*

A: Well, I wasn't very popular about the time that talking pictures came in. The head of Fox was a former police commissioner, and I made a picture kidding policemen—*A Girl in Every Port* [1928]—and this guy came out of the theatre and said, "Well, that's the worst picture that Fox has made." And I said, "You're just a goddam fool." It got its cost back in one theatre! But he never forgot that I called him a goddam fool. I couldn't get to do a picture. He'd turn down every story. I asked the lawyer about it and he said, "He's got a pretty good defense if he says that you were not capable of making a good picture. I'd wait a little bit." So I wrote the story and the scenario and the dialogue of *The Dawn Patrol.* I paid John Monk Saunders $10,000 to put his name on it, because I didn't think *I* was going to do too well; I was just a beginner. Barthelmess took *Dawn Patrol* and insisted I make it. It was my first talking picture. [*The film was made at Warner Brothers; Hawks did not return to Fox Films, although he eventually got his back salary.*] Barthelmess stuck by me, and it was the biggest-grossing picture of the year. I had no trouble after that, and he'd done a great deal for me.

Q: *Do you remember that song in* The Dawn Patrol—*"stand by your glasses, steady . . ."?*

A: You're goddam right I remember it. . . . My brother and I were just discharged from the First World War and we were in New York. We went into a restaurant, bar, something. Young fella there, about four cops around him, and in a quiet voice he was just telling them what sons-of-bitches they were. Boom! they knocked him down. I went over to the sergeant and said, "What the hell did you beat up on that kid for?" He was drunk, had been in the war and everything. "Well, we can't control him. Do you think you can?" I said, "Well, we can try." So my brother and I took him over to the Deke house—we were both Dekes, from Cornell and Yale—and we put him to bed. My brother said, "That guy certainly started something." And this figure came out of the bed and said, "Well I'll finish it now!" and boom! we had to knock him out. He turned out to be the editor of the paper at Princeton, and he'd been at all the fronts since Verdun, and he told me about how he'd get back for a leave and he had this little French girl and he'd stay with her and drink brandy and then go back and get in the thing again. So that's where this whole idea came from, because he told me the song. And my brother could play the piano a little bit, and he could remember it. So when I was making the movie I said to him, "Do you remember that song?" and he played it, and we could remember the dialogue between the two of us, and we put it in the picture. And I was asked to sign a release by Warner Brothers for the song, and I said, "I can't sign a release." I told them where I got it. It was a number of years before I found out who wrote it. It was Rudyard Kipling. [*Pause; then, speaking quietly*]

> We meet 'neath the sounding rafters,
> The walls all around us are bare.
> They echo the peals of laughter,
> It seems as though the dead are there.
> So stand by your glasses steady,
> This world is a world of lies.
> Here's health to the dead already
> And hurrah for the next man that dies.

That was Kipling.[1] And we were never sued.

---

[1] The lyrics are from Kipling territory but not Kipling—specifically, Bartholomew Dowling's "The Revel," a poem "commemorating those who died in a great cholera epidemic in India," according to *Bartlett*. They are somewhat altered in Hawks's film—another writer rewritten.

Come and Get It and Frances Farmer

Q: *Do you remember what you had in mind for the ending of* Come and Get It? *I gather that your ending didn't please someone at the studio and William Wyler had to take over and finish the film . . .*

A: Well, [Edna Ferber] wrote a story. . . . First place, [Sam] Goldwyn was going to the hospital so he said, "I want you to make this. Do anything you want to do." And then I talked to her, and I said, "That isn't such a good story that you wrote. You really ducked around all the issues." And I talked to her a little while, and she said, "How come you know so much about it?" and I said, "You're writing about my grandfather and all the people in his class—they were the lumber barons of the time—and your mother kept a little antique store in Oshkosh, Wisconsin, and it was so crowded that everybody knocked a dish off when they went in, and then they had to pay for an antique." [*Laughter*] "My God!" [said Ferber,] "What were you going to do?" "Well, for one thing this poor little lame girl that you make all the lumbermen laugh at, I'm gonna turn into a good lusty whore." "I wish I had," she said.

Utilizing all that I knew about logging drives and stuff like that, we did that picture until Sam Goldwyn came back. And I said to his wife, "I won't finish it for about four or five days. You better keep him outa there." "Why?" " 'Cause he's gonna faint!" Finally she comes to me and says, "I can't keep him out, Howard. What are we gonna do?" "Well, get ready to help him if he faints." And I went to see him. He wanted to see me the next day at his house. He was sitting back in the chair with his legs covered like an invalid. He started talking. I said, "Wait a minute. Are you a sick man?" "Yes." I said, "OK, then we ought not to talk. Have you got any ideas about what you'd like to have done with this picture?" He said yes. I said, "Tell 'em to somebody that you trust and let me communicate with him, 'cause I don't want to argue with you if you're a sick man." So a very nice guy that used to work for *Saturday Evening Post* was working for him. He said, "I don't understand the difference, what he wants compared with . . ." "Well, tell me what he wants," and he told me, and I said, "Well, I think that's easy to fix up," and I wrote some scenes. Then he [Goldwyn] wanted to see me and he said, "Now these scenes are just what I want. Just perfect. Who wrote 'em?" I said, "I did." And he said, "Directors shouldn't write." And I said, "You stupid son-of-a-bitch, I don't want to work with you any longer." And I quit. And he had everybody in town call me to come back. And I said, "I won't come back." So Wyler came in and they tried to write some scenes and finally Wyler found the scenes I wrote and said, "This is the scenes we ought to use." He didn't make 'em the way I'd have made 'em, but they had the same effect.

Q: *Would you have had the father and son [Edward Arnold and Joel McCrea] split at the end and go their separate ways? I often thought that maybe you'd have had it end like* Red River . . .
A: Oh, I would have, sure. Underneath it, you know, is the feeling, and I think that the father loved an image, and felt very guilty about what he'd done, and I think when it was all over that he'd have been very happy that his boy fell in love with her. Otherwise it would have separated them completely over such a little thing.

Q: *Did you like Frances Farmer?*
A: Mm-*hmm.*

Q: *I thought she was tremendous in that.*
A: Ah, God, she was so good.

Q: *Just beautiful. Really sad what happened to her.*
A: She came into my office and I talked with her for half, three-quarters of an hour, about a little part. And finally I said, "You oughta be playing the lead." She said, "I can do it." "Well," I said, "we'll try a test." And we made a test. And she, like any kid, you know, get theories what they should do and all, how they're gonna age and everything. All I wanted was mannerisms. We made a test. She had to cry in it. I told the makeup man to get some stuff to blow in her eyes. "I don't need that." I said, "OK." She didn't realize she had to do it four times in different shots. She dried up. So finally I said, "You'd better let me help ya," and she did. She saw that and she said, "You were right." And I said, "But you weren't right. You didn't have the right attitude. You didn't take it right. Where do ya live?" She told me and I said, "I don't know where that is. Where is it near?" She said, "Schwab's drugstore."

I said, "I'll pick ya up there at eight-thirty tonight, and we're going hunting until we find some little joint that's got somebody that will show you how to play this thing. And we saw this marvelous dame singing—she was talking with some friends of hers and they hit the chords for her to start—"I'll be with ya in a minute" and she goes on talking. And I said to Frances, "Now look. It's gonna cost ya about fifteen dollars. Sit her over a beer or two. You won't get hurt, you're a big husky girl, you may get your leg felt a little bit, but just watch. Whoever sits down and picks you up, mimic this girl." She came back in about ten minutes and said, "I'm ready to do the part." No makeup. Just a different-color hair and this marvelous attitude. And she sang. And I said to Eddie Arnold, "This girl's new, this is her first picture." Very first scene, she said, "Mr. Arnold, if you'd answer me just a little quicker we could keep up the speed of this scene, we could keep it going." He come and said, "Hey, she's pretty good, isn't she?" I said, "She's so damn good that you better *really* go to work or she's just gonna take it right out from under you." And she was fabulous. And I paid off the other girl, 25, 30,000 dollars, that they'd engaged; put her in at $75 a week.

I had a boat at that time. Be going out in the boat for the weekend. She'd show up with a—blue denim trousers, bare feet, toothbrush stuck in her pocket—and the cleanest, freshest-looking girl ya ever saw in all your life. And probably spoiled her in a way, because they gave her some boys didn't know how to direct, and then some bad stories, and she'd been used to working the other way, and she became a pain in the neck to the poor directors that had to work with her because they couldn't keep up their schedules. I tried to reason with her. Then she met Clifford Odets, and fell in love with him; and he was a nasty man. And he put her really through the wringer. And she ended up a drunk, and she didn't even take a drink before she met him. And every time they'd let her out of the hospital she'd come and see me, but my God!

I think she had more talent than anybody I ever worked with.

Joan Crawford and *Today We Live*

A: Joan Crawford was probably one of the . . . I used to go around with her when she was just a beginner; tried to teach her some of the things and taught her pretty well. But when Bill Faulkner wrote a story, a script for me, we didn't have any woman in the story. And they told me, "Have you got your cast?" and I said yeah—Gary Cooper, and Bob Young, and Frank, Franchot Tone. "Oh," they said, "you've got Joan Crawford" and I said, "Oh, you've got the wrong place, there's no girl in this," and they said "There is now." And they said, "Look, we've discussed this and we haven't got a picture for her and we'll lose a million dollars if we haven't got a picture so you're stuck." And well, there wasn't anything I could do. I didn't have anything in my contract that allowed me to say no to them. And I said, "Have you told Joan?" "Yeah, she's down in the commissary waiting for ya." I went down there, she saw me and she started to cry, the tears started falling. "Howard, I—I read that thing and there isn't a part for a girl in it!" [*Chuckles*] I said, "Look, Joan"—I told her about what happened—"you're under contract, I'm under contract. This can be the worst thing and we can both have the worst time, or we can have some fun. We don't have to start going out again, but you can kiss me when I come on the set or something like that, and you've just gotta take it." "OK," she says, "I will." And she gave me a flower and a kiss every morning, and drove me half nuts about some of the thing, y'know. She wanted to talk like the boys talked. Well, I couldn't blame her for wanting to talk that way because it was very special. Some of the clothes she got on were really . . . But she was a marvelous kid, dame, y'know, to go through this thing, with me handing her a scene each day and . . .

Actresses in General

A: When I see a girl that I think has possibilities, by the time she's in a TV show that's pretty good and by the time she's finished so that I can use her, she's got the cutes. All these people hear these laugh tracks that they attach to the thing, and they begin to think they're funny and that they're cute. Just messes them all up.

Q: *I was wondering why, for instance, you've worked through the years with Walter Brennan and John Wayne and Cary Grant, people like that, actors like that, but I know of only three actresses that you've used more*

than once: Bacall, and Ann Dvorak, and Charlene Holt. And I was wondering
why you don't use, or you haven't used, actresses more than once.

A: Well, to be truthful about it, usually they've done pretty well when
they become stars, and then they think "My public likes me to be this
kind of a person" and they don't want to try anything.

I made a test of a girl once. She was just fabulous. She was a rebel in
everything she did. The way she wore her hair, the way she wore her
clothes, the way she'd read lines. I signed her for a movie to play the
part of a girl who thought that if she slept with somebody she brought
bad luck and they got killed. When I told her she had the part, she said,
"I'm a movie star. Now everybody's gonna love me"—and she started
changing. She was *lousy* in the picture. Matter of fact, I didn't make any
close-ups of her. I was going to leave them, hoping that she'd get better
toward the end of the thing and I'd get the close-ups then. She never
got anyplace; she just spoiled the picture.

Well that's one of the things—for instance, you take Charlene Holt.
Charlene was really a good actress but she'd been brought up and—the
clue came one day when she said, "I used to watch So-and-so and she
was *so* lovely, just *lovely*" and I said, "I don't *want* you to be lovely, I
want—" you know. Now she was pretty good in *El Dorado* but she was-
n't so good in the other picture before it. Now in real life you get a couple of drinks in her and look out! I mean, she's *dangerous*!—and
attractively so. But she thought that she ought to be "liked" . . .

Walter Brennan

Q: *Was that moment at the end of* Rio Bravo *when Stumpy imitates*
Chance and says "Ah told you to get back in thar!"—how did you do that?
Was that improvised or—?

A: You do that by a very simple thing and that is you're making fun
of the star. Walter Brennan was ideal for me to do that with, and he did
it in everything I ever did. I don't know if you ever heard about this. I
had a very smart production master, and he said, "When you were
telling us the story, Mr. Hawks, about one character, I know a fellow
that's so near the man that you told us about. Ah but hell, he's just an
extra." I said, "Look, if you think that he's good, bring him in, but do

one thing for me. Give him some pages of dialogue and get him in costume so I don't have to see him two or three times, and when he knows the dialogue bring him in here." And he brought in Walter Brennan. And I laughed the minute I looked at him. And I said, "Mr. Brennan, they got some lines for you to read?" and he said yeah. I said, "D'ya know 'em" and he said yeah. "Well, let's you and I read 'em. I'll read one part and you read the other" and he said, "With or without teeth?" I said—started laughing—"Without." He turned around, took his teeth out, put 'em in his pocket, turned around, [*imitating toothless Brennan*] started talkin'. I hired him; he was supposed to work three days; I kept him six weeks, and he got nominated for an Academy Award.

Everything Brennan did, he did so easy, and so well. . . . In *Red River*, I called him up, said "Walter, I got a story." "I'll be right over." He came over, sat down [*rubs his hands together*]—"What are we gonna do?" "Well, I said, "I want you to read this script." Had one line in it—the cook's name is Groot—that's the only thing it had; didn't even have a scene with him. "Well," he said, "where's the contract?" And I said, "Well, the contract isn't here." [*Rears back*] "Well, I don't read anything until I get the contract signed"—which is the directly opposite from the usual. So he came in the next day, I said "Here's the contract," he signed it [*slaps hands together and rubs them*]—"Now I wanna hear about the story." I said, "*Now*, you son-of-a-bitch, you're *signed*! I don't have to tell ya the story—*read* it!" And he came in the next day and he read the script and he said, "Jeez that's a good story. What are we gonna do?" I said, "Remember the first time we met, you were gonna read the scene for me?" "Ah, you mean that thing about the teeth?" I said "Yeah. You're gonna lose your teeth to an Indian in a poker game and then all the way through the picture, every time you wanna eat you're gonna have to get 'em back from the Indian." "Ah, Howard, ya can't do that" and I said "Yes we can." So that's all we started with. Every scene that he did like that, he played with the Indian, I wrote. Then I found out he was so damned valuable in making scenes, as a judge, y'know, as a . . . to condemn Wayne or anything, and to buck against Wayne. He got an award out of the damn thing.

But he was a hell of an actor. He was so funny in making *Rio Bravo* . . . [*Reverie interrupted to let a dog outside . . .*]

Scarface, Re-release, Paul Muni, Actor's Vanity

A: If you were going to do [*Scarface*] again today, you'd make it about the same way.

Q: *It's a completely modern film. It really is. What about the re-release? Is* Scarface *going to be re-released now that Hughes is gone?*
A: We were just in the middle of correspondence where he'd asked me what I would do. He's got a motion picture division and I sent them some correspondence and I said, "Do you want to do this?" and I think that they want—it would mean that I'll release it.

Q: *It would be good if people could get to see it again in this country. There was a showing of it in Seattle a few months ago in a classic films series, and I noticed on a poster at the top of an escalator where most of the people go by who are coming to campus in the morning, and the next week after it had been shown somebody drew a big ring around* Scarface *and wrote "Best Film of 1976."*
A: Well, it's amazing the reactions . . . Hughes didn't have a negative on it, so when I wrote him I said, "I've got a negative, perfectly good negative; I can make all the prints that I want. I'd change the [fore-word] titles and take out the silly scene about the mayor of a city [publisher] in the middle, and put back the old ending where [Tony Camonte] ends up in some horse manure in the gutter."

Q: *I wanted to ask you about the ending, what you felt was going on. Early in the picture someone predicts "Someday we're gonna take your gun away from you and you'll squeal like all the other rats." And then at the end they bust in, shoot the gun out of his hand, and Camonte goes into this "Don't shoot!" and appears to be acting like the rat as predicted. But when he has his chance he bursts through the cops and runs outside, and of course is killed. Was he putting on an act, looking for a last chance, or was he literally "no good alone" as he was saying and he'd just gone to pieces—?*
A: I think he'd just gone to pieces. Muni was very funny. He was a good actor, played a marvelous part. But he wasn't a bit happy about going to pieces and being a yellow bastard, you know. And we rehearsed it and I said, "This the way you're gonna do it?" He said,

"I think it's the best way." I walked back and started playing cards with somebody. He said, "When are we gonna shoot the scene?" I said, "Whenever you stop being an actor and start being a real good one." Finally he came over and he said, "I'll do it."

Too many times an actor realizes that he's had a hell of a part, and the better he acts his finish, the more he loses the sympathy of the audience. I asked—who was the English actor? So good an actor, did *Elizabeth Browning [The Barretts of Wimpole Street/Forbidden Alliance]*—Charles Laughton. Vic Fleming and I met him one night. We sat alongside him and he got further down in his chair, you know, asking him questions. And I said, "Charlie, what are you gonna do with this scene?"—he told me what he was gonna do next day—I've forgotten the scene, but anyway he had his choice of playing it *honestly* or playing it as an actor playing, a role. He was quite a bit fairy-like, you know. "Well, I don't know—" I said, "Are you gonna have the guts to play it honestly?" "Well, I don't know. I won't know till I get there." I said, "In other words you're afraid what the answer is." "Well," he said, "maybe that's true." He was quite funny about it.

Today's Actors

Q: *One of the things that it seems to me is happening now, both onscreen and off-, is distinctions between men and women are blurring. You can hardly tell boys from girls a lot of the time. It seems to be the fashion for everybody to kind of be "people," not individuals—sexual individuals. And a lot of your men and women get together through sexual antagonism/attraction, which has a lot to do with being a man, being a woman, and being individuals. Do you think you'd find it difficult to do something like that now in a film. Who would you get to play parts like that?*

A: The trouble is to get people to play parts like that. Let me ask you a question. If you had a good tough hero, who would you sign today to play it? A lot of them are more effeminate than the women.

Q: *Maybe Jack Nicholson.*

A: Maybe, but I doubt if you could do anything with Jack Nicholson that's different than what he's done, because I think he was the same in the picture before *One Flew over the Cuckoo's Nest* as he was in that.

I think he's gonna play that kind of man, and that isn't the kind of guy I want.

Q: *How about James Coburn? Do you like him at all?*
A: Yeah, I like him, he's pretty good. But it's awful hard to . . . They wanted me to make a picture, they were stealing *Winchester '73*, something like that, and doing it in Turkey, with gunrunners. And I said, "I'll only make this if I can rewrite the whole story, if I can get who I want to play in it." "Who do you want?" I said, "I'd like to have James Coburn and"—oh, who was the fellow, the famous quarterback, the black-haired guy?—"Joe Namath." And the guy in charge said, "Who's Joe Namath?" I said, "I don't want to work for you."

But that's how hard it is to cast. I've made pictures with Bogart, and all the westerns I've made with John Wayne; and you start thinking who you're going to put into a movie; and these fairy-like people that are running around—I mean, there's no strength or guts to them, they don't do scenes . . . The only one that's worth anything today is Robert Redford. He's pretty good. Redford *and* another combination usually works out pretty well . . . I've got a great story about two guys, two really good tough guys, going around the world getting into scrapes—women every place they go. I haven't started it yet because I can't find anybody I think's good enough to put in it. . . .

The Industry Today

A: I had a funny experience with Peter. I was talking to the fellows at CBS. I said, "I know a fellow who, if things go right, 'll probably be one of the best of the young directors, Peter Bogdanovich." They called me and they said, "Look, he doesn't want to do stories that we want to do." I said, "Well I told you he was smart." And they said, "What are we gonna do?" and I said, "How'd you like it if I produced them and he directed them and then I would choose the stories?" Well that'd be OK, and I said, "I'll talk to Peter," and I talked to Peter, and I said, "We'll do four pictures for you. You're looking for four. But we don't want to be stuck with casting, so when we're making the first one we can be preparing the second one and we can get it cast well." They said OK. Peter and I picked four stories. And I said to Peter, "Look, this is all too easy. I think we oughta give 'em something . . . let's give 'em five stories and let them eliminate one of 'em." They took the turkey that we handed them, chose that and didn't want the others! And so Peter said "I won't work for them" and I said "Neither will I."

There was one very nice fellow running a studio. He asked me to come in and talk to him. When we started to talk he said, "You've got a story you'd like to do?" and I said yeah. He said, "Do you mind if I ask somebody to come in?" I said, "No, go ahead." I told him the story and he said, "Gee that's a good story. Really good one. Who have you got an idea of putting into it?" and I said, and they said "Oh we've got him. We could put in another person." "Well we have a commitment," the other fella said, "with So-and-so." "Yeah, we could put him in with him." And pretty soon they were casting the whole picture with people they had something going with, until they said, "Where are you going?" and I said "Home. You're just wasting my time." And I said, "Who the hell are you?"—the fella he'd brought in. "You ever direct a picture?" No. "Ya ever written one?" No. "Ya ever produced one?" No. "What are ya?" "An agent." And I said, "I hate agents." And I said to this fella, "Now you know why I'm walking out. If I'm gonna deal with people who just hear a story that I've been working a long time on, and then they know how to cast it and how to make it—I thought you told me you wanted me to make the picture?" He said, "I did." I said, "You want to make 'em right now and you don't know anything about 'em." And he called me after I got home and he said, "Look, I made a mistake in asking that fellow in"—he was trying to blame it on somebody. "I'd like to have you do this picture," and I said, "You're too late. I went from you to somebody else and they wanted to do it and it's all set-tled." "Well," he said, "whenever you've got a story, phone me, will ya?" and I said, "Whenever you *need* somebody, phone me."

INDEX

CONVERSATIONS WITH FILMMAKERS SERIES
PETER BRUNETTE, GENERAL EDITOR

The collected interviews with notable modern directors, including

Robert Aldrich • Woody Allen • Pedro Almodóvar • Robert Altman • Theo Angelopolous • Bernardo Bertolucci • Tim Burton • Jane Campion • Frank Capra • Charlie Chaplin • Francis Ford Coppola • George Cukor • Brian De Palma • Clint Eastwood • John Ford • Terry Gilliam • Jean-Luc Godard • Peter Greenaway • Alfred Hitchcock • John Huston • Jim Jarmusch • Elia Kazan • Stanley Kubrick • Fritz Lang • Spike Lee • Mike Leigh • George Lucas • Sidney Lumet • Roman Polanski • Michael Powell • Jean Renoir • Martin Ritt • Carlos Saura • John Sayles • Martin Scorsese • Ridley Scott • Steven Soderbergh • Steven Spielberg • George Stevens • Oliver Stone • Quentin Tarantino • Lars von Trier • Liv Ullmann • Orson Welles • Billy Wilder • John Woo • Zhang Yimou • Fred Zinnemann